SOUL OF THE COURT

The Trailblazing Life of Judge William Benson Bryant Sr.

Tonya Bolden

FOR THE HISTORICAL SOCIETY OF THE DISTRICT OF COLUMBIA CIRCUIT

University Press of Mississippi / Jackson

Margaret Walker Alexander Series in African American Studies

The University Press of Mississippi is the scholarly publishing agency of the Mississippi Institutions of Higher Learning: Alcorn State University, Delta State University, Jackson State University, Mississippi State University, Mississippi University for Women, Mississippi Valley State University, University of Mississippi, and University of Southern Mississippi.

www.upress.state.ms.us

The University Press of Mississippi is a member of the Association of University Presses.

Any discriminatory or derogatory language or hate speech regarding race, ethnicity, religion, sex, gender, class, national origin, age, or disability that has been retained or appears in elided form is in no way an endorsement of the use of such language outside a scholarly context.

Manufactured in the United States of America
∞

Library of Congress Cataloging-in-Publication Data

Names: Bolden, Tonya, author.
Title: Soul of the court : the trailblazing life of Judge William Benson Bryant Sr. / Tonya Bolden.
Other titles: Margaret Walker Alexander series in African American studies.
Description: Jackson : University Press of Mississippi, 2025. | Series: Margaret Walker Alexander series in African American studies | Includes bibliographical references and index.
Identifiers: LCCN 2024045111 (print) | LCCN 2024045112 (ebook) | ISBN 9781496832924 (hardback) | ISBN 9781496852694 (trade paperback) | ISBN 9781496852472 (epub) | ISBN 9781496852465 (epub) | ISBN 9781496852458 (pdf) | ISBN 9781496852441 (pdf)
Subjects: LCSH: Bryant, William B. (William Benson), 1911–2005. | African American judges—Biography. | Criminal defense lawyers—Biography. | African American lawyers—Biography. | Lawyers—United States—Biography.
Classification: LCC KF373.B79 A5 2025 (print) | LCC KF373.B79 (ebook) | DDC 347.73/2234 [B]—dc23/eng/20240925
LC record available at https://lccn.loc.gov/2024045111
LC ebook record available at https://lccn.loc.gov/2024045112

British Library Cataloging-in-Publication Data available

In Memory
of
Stephen J. Pollak (1928–2024)

CONTENTS

ACKNOWLEDGMENTS

Great thanks to Lisa McMurtray, acquisitions editor at the University Press of Mississippi (UPM), for embracing the project, for being so eager to see Judge Bryant's story reach a wider world. I am also grateful to Lisa's former assistant, Michael C. Martella, project editor Laura Strong, and, of course, to the UPM Board of Directors.

There are others at UPM worthy of thanks for their fine work. Thank you, Steven B. Yates, associate director/marketing director; Joey Brown, marketing assistant and exhibits coordinator; Amy Atwood, marketing aide; Courtney McCreary, senior publicity and promotions manager; Kristin Kirkpatrick, electronic and direct-to-consumer sales manager; Todd Lape, former assistant director/production and design manager; design and production manager Pete Halverson, and Lisa Williams, copyeditor.

And thank you, my literary agent, Jennifer Lyons, for all the time and hard work you invested in finding just the right publisher.

Long before that happened, there was the exuberant Linda Ferren, executive director of the Historical Society for the District of Columbia Circuit from 1990 to 2021. It was in Linda that the idea—the dream—of a biography of Judge Bryant was first born.

In making that dream a reality, there was Stephen J. Pollak, the engineer of it all.

Following a referral from one of my fellow authors, Ellen Butts, in early 2016 Steve, a warrior for social justice and at the time president of the Historical Society of the District of Columbia Circuit, contacted me about writing the book, sharing with me highlights from Judge Bryant's life. I was intrigued. After some preliminary research, I very much wanted to tell Judge Bryant's story. I had recognized that there was a quiet but mighty positive power to this man. His overcoming, his courage, his integrity, his humanity, and his absolute commitment to justice put him in the pantheon of great souls who over time have called the nation to be a more perfect union, to be its best self. The more I learned about Judge Bryant, the more I wished that I had met him—or just been in his presence—at least once. And the journey began.

It was a journey indebted to the generosity of twenty of the judge's former law clerks. They responded with gusto to the society's 2017 request for assistance in funding the project. Had time permitted the society to reach out to all the judge's former law clerks, surely more would have contributed to the cause out of respect, reverence, and love for their former boss.

Of course, the journey would never have begun were it not for the society, an organization doing such important, meaningful work. Bless you, and bless all your financial supporters over the years.

During my journey with the life of Judge Bryant, there were setbacks, roadblocks, delays, and a pandemic, and at times I gave Steve Pollak fits with my process. But in the end, he kept the faith.

Steve's passion, his commitment to the project, knew no bounds. I will always remember how much he extended himself during one of my visits to DC to interview people who had known Judge Bryant. It was not enough that Steve arranged and organized the interviews—down to lining up ideal places to meet (and in one case, lunch). On top of all that, he made time to drive me around the city to take in places of significance to Judge Bryant, from Howard University to the stretch of Seventh Street, NW, that was home to young Bryant's first favorite pool hall. Steve also gave me a tour of the E. Barrett Prettyman United States Courthouse that included a visit to Courtroom 16, where Judge Bryant presided for forty years. After that came a stroll around the stunning William B. Bryant US Courthouse Annex.

Most endearing of all, Steve coaxed a doorman into letting us have a quick look around the lobby of 2029 Connecticut Avenue, NW, where college student Bill Bryant had worked as an elevator operator.

It pains me that Stephen J. Pollak did not live to hold a copy of *Soul of the Court* in his hands.

Steve's extraordinary leadership on the project included heading a wonderful committee, men and women who served over the years, at different times and for different periods. Their edits, suggestions, and answers to miscellaneous questions—priceless. Thank you: Michelle Coles, Linda Ferren, Jack Geise, Carrie Johnson, Colbert King, William B. Schultz, Carl Stern, Karen Stevens, Annamarie Steward, and Stuart Taylor.

Committee member William B. Schultz, who clerked for Judge Bryant, was exceptionally hands-on—doing deep reads of chapters, providing rapid, thoughtful responses to questions, offering clarity on matters of the law and significant insights on Judge Bryant. The same was very true of James E. Rocap III, who became president of the society in 2019. Thank you, Bill. Thank you, Jim. It was such an honor and a pleasure to work with the two of you. (And, Bill, the series of interviews you conducted with Judge Bryant on behalf of the Historical Society of the District of Columbia Circuit's Oral History Project were invaluable.)

And thank you, Leith Alvaro, the society's executive director beginning in January 2022, for the vital role you have played in the book's postpublication life.

It was an honor to communicate with people who knew Judge Bryant well. For their time and insights, I am grateful to Linda Ferren, Judge Joyce Hens Green, Judge Henry F. Greene, William R. Hyde Jr., Judge Henry H. Kennedy Jr., Judge Theodore R. Newman, Jacob A. Stein, Senator John W. Warner, and Robert P. Watkins III. On this list, too, is Judge Bryant's dear friend historian Dr. Michael R. Winston. He not only granted me an interview but also took the time to do a careful reading of an early draft of the manuscript, providing truly usable feedback along with historical facts that were news to me.

I also learned a great deal about Judge Bryant's intellect, character, personality, and spirit from others: Thank you, Diane Steed, Judge Bryant's secretary for more than twenty-five years. Thank you, Deborah "Debbie" Jones Taborn, his great-niece. Thank you, Vaughn and Lauren Stebbins, his grandchildren.

Last—and certainly not least—I will be forever grateful to Judge Bryant's daughter and son: Astaire A. "Penny" Bryant and William B. "Chip" Bryant Jr. They generously shared so much information about their dad, their mom, themselves, and other family members. They responded—usually rather quickly—to a multitude of questions. They reviewed chapter after chapter after chapter, advising me of any wrong turns. They trusted me.

I will never forget that bright and shining September day in 2016 day when I was in DC for an event, and Steve Pollak had arranged for a quick meeting in his office. You were both so gracious—and I was so nervous.

Penny, I will also never forget our splendid dinner, in early June 2017, at one of your dad's favorite restaurants, Clyde's Chevy Chase, where we talked ourselves to pieces. A few weeks later, you welcomed me into your home, where you shared family photographs and other memorabilia, and we had a wide-ranging conversation. You then facilitated my interview in your home with the wonderful Diane Steed, your dad's secretary for so many years.

And, Chip, what can I say about your prodigious memory? Your ability to recall events in such detail is truly astonishing. At times I think you wondered if you were giving me too much information. Never. Never. Never. I will never forget the time and attention that you gave to each and every question.

Thank you, Penny.

Thank you, Chip.

Without your steadfast, extraordinary cooperation, this book would not be.

SOUL OF THE COURT

PROLOGUE

"You crazy?"

That was plainspoken, strong-willed sixty-eight-year-old Charlie Wood in the summer of 1933 when his twenty-one-year-old grandson hit him with the news that he was seriously thinking about going to law school instead of playing it safe. Playing it safe is exactly what Charlie had done in DC, securing government jobs, one of which was as a messenger for today's Government Accountability Office.

Grandson Bill had yearned to go to law school before he graduated from Northwest DC's Howard University in the spring of 1932, but he had no money to speak of and no one to finance the venture. Since graduation he had been supporting himself as a laborer, but then, in the summer of 1933, came a shot at a better-paying and relatively safe, secure job.

An aunt was dating a fellow who was tight with the head of the National Alliance of Postal Employees, a Black union, and this boyfriend arranged for Bill to meet with this union official at his office in Northwest DC's U Street District, once the heart and soul of Black DC. Bill showed up at the guy's office on the appointed day, at the appointed hour, but the man wasn't there. After about an hour's wait, Bill left.

Another appointment was arranged. This time Bill was within a few blocks of the place when he muttered to himself, "I'm not going down there. I don't want this job, the hell with it." He made an about-face.

Law school or bust.

You crazy?

Black lawyers in DC—indeed around the nation—were pretty rare, with most barely scraping by. They were largely limited to a Black clientele, and the Black middle class was not all that large. Most Black folks simply could not afford to pay a lawyer much, if anything.

Some lawyers received produce from vegetable gardens in lieu of cash and held down part-time jobs, at the post office, for example. Many Black men would never have been able to embark on a life in the law had they not been married to women with solid jobs, such as schoolteachers.

"Negro lawyers don't amount to a damn," Charlie Wood declared.

Bill dearly loved and respected his grandfather—his "Papa." Nevertheless, the equally strong-willed grandson pushed past Papa's "You crazy?" With raw determination and money saved up from laboring jobs, he entered Howard University School of Law in the fall of 1933.

Bill Bryant's road to a life in the law was not easy. There were disappointments and delays, but there was also his tenacity, his absolute immersion in the law, and his razor-sharp mind that eventually earned him a reputation as one of DC's most outstanding criminal defense attorneys; one who, on April 1, 1957, stood before the US Supreme Court fighting for a client's life.

That client was Andrew Roosevelt Mallory, a young, poor, Black South Carolinian classified as a moron by one psychiatrist. Mallory was languishing in the DC Jail, on death row for the rape of a white woman three years earlier.

When Bill Bryant stood before Chief Justice Earl Warren, Associate Justice Felix Frankfurter, and the other seven justices, he methodically and masterfully fought for Mallory's life on several grounds. Chief among them was the very long delay between his client's arrest and arraignment. During that delay, the police extracted a confession from hapless Andrew Roosevelt Mallory.

With an array of facts at his command, forty-five-year-old Bill Bryant, a low-key, wiry guy, maintained that the police had no excuse for not arraigning Mallory immediately after his arrest in keeping with the federal statute that mandated that arrestees be arraigned "without unnecessary delay."

Mallory's delayed arraignment was not necessary, said Bryant. It was "*chosen*"—chosen so cops could interrogate Mallory long enough to get a confession.

Justice Frankfurter seemed to savor that word "chosen." He soon remarked, "You said that the delay was *chosen*. It was designed—"

"Delay was *chosen*."

"A designed delay."

"That's right, Your Honor."

Two and a half months after Bryant's oral argument, on June 24, 1957, the high court overturned Mallory's conviction in a unanimous decision. A new trial was ordered, one in which Mallory's confession would be inadmissible because it was the fruit of an illegal detention.

Doubting that he could land a conviction without that confession, US Attorney Oliver Gasch had the case dismissed.

At half-past noon on Wednesday, June 26, 1957, twenty-two-year-old Andrew Roosevelt Mallory was released from the DC Jail. "No pictures, no pictures," he pleaded. When a reporter asked what was next for him, Mallory said he planned to "start a new life" in Greenville, South Carolina.

The next day, South Carolina's Senator Strom Thurmond blasted the Mallory decision. This arch-segregationist contended that it would "give greater protection to such heinous criminals as rapists and murderers." He called for legislation "to curb the Supreme Court in its reckless exercise of power."

Months later the Mallory decision was still in the news. Fulton Lewis Jr., a prominent right-wing columnist and radio broadcaster, condemned it as another of the high court's "hooligan decisions."

Though denounced by conservative politicians and many members of law enforcement, the Mallory decision was, without a doubt, a milestone moment with regard to defendants' rights. It was one in a line of cases that culminated in the Miranda Rule, which mandates that if you are arrested, before you can be interrogated you must be told, "You have the right to remain silent. Anything you say can and will be used against you in a court of law. You have the right to an attorney. If you cannot afford an attorney, one will be appointed for you."

The Mallory decision was certainly a milestone moment for Bill Bryant. It thrust into the national spotlight a man from humble origins, born in a place he called "just a wide spot in the road."

Chapter 1

WIDE SPOT IN THE ROAD

Wetumpka, Alabama, was that "wide spot in the road," a town on the banks of the Coosa River and with a name derived from a Creek phrase for "rumbling waters."

Home to a nearly five-mile-wide, roughly eighty-million-year-old impact crater and Alabama's first state prison, nicknamed "the Walls" (completed in 1841),[1] Wetumpka wasn't the luckiest of towns. In 1886 it was hit hard when torrential spring rains slammed Alabama, Georgia, and Tennessee. Cresting over sixty feet, floodwaters destroyed the covered bridge that connected Wetumpka's east and west sides of town. Before that wooden bridge was replaced with an iron one, Wetumpka was rocked by an earthquake. Decades earlier Wetumpka was twice ravaged by fire. Too, the town's pride had been wounded back in the 1840s when politicians decided to move Alabama's capital from Tuscaloosa. Wetumpka lost out to Montgomery, some twenty miles away.

It was about a mile outside Wetumpka that, at about half-past midnight on October 3, 1900, a mob of more than a hundred "determined" white men, with the help of bay dogs, finally caught up with Winfield Townsend. One of those determined white men fired a pistol that brought this young Black man down from atop a small tree. Townsend, only fifteen or sixteen, had allegedly tried to "outrage" a white woman in nearby Eclectic.

Hours after his alleged confession to authorities, the mob said to hell with the legal system and dragged Townsend into a graveyard, where a large oak tree was readied for a hanging. Then came a halt.

1. Its first inmate (1842) was a man sentenced to twenty years for sheltering someone who had escaped slavery. "Alabama Department of Corrections Convict Record from the Walls (Wetumpka Penitentiary), 1888–1896," Alabama Department of Archives and History, https://archives.alabama.gov/research/finding-aids/GRCOR50.pdf.

A discussion ensued on the best way to kill their captive. Finally, a vote was taken.

Burning him at the stake won out over a hanging.

"The stake was prepared and the negro was bound to it with chains," reported the *Augusta Chronicle*. "Pine knots were piled about him and the flames were fired by the husband of the negro's victim. As they leaped to the wretch's flesh his wild cries upon God for mercy and help could be heard for miles. The crowd looked on deaf to his cries and in an hour the negro was reduced to ashes."

Such was the type of brutality legions of Black people throughout the South feared facing in 1900 and in 1911 when William Benson Bryant was born on September 18, joining Wetumpka's population of about a thousand souls.

In all likelihood, the baby boy's young mother, Alberta, small, brown-skinned, and with high cheekbones, gave birth to him in the home of her parents, Lizzie and Charlie Wood. Lizzie was, for a time, a washerwoman for a family. Papa Charlie, a shoemaker by trade, operated a general store.

The baby's father, Benson, who had married Alberta seven months before their child was born, was not in the picture. Right before or shortly after the baby's birth, this short, slender young man with light brown eyes, at one time a porter for Southern Express, left town.

Benson and Alberta's son was about three months old when an incident that changed the trajectory of his life occurred.

One day a bunch of white teenaged boys were hanging out at Papa Charlie's store, and one of them said something vulgar to one of his precious, good-looking teenaged daughters. With a buggy whip in hand, Charlie chased that boy away from his store and down the street. As his grandson later said, Charlie, a small, slight man, had "a lot of temper and he was a little defiant." He was especially insolent toward white folks when "fortified with whiskey."

For the longest time Charlie got away with sounding off to or about white folks because he had a white benefactor: Cap Pennington, a veteran of the Confederate Army and an influential planter. Charlie, born in May 1865, shortly after Robert E. Lee surrendered to Ulysses S. Grant, was known around Wetumpka as "Cap's boy." People didn't mean "boy" in the derogatory sense, but as in "son." Charlie was a child Cap had fathered by a Creek woman, likely a Black one. Cap Pennington's displays of affection for Charlie had included taking his children for buggy rides in the countryside some Sundays and setting him up in that general store, which sold the likes of coffee beans and flour, crockery and buggy whips.

We do not know if Charlie had been drinking when he lashed out at that white boy—probably hurling a few choice words at him—but we do know that there were folks who felt that this time Charlie Wood had gone too far. White men showed up at his house.

One shouted, "Charlie, come on out now. We don't want to hurt the rest of the family. You might as well come on out now."

The brazen Black man responded with one gunshot through his front door and another through his side door. Cussing mad, he soon stepped outside.

"All right, goddamn it, here I am!"

Those white men were gone but not done with Charlie Wood. It wasn't long before a mob formed in that place of rumbling waters. When Charlie got wind of it, he slipped quick into women's clothing and made haste to the L&N Railway depot, where he caught a train up to Birmingham. From there, he headed to Washington, DC. After he got himself settled, Charlie sent for his wife, their daughters and sons, and their eleven-month-old grandson forever abandoned by his own father.

Chapter 2

FEEL YOURSELF GROW

When Charlie Wood's family arrived in the nation's capital in the summer of 1912, the city's colossal white granite Union Station was only four years old. The marvelous marble Columbus Fountain in front of the train station had just recently been unveiled. The only wonders on the National Mall were the Washington Monument, the Smithsonian's red sandstone "Castle," the National Museum (now the Arts and Industries Building), and the two-year-old National Museum of Natural History. With no Lincoln Memorial, no parade of museums, America's Front Yard was just a lot of open space in a city of roughly 330,000 people. About 30 percent of them were Black.

Charlie Wood initially had his family living out on Benning Road, NE. "That area out there was all country," recalled his grandson, remembering horse-drawn ice and produce wagons, kerosene lamps, and outhouses.

The boy—"Willie Benson" to the family—was about five years old when his quiet, retiring, and overprotective mother, then in her mid-twenties, married widower George S. Washington. About twelve years older than Alberta, George had a good job as a porter at Union Station. Not long after they married, the new family moved to 1507 B Street, NE (now Constitution Avenue). They lived among workaday Black folks—dressmakers, servants, unskilled laborers.

Young Bill's stepfather, a nice, kind man, was a devoted reader of the *Star*, DC's leading daily at the time. "My stepfather used to sit down after dinner," Bill recalled, "and open it up and read items out of it out loud." George's stepson vividly remembered him reading reports of lynchings—"that some Negro had been burned to death or hanged." Because most white-on-Black mob murders occurred in the Deep South, the boy developed a mortal fear of the region. Amplifying his fear was the knowledge that his beloved Papa had narrowly escaped a lynch mob down there. Alberta had taken her son to Wetumpka twice by the time he was nine. He had been to the old Wood home, seen those bullet holes for himself.

The kid had cause to fear for his safety right in DC in the summer of 1919 when white men set off a race riot. It happened after a white woman claimed that two Black men had accosted her and tried to steal her umbrella. A suspect was arrested but then released.

On Saturday, July 19, 1919, a hot, sticky night, word of the suspect's release spread in downtown bars packed with white World War I veterans. Especially outraged because the woman's husband was a Navy civilian worker, waves of determined white men, many of them drunk, flooded predominantly Black (and poor) Southwest DC. They took to the streets with guns, pipes, clubs—whatever weapons they could lay their hands on. Black people were shot, kicked, cut, and beaten bloody. And the violence was not limited to Southwest DC. "Before the very gates of the White House," reported the *New York Tribune* on another night of violence, "negroes were dragged from streetcars and beaten up while crowds of soldiers, sailors and marines dashed down Pennsylvania Avenue . . . in pursuit of the fleeing negroes. In one instance a restaurant, crowded with men and women diners, was invaded by a crowd of uniformed soldiers and sailors in search of negro waiters."

This was not all that far from young Bill's home.

The violence lasted for several days, until President Woodrow Wilson dispatched troops, and Mother Nature sent down a heavy rain.

This riot was one of more than twenty that rocked the nation in the summer and fall of 1919. Whatever the initial spark, these riots were rooted in white resentment of post–World War I job competition from Blacks. Many whites were also incensed over the rise in Black assertiveness and unabashed pride. This was evident a few months after Armistice Day in November 1918, when three thousand members of the 369th Infantry Regiment—the Hellfighters—enjoyed a triumphal march from New York City's 23rd Street up to 145th Street and Lenox Avenue in Harlem. This Black regiment had proven itself battle-brave when it fought under French command during the Great

War—as had another Black regiment, the 372nd Infantry Regiment, which included the District of Columbia First Separate Battalion.

Because the worst riots of 1919 erupted during the summer months, the period became known as "Red Summer." The term was coined by civil rights activist James Weldon Johnson, who wrote the lyrics to "Lift Every Voice and Sing," the national Black anthem. The racially tense times had inspired Jamaican-born writer Claude McKay to compose the sonnet "If We Must Die," which ends with this: "Like men we'll face the murderous, cowardly pack, / Pressed to the wall, dying, but fighting back!" Black people did indeed fight back during Red Summer. In DC men armed with shotguns and pistols opened fire on whites from alleyways and rooftops.

We do not know what Bill, going on eight, heard, witnessed, felt during those frightful, bloody days in DC, a city with a long history of white-on-Black oppression, a city where Jim Crow long reigned by law and custom.

The capital had become more segregated several months after Charlie Wood's family arrived. In April 1913 President Woodrow Wilson signed off on the segregation of the federal workforce. This was shortly after he took the oath of office on March 4.[2]

Black people who had supported Wilson's bid for the presidency were livid over his pro–Jim Crow action. One of them was scholar-activist W. E. B. Du Bois, a founder of the NAACP and editor of its magazine, *The Crisis*. On the campaign trail, Wilson had promised Black Americans "not more grudging justice but justice executed with liberality and cordial good feeling."

After Wilson's rank betrayal, Du Bois called out the president in an open letter: "Sir, you have now been President of the United States for six months and what is the result? It is no exaggeration to say that every enemy of the Negro race is greatly encouraged; that every man who dreams of making the Negro race a group of menials and pariahs is alert and hopeful."

Jim Crow reigned in the War Department, the Navy Department, the Treasury Department, the Post Office, and in other government

2. In 1933 Congress moved Inaugural Day to January 20, effective in 1937.

agencies. There were separate-and-unequal restrooms, cafeterias, offices. Where separate offices could not be arranged, screens went up between Black and white workers. Moreover, many Black employees suffered an economic blow. Scores were fired, and many in supervisory positions were demoted.

For young Bill, growing up in DC meant that while he and his mother could sit wherever they wished aboard a trolley car and visit any public library—including the Library of Congress—his mother couldn't take him to any park or swimming pool of her choosing. Alberta couldn't shop in certain downtown department stores, such as the palatial Garfinckel's on the corner of Fourteenth and F Streets, NW, where her sister Emma worked as a seamstress for a time. While Alberta *could* shop down the street at Hecht's, she couldn't try on any clothing she may have wished to purchase. If her stomach growled while downtown, she could not get a bite to eat, not even at a hamburger joint.

But Alberta did not necessarily have to leave the Black community for many of her needs. As elsewhere in the nation, enterprising, determined Black people had turned insult into opportunity. The U Street District teemed with Black-owned businesses, from banks and pharmacies to restaurants. It was also home to DC's first Black-owned department store, Ware's. What's more, Alberta had no reason to bemoan the fact that her son couldn't attend school with white children. Young Bill was not relegated to ramshackle affairs like those legions of Black children attended elsewhere in the South. His schools' facilities were of quality, and many of his teachers were highly educated.

Young Bill was a natural, hungry learner, first at Lovejoy Elementary on Twelfth and D Streets, NE, then, after his family moved into an apartment on U Street, NW, at nearby Garnet.[3] At Garnet he took pride in earning high marks and was often too eager for at least one teacher, Miss Daley. "I would always try to sit up front," Bill said, "but the teacher sometimes would sit me in the back row." When Miss Daley asked a question—"I would start holding my hand up and

3. Lovejoy was named after white abolitionist Elijah Parish Lovejoy, and Garnet after Black abolitionist Henry Highland Garnet.

shaking, and I would end up in the front of the room, trying to get her attention." Not until years later did he understand that Miss Daley had nothing against him but was merely trying to give other students a chance to demonstrate what they knew.

"I loved her like I loved my mother," he declared of Clotill Houston, who taught him history and geography in the fifth grade. He remembered Lovejoy and Garnet as places where "you could feel yourself grow."

Young Bill was never in better spirits than when in school. His love of learning was not the only factor. School was his number-one social outlet. He was an only child, and one without any cousins his age nearby. Moreover, Alberta didn't allow any after-school or weekend ripping and running with other kids in his neighborhood. So the boy made the most of shooting marbles, pitching horseshoes, and taking part in other playground pastimes during recess. While at Garnet he didn't always head straight home after school as ordered but indulged in "a little loitering": playing a little baseball or basketball. Once home, with no telephone, no television, Bill threw himself into his homework. He also became a voracious reader.

It was during these early school days that the boy made a name for himself. His biological father's surname was *Bryan*, not *Bryant*. When someone at school mistakenly listed him on a roster as "William Bryant," he let the error stand, embraced it, "out of resentment toward his father," explained his daughter, "and his wish to be independent of his father and be his own man."

After Garnet, Bill Bryant attended Dunbar High, the nation's first Black public high school. When it opened in the basement of the Fifteenth Street Presbyterian Church in 1870, it did so as the Preparatory High School for Colored Youth. Some twenty years later, when it moved into its own building at 128 M Street, NW, the school was renamed M Street High and became renowned for its rigorous curriculum and its insistence that students not only strive to be credits to the race but also devote themselves to advancing the race. This was still the case in 1916 when the school moved into a brand-new building on First and N Streets, NW. That's when it became Dunbar High.

Named after Paul Laurence Dunbar, the most celebrated Black poet at the turn of the twentieth century, Dunbar High was an imposing red-brick, stone-trimmed Elizabethan-style building with two crenellated towers. The school boasted a 1,500-seat auditorium, a swimming pool, two gyms, a printing plant, and a bank for accounting and bookkeeping classes. On top were a greenhouse and roof garden, and beneath the auditorium was an armory for the Cadet Corps. Shortly after Dunbar opened, *The Crisis* hailed it the "Greatest Negro High School in the World."

Dunbar was not a neighborhood school. It accepted students from all over the District, so Bill mixed and mingled with the sons and daughters of laborers along with those of physicians—and with teens who wanted to be physicians, such as his good friend Burke "Mickey" Syphax, who would become an eminent surgeon. Mickey, whose great-uncle William Syphax founded the school that became Dunbar, was a member of one of DC's most prominent Black families.[4] Mickey lived near Howard University in LeDroit Park, a neighborhood of charming Gothic cottages and gorgeous Victorian mansions.

Eager to get ahead in life, Bill was himself thinking of becoming a physician when he entered Dunbar in 1925. "If a Black doctor got a toehold, he could make some money," he said. Moreover—and perhaps most important for Bill—doctors in private practice represented independence, the kind of independence his Papa Charlie had enjoyed when he was a shoemaker, then a shopkeeper down in Wetumpka. The young man's interest in becoming a doctor may also have been piqued by the fact that one of his mother's sisters, Aunt Josephine, was dating a student at the Howard University College of Medicine, John W. Edwards.

Whatever profession Bill chose, he was rooted and grounded in the axiom that legions of Black men and women instilled in their young people when readying them for reality: "You will have to be twice as good to get half as far." Bill heard this over and over again from family members as well as from his teachers.

At Dunbar, Bill had an array of exceptional teachers, people "who I think would necessarily leave a mark on anybody," he said. One was

4. The Syphaxes had a connection to the nation's first First Family. Charles Syphax (born c. 1790) was enslaved by George Washington Parke Custis, Martha Washington's grandson by her first marriage and President Washington's adopted son. Syphax's wife, Maria, was the daughter of Custis and an enslaved woman.

English teacher Bertha McNeill. In his 2006 autobiography, former Massachusetts attorney general and US senator Edward W. Brooke III, a student at Dunbar in the 1930s, credited McNeill with teaching him how to write effectively and organize his thoughts—"skills that were invaluable in law and politics." Another teacher who left a mark on Bill was English and Latin teacher Eva Beatrice Dykes, an M Street High alumna and one of America's first Black women to earn a PhD (in English philology from Radcliffe in 1921). Bill would also never forget history teacher Neval Hollen Thomas, who had earned a bachelor's degree and a law degree from Howard. Because Thomas had a high, nasally voice, students called him "Cat Thomas."

Along with Thomas's voice, etched in Bill's memory was the man's fervor for social justice. He remembered that Thomas, head of the NAACP's DC branch from 1925 to 1930, talked "incessantly about the evils of segregation and discrimination." Bill needed no convincing. He once declared that as a child he had a "deep hatred" of what he called "the system." He also stated, "from the day I was born I remember resenting the pattern of race relations in the United States." And in his mind the campaign for desegregation did not stem from a desire "to rub elbows with white people" but from a centuries-old desire for equality of opportunity. For justice, plain and simple.

In teaching his students to take pride in themselves, in their history, Thomas's primary text was the four-hundred-plus page *The Negro in Our History*, a staple in Black schools since its publication in 1922. Its author was former M Street High French, Spanish, English, and history teacher Carter G. Woodson, the second Black American to earn a PhD from Harvard (in history in 1912), following Du Bois, who had earned his in 1895.

Along with the rest of Black America, Bill had Dr. Woodson, the "Father of Black History," to thank for Black History Month's precursor, Negro History Week. It was launched in 1926 when Bill was a freshman. The inaugural celebration in DC included a program at Dunbar on February 7. Speakers included Dr. Woodson and Neval Hollen Thomas. Thanks to Dr. Woodson and teachers like Thomas, Bill knew that he was "somebody."

Studious Bill was something of a cutup in high school and "a bit irreverent when it came to old-school uptight authority figures," said his son. He remembered a summer day when he, in his teens, and his father were walking downtown and encountered two elderly ladies, one of whom had taught Bill at Dunbar. After introductions were made, Bill's former teacher turned to him and, said his son, "not with humor but with total disdain declared, 'I must say, I never thought you'd amount to anything!' Without skipping a beat, my dad replied with a smile, 'Well, 'tweren't none of your doing!' He bid them good day and we continued on our way." Though Bill may not have liked all his teachers—and at least one could not stand him—he "loved his overall experience—he loved Dunbar!" said his son.

Being a member of the Cadet Corps was a highlight. In her book *First Class*, a history of Dunbar, Alison Stewart stated, "More than an after-school military training activity or club, the Corps was a life experience, one that fed the Dunbar ecosystem of excellence." That Cadet Corps excellence included suiting up in a uniform properly pressed, putting on black shoes polished to a high shine, donning gloves white as snow, and, most thrilling of all, mastering the precision rifle drills, which "required focus and instant recall," wrote Stewart. "Upon hearing the booming command 'Port Arms!' it was second nature for a cadet to snap his rifle to a diagonal position in one swift movement, using the right hand to carry the firearm across the front of the body, with the butt of the rifle in front of the right hip, the barrel of the weapon perfect[ly] aligned between the neck and left shoulder and the gun held four inches from the body. And this was one of many sequences to remember." Such drills were hardly for the faint-hearted, and Bill was anything but faint-hearted. Focus, instant recall, and precision became hallmarks of his life.

While more than a few Dunbar students were snobs, Bill was not. There was more to his life than Dunbar's "ecosystem of excellence." It probably worried Alberta to no end when her Willie Benson, feeling his oats, started hanging out in barbershops and pool halls on Seventh Street, NW. This was an area that inspired Langston Hughes when he lived in DC in the early 1920s, working an assortment of jobs (including as a busboy and as an assistant to Dr. Woodson) while he labored over his first book of poetry, award-winner *The Weary Blues*.

Looking back on *The Weary Blues*, Hughes reminisced, "I tried to write poems like the songs they sang on Seventh Street—gay songs, because you had to be gay or die; sad songs, because you couldn't help being sad sometimes. But, gay or sad, you kept on living and you kept on going." Those Seventh Street folk who kept on living, kept on going, worked "hard for a living with their hands." They "played the blues, ate watermelon, barbecue and fish sandwiches, shot pool, told tall tales, looked at the dome of the Capitol and laughed out loud." Seventh Street was also a hot spot for numbers runners, bookies, and, with the advent of Prohibition in 1920, bootleggers.

Bill's favorite haunt was a pool hall on Seventh and T Streets, Frank Holliday's place, a joint well remembered by one of DC's most famous native sons, Duke Ellington. Holliday's place was "the highspot of billiard parlors," Ellington wrote in his memoirs. It attracted "the great pool sharks from all over town"—and from out of town, too, for championship matches. After Bill started shooting pool at around age fourteen, he never wanted to stop—and he eventually became a phenomenal player known to win some games playing one-handed.

In hanging out at Seventh Street pool halls and barbershops, no doubt chowing down on his fair share of barbecue and fish sandwiches and shooting the breeze with guys with nicknames like Lefty and Red, Bill certainly became more streetwise. Rubbing elbows with Seventh Street folk, as Hughes and Ellington did, gave Bill an appreciation of everyday people's challenges, their homespun wisdom, and their strategies for survival (legal and illegal). But Bill did not get caught up in the streets. He was seriously focused on making the most of his hungry mind. He wanted nothing more than to continue to feel himself grow.

Having twice taken advantage of summer school, Bill finished high school in three instead of the usual four years. And when this sixteen-year-old graduated from Dunbar in June 1928, he no longer wanted to be a physician. Thanks to two fantastic teachers of history and civics, Frank Perkins and James Saunders, he had developed a serious interest in political science and in the law, both pathways to taking on "the system" and advancing the race.

Chapter 3

SCHOOLBOY

Determined to go to college and itching to get away from home, Bill had toyed with the idea of applying to Lincoln University, near Oxford, Pennsylvania. Another historically Black college or university (HBCU) he considered was Morgan State in Baltimore. He had also thought about applying to one Ivy League school, the University of Pennsylvania. He never considered an HBCU in the Deep South such as Morehouse or Tuskegee. "Going South was a 'no, no' to me."

In the end Bill scrapped the idea of going away to college, because he could save on room and board if he went to school in DC. Because he was Black, Bill had only two options: Miner, a teacher-training school, which two aunts, Josephine and Elizabeth, had attended; and Howard, the nation's leading HBCU.[5] With no interest in becoming a teacher like his aunts, Bill enrolled in Howard, with its magnificent Main Building, a mashup of Gothic and Second Empire architecture perched on a hill 185 feet above the Potomac River and visible from all sections of the city.

When Bill entered Howard in 1928, the Reverend Mordecai Wyatt Johnson, one of the greatest Baptist preachers of the day, was in his second year as the university's first Black president since its founding in 1867. And this rather autocratic man was on a mission to make Howard even greater—the Black Harvard. If anyone could make that vision a reality, it was the very driven Mordecai Johnson.

5. Miner Normal School grew out of a school for Black girls founded in 1851 by white abolitionist Myrtilla Miner. In 1929 the school became the four-year degree-granting Miner Teachers College. In the 1950s it merged with the once all-white Wilson Teachers College, forming the DC Teachers College. In the 1970s this institution became part of the making of the University of the District of Columbia (UDC). Judge Bryant was a member of the board that created UDC. Astaire A. Bryant, email to author, February 14, 2024.

Johnson, whose parents had been born into slavery, had earned two bachelor of arts degrees, one from Atlanta Baptist College (now Morehouse), another from the University of Chicago. After that, he earned a bachelor's of divinity degree from Rochester Theological Seminary, then a master's of sacred theology from Harvard.

In earning his bachelor's degree, Bill was on his own financially. Depending on the course of study and whether one lived on campus, Howard cost roughly $150 to a little over $200 per quarter. Bill was able to keep up with college costs and take care of his personal expenses because, thanks to his friend Ed Simon, within days of graduating from high school, he landed a job as an elevator operator at the swanky Bates Warren Apartment House, today the still swanky low-rise Beaux Arts apartment building known only by its address: 2029 Connecticut Avenue, NW.

When Bill worked at Bates Warren, its tenants included Eleanor Pusey, a Dodge Motor Company heiress. The building was also home to two US Supreme Court justices: George Sutherland and Edward Terry Sanford. Bill remembered the justices stepping out evenings for an after-dinner cigar and stroll. Given his interest in law and political science, did Bill ever converse with these two eminent men?

"No. You didn't talk to anybody," he said.

Even if it were permitted, Bill would not have had many opportunities to chat with tenants. Ed ran the passenger elevator. Bill was posted to the freight elevator; the only time he shuttled tenants up or down the building was when Ed needed a bathroom break or relief for some other reason.

Bill worked seven days a week, from 4 p.m. to 11 p.m. After 8 p.m., he handled the switchboard as well. The pay was sweet: forty-five dollars a month (at a time when he could buy a dozen eggs for about fifty cents). Moreover, the job was not physically taxing. "There was a lot of dead time after the servants went home, unless there was a party or something going on upstairs. After about 8:30 there was hardly anything for me to do running a freight elevator." During that dead time all Bill could do was twiddle his thumbs and think. Studying on the job was not allowed. And Bill was not about to do anything to jeopardize that job, especially not after Wall Street crashed in October 1929. He was two months into his sophomore year.

As the Great Depression set in—as thousands of banks failed, as countless hardware stores, shops, factories, and other businesses shuttered, as joblessness soared, as the ranks of the homeless swelled—Bill not only kept his job at Bates Warren. In the summers he hustled up jobs as a laborer on construction crews. There he earned about three dollars a day. Some coworkers called him "Schoolboy," and some of the construction work he did was at his school. He laid bricks for one of Howard's new buildings.

As required of all male students during their freshman and sophomore years at Howard (and at many other universities), Schoolboy did ROTC. At Howard the only option was Army ROTC. And Bill excelled at it. He made the grade to be a member of the Sabers, "a club open only to men in good standing in the Second Advanced Class of ROTC," his yearbook states. "The ideals of the Sabers are primarily the development of patriotism, good citizenship, and military discipline. The organization stands for leadership, punctuality, truth, and respect for self and others."

Bill would adhere to these ideals beyond his days at Howard, which he remembered as quite a "cosmopolitan place." Students, he said, "came from everywhere in the country, the Virgin Islands and even Africa." And there was "a good contingent of West Indians from all the islands." One international student Bill remembered quite well was the Nigerian Nnamdi Azikiwe, who would play a crucial role in his people's fight for freedom from British rule and serve as the first president of an independent Nigeria (1963–1966).[6]

With so many students from different parts of the nation and the world, Howardites definitely compared notes on race matters, engaging in what folks would later call "rap sessions." "There was a whole lot of that," remembered Bill. "I mean kids from Connecticut, New York, places that weren't segregated completely—you know, theaters and what not and public facilities—they would always talk about the complete separateness [in DC] and points further south, and they resented it. And of course those here resented it."

It is inconceivable that there weren't rap sessions about the legal lynching of nine young Black men, the youngest twelve or thirteen,

6. Nnamdi Azikiwe enrolled in 1927 but transferred to Lincoln University in 1929.

the oldest nineteen, arrested in late March 1931 in Paint Rock, Alabama, charged with raping two young white women aboard a freight train. One of the nine, Olen Montgomery, was nearly blind. Ozie Powell had the IQ of an average eight- or nine-year-old. So did Willie Roberson, who would have found sex an ordeal due to complications related to the venereal diseases from which he suffered. When arrested he was heading to Memphis, Tennessee, for treatment.

Bill was a junior when the trials began in Scottsboro, Alabama, on April 6, 1931. By sundown on April 9, all-white juries had found eight guilty and sentenced them to death. The trial of the youngest defendant, Roy Wright, ended in a hung jury.

Justice-loving Americans cried foul! Constitutional rights had been trampled. For one, the defendants had been denied their Sixth Amendment right to effective counsel. The ordeal of the "Scottsboro Boys" lasted for years, and in the end the world learned that when they were arrested, they had been guilty of nothing other than hopping a ride on a freight train.

Had Bill been raised in his birth state of Alabama, could he have been a Scottsboro Boy? Probably not. But in 1931 he no doubt thanked his Maker that he was raised in Washington, DC, where he had the privilege of attending Howard University.

Along with remembering Howard as a cosmopolitan place, Bill remembered the university as "a mecca for top-flight" Black professors. No surprise there, given that Howard was the premier HBCU and that Black intellectuals who wanted to teach were rarely hired at predominantly white institutions. Of course, for some Black intellectuals, an HBCU was not a school of last resort but a first choice.

When Bill attended Howard, those top-flight minds included Bill's high school teacher Dr. Eva Dykes, who joined Howard's faculty in 1929. Once again Bill thoroughly enjoyed studying English under her, but the person who topped the list for him was the debonair Ralph Bunche, a summa cum laude and Phi Beta Kappa graduate of UCLA, where he majored in international relations. After college, Bunche had gone east, to Harvard, where he earned a master's degree in political science.

Bunche launched Howard's political science department in 1928, the year Bill arrived. While getting his department off the ground, twenty-four-year-old Bunche was working on his PhD in political science from Harvard, which he would achieve in 1934, becoming the first Black person to earn a doctorate in that field from an American university. At Howard the courses Bunche taught included "Popular Government in the US: Its History, Organization, and Practice," "Elements of International Law," "History of Political Theory," "American Political Thought," "Principles of American Diplomacy," and "American Constitutional Law." Bill devoured Bunche's courses, always having "a feeling of growth with him." He declared Ralph Bunche "the greatest thing. That's the memory I have of Howard University. When I think of Howard University, I think of him."

Given Bill's interest in law, one cannot help but wonder if in the winter of 1931, he attended any of the guest lectures by legendary criminal defense attorney Clarence Darrow, best known for the 1925 "Scopes Monkey Trial," in which he represented science teacher John Thomas Scopes, charged with teaching evolution in violation of a Tennessee law. It was in early January 1931 that Darrow delivered a series of morning lectures at Howard's law school. They included "Preparation for Trial," "Examining Witnesses," "The Lawyer and Public Service," and "The Constitution."

"And in college," remembered Bill, "I got involved deeply in constitutional law as a very attractive subject," one that appeals to anyone seeking a firm grasp of the separate powers of the legislative, executive, and judicial branches of government and the rights of "we the people"—along with various ways of interpreting and applying this supreme law of the land.

When he graduated from college in 1932 with a bachelor's degree in political science, having minored in English, Bill longed to attend Howard Law, but there was no financial aid available, and while unlike a multitude of Americans in these deepening days of the Great Depression, Bill may not have been flat broke, he definitely did not have sufficient funds to start law school.

As it happened, the commencement speaker for Howard's class of 1932 was the person presiding over the economic debacle: Herbert Hoover, a man hoping against hope for a second term—and after whom shantytowns were named. When President Hoover addressed some four hundred Howard graduates on Friday, June 10, 1932, he delivered a bland speech that lasted all of three minutes.

"He had nothing to say," remembered Bill.

As for him, on the Monday after graduation he went to work as a laborer. About a year later—

"You crazy?"

Many people would have agreed with Charlie Wood that Bill's determination to go to law school was crazy—and not merely because Black lawyers were rare, and financially successful ones even rarer.[7] Enrolling in law school would have also struck many people as crazy because in 1933 the nation was still in the grips of the Great Depression. True, during his first hundred days, Hoover's successor, Franklin Delano Roosevelt, had managed to get through Congress an unprecedented amount of legislation to alleviate the suffering—and give Americans a "new deal." This legislation included job-creating agencies such as the Civilian Conservation Corps and the Public Works Administration. Still, happy days were a long way off.

But that didn't deter Bill Bryant. Just as his interest in law had only intensified, so had his desire to be independent. "I had worked menial jobs and what not, and I had a strong desire to be independent," he said. "I was tired of being under somebody's thumb." So despite the hard times, the precarious existence of most Black lawyers, and Papa designating him a "prime fool," in the fall of 1933 stubborn Bill Bryant enrolled in Howard University School of Law, where the tuition was $135 a year. Not only did he have savings from a year of doing menial labor, but he also had the benefit of still living with his mother and stepfather, and so he had no rent to pay. (Having moved several times, the family was living in an apartment on Fairmont Street, NW. Bill called his mother "nomadic.")

When Bill entered Howard Law, the person at its helm was Charles Hamilton "Charlie" Houston, whose Aunt Clotill had taught him

---

7. In 1930 DC had a little over 3,300 lawyers. Of that number, ninety-four were Black, and only four of them Black women. Nationwide there were 160,605 lawyers; 1,247 of them were Black. J. Clay Smith Jr. *Emancipation: The Making of the Black Lawyer, 1844–1944* (Philadelphia: University of Pennsylvania Press, 1993), 631–33.

history and geography at Garnet. Thirty-eight-year-old Charlie Houston, a six-foot-tall hulk of man, was the only child of a doting Mary Hamilton Houston, a former teacher and hairdresser, and attorney William LePre Houston, a graduate of Howard Law (1892).

Son Charlie, a graduate of M Street High, attended Amherst, where he graduated magna cum laude and Phi Beta Kappa. Following a stint as a teacher at M Street High and army service during World War I, he headed to Harvard Law. There, he was mentored by future US Supreme Court Associate Justice Felix Frankfurter, specialized in constitutional law, and became the first Black member of the *Harvard Law Review* editorial board. Houston earned his LLB in 1922 and his SJD the following year. He then studied civil law at the University of Madrid for a year on a Sheldon Fellowship. Back in the States, after passing the bar he joined his father's firm, making it Houston and Houston. Charlie Houston also began teaching at Howard Law, then located about a mile from Howard's campus, in a three-story row house at 420 Fifth Street, NW.

In President Mordecai Johnson's mission to make Howard the Black Harvard, he was not about to leave its law school behind. Howard Law had produced many fine lawyers, but it had very low admissions standards. Many students entered with only a high school diploma. Moreover, because the law school was a part-time night school (three evenings a week), it was not accredited. In 1928 Johnson and the board of trustees had decided to make the school a full-time day school and a training ground for first-rate civil rights lawyers. In 1929 the board put Charles Hamilton Houston in charge of this endeavor.

Part steamroller, part bulldozer, Houston raised admissions standards, revamped the curriculum, recruited the brightest minds he could find to join the faculty, and secured funds to bring in guest lecturers (like Clarence Darrow). A Thursday, February 5, 1931, memorandum to the faculty reveals just how demanding Houston could be. "I am planning to make a study of the entire curriculum for the purpose of co-ordinating the subjects and eliminating waste. For example, the matter of Juries could probably be handled in Criminal Procedure, Criminal Law Laboratory, Common Law Pleading and Moot Court." He asked the faculty to submit a list of "the case and text material used during the first semester in each course," a list of "cases assigned and covered during the first semester, grouping them by chapter and section," and a list of "any special mimeographed or review work done." He also requested "an informal short memorandum of your opinion [on] how much work can profitably be covered in the semester, and the best way to cover the same" and any "suggestions for the current semester." Faculty members were to respond no later than Tuesday, February 10. Satisfying Houston's requests probably ruined some weekend plans.

That same year Howard Law was accredited by the American Bar Association and gained membership in the Association of American Law Schools. A building on Howard's campus with a well-equipped law library was on the drawing board.

Charlie Houston had not always planned to become a lawyer. He claimed that his experience in the army drove him to it. "The hate and scorn showered on us Negro officers by our fellow Americans convinced me that there was no sense in my dying for a world ruled by them. I made up my mind that if I got through this war I would study law and use my time fighting for men who could not strike back."

Bill Bryant didn't buy that. He believed that people like Charlie Houston "weren't so outraged at first about the fact that whites discriminated against Blacks." What really rankled them, he believed, was "the fact that whites didn't discriminate enough to draw the line between them and the rest of Blacks." Bill thought the same of W. E. B. Du Bois. "A degree from Harvard entitled the recipient to certain privileges in the society. I assume that he was naive enough to think that he could lay claim to them, and then realized that as the setup was then, after he had counted the last white man on earth, then you might count him. And that was a two-edged blow. I think that was a shock to him." After Du Bois became the first Black person to earn a PhD from Harvard in 1895, his first teaching post was at one of the oldest HBCUs, Wilberforce in Ohio.

Bill believed that Charlie Houston was similarly shocked by his post-Harvard prospects. After graduation, white classmates went off to prominent law firms, but he, said Bill, had "no entree. He came back to his father's law office, which wasn't a teeming law office." In

Bill's mind, Houston and Du Bois became such stalwart race men only after they had an epiphany: "I can't be free until all of us are, because we are looked upon as 'all of us,' and the only way I am going to get out of this box is to get everybody else out of the box with me."

Whatever his initial motivation, Charlie Houston became a brilliant legal tactician and trial lawyer. The first Black US Supreme Court justice, Thurgood Marshall, Houston's principal protégé, called him the "engineer of it all," referring to Houston as the mastermind behind numerous lawsuits (including several US Supreme Court cases) aimed at killing Jim Crow—overturning the infamous 1896 decision in *Plessy v. Ferguson*. In it the US Supreme Court had ruled, 7–1, that Jim Crow laws did not violate the Fourteenth Amendment's equal protection clause under the "separate but equal" doctrine. In *Plessy*, the Court upheld lower court rulings that found segregated railroad cars constitutional. The reasoning of the decision applied to schools and other public facilities when in fact such facilities for Black people were rarely equal to those for white people.

In his zeal to develop masterful attorneys, Houston was tough, for sure. (Students called him "Iron Shoes" and "Cement Pants.") However, Thurgood Marshall also found him to be a "sweet man once you saw what he was up to. He was absolutely fair, and the door to his office was always open." When Bill entered Howard Law, the gangly, gregarious Marshall was a year away from graduating first in his class, after which he went into private practice in Baltimore, his hometown.

Unlike Thurgood Marshall, Bill Bryant did not find Houston sweet. In fact, he crossed swords with him by violating Houston's unwritten rule that students dare not have full-time jobs. "The law is a jealous mistress," Houston cautioned.

Bill had landed a job at Howard as a switchboard operator, working from midnight until 8 a.m. He called that job "manna from heaven." He added, "After one o'clock at night, you could hear a rat walk on cotton. Nothing happened except the watchman would come in about every forty minutes and stay around until he went back out on his watch. No phone or anything." Unlike at Bates Warren, Bill could study on this job that he refused to give up.

"You can't do this and get the law," Houston warned.

Bill stood his ground with this Charlie just as he had with his Papa Charlie. "I told him his job was to put the law in the classroom and my job was to get it and that I wasn't asking any special favors from him or the school." Bill was not only stubborn but also, as he later admitted, "so cocky back then that when I spit, I thought it would bounce!"

For defying Houston, Bill paid a price. Howard Law did not grant scholarships on the basis of need, only on merit. So there were no scholarships for first-year students, but there were scholarships for students who came in first and second in their first year. Having come in first in his class in his first year, Bill eagerly looked forward to a scholarship, but it never materialized. The rules were suddenly changed in his case. He was told that there was no scholarship for him because he had a job and so was not in need.

Like those folks on Seventh Street with their barbecue and the blues, Bill Bryant, spitting-mad, kept on living, kept on going.

Howard Law was small, with a student body of about forty. The caliber of the students trumped high enrollment. Professors "had no hesitancy to fail students who did not perform," Bill recalled.

One of those professors was George E. C. Hayes, who taught courses in criminal law. This M Street High alumnus had earned his bachelor's from Brown University and his law degree from Howard. Hayes, whose practice was located at 613 F Street, NW, next door to the Houstons' firm, was one of DC's handful of successful Black attorneys. Folks around town summed him up, said Bill, as a "hell of a lawyer."

The courses Charlie Houston taught included "Common Law Pleading," "Conflicts of Laws," "Evidence," and "History of Law." Houston was an excellent teacher, and Bill gave credit where credit was due. While Houston "wasn't a magical teacher," he was always "thoroughly prepared." He could "swim through any length of the pool" on any given subject. What's more, said Bill, Houston "seared your soul, put the branding iron on you to have a dedicated, determined faith that the law could solve man's problems." (Houston drilled the mantra "a lawyer's either a social engineer or he's a parasite on society" into the minds of his students.)

Bill also remembered that Houston "was obsessed with the concept of excellence, there was no question about his standards." And there was no curve. "You were marked on the basis of 100 and if you got less than 70 you failed." Some of the highest grades he earned were in Houston's classes.

When Bill started law school, he was in a serious relationship with his first real girlfriend, Astaire Gonzalez. This petite, very pretty, olive-skinned young woman with long black hair was a graduate of Armstrong, DC's vocational high school for Black youth. The two had met in the summer of 1932 in the home of Bill's friend Ed Simon, by then a postal worker. Astaire was a friend of Ed's wife, Lucy, with whom Bill had gone to elementary school.

For Bill and Astaire, born about two weeks apart, it was truly love at first sight. "It was just like we [were] kind of made for each other," said Bill. The two were soon inseparable.

The couple occasionally took in a movie or headed to the Howard Theatre to catch a show headlined by Noble Sissle, Lionel Hampton, Ella Fitzgerald, Lena Horne, or Duke Ellington. Mostly, Bill and Astaire hung out at her home with her family: her father Frederico Lopez de Gonzalez Sr., a native of Spain raised in Cuba and St. Lucia, and at one point a laborer for the Department of the Interior; her Maryland-born Black stepmother, Rebecca, a homemaker; her older sister, Clauzelmin; and her younger brother, Frederico Jr.

After a two-year courtship, and shortly before they turned twenty-three, on August 25, 1934, with Bill banking on that scholarship he would never get, he and Astaire took their fine romance to a higher level, eloping to Baltimore. They figured that if they told their families of their desire to marry, they would have tried to talk them out of it. Bill's family had nothing against Astaire. Hers nothing against him. It was the economy. Conventional wisdom said that it was a mistake to get married during hard times. Indeed, between 1929 and 1933, America's marriage rate fell by a little over 20 percent.

The couple, whose nickname for one another was "Dopey," started married life in a rented room in the Simon home, a townhouse at 1034 Park Road, NW. Without that scholarship Bill and Astaire were still better off financially than many Americans. They had jobs. He recalled that he was earning $90 a month, and she about $120 as a clerk at the Civil Service Commission.

On Friday, June 5, 1936, Howard University conferred 243 degrees during its commencement exercises, four to law school students—with Bill Bryant graduating at the top of his class. It may well have galled Charlie Houston that Bill pulled that off while holding down a full-time job.

Houston was no longer at Howard in 1936. The year before he had signed on as special counsel to the NAACP, headquartered in New York City. He was laying the groundwork for the nation's first civil and human rights law firm, one that would be established under Thurgood Marshall's leadership: the not-for-profit NAACP Legal Defense Fund (LDF).

The commencement speaker for Howard's class of 1936 was George F. Zook, president of the American Council on Education. Bill, however, was not on hand to hear whatever words of wisdom and encouragement Dr. Zook had to offer. Still steamed over that scholarship denial, he boycotted graduation.

"I sat on my front porch."

And his next pursuit was not a life in the law.

Chapter 4

IF I CAN CUT THE MUSTARD

While a few years earlier he had turned his back on the opportunity to land a safe, secure job at the post office and defied his Papa Charlie's take on going to law school, Bill was not a prime fool. Financially conservative by nature, he was not about to pursue a life in the law on a wing and a prayer—especially now that he had more than himself to think about. And he didn't have only Astaire to consider. By the time that he graduated from law school, he and Astaire had adopted their niece, Beatrice.

Beatrice was the daughter of Astaire's older sister, Clauzelmin, who, tragically, died from heart disease at age twenty-five in 1931. At the time Clauzelmin, a housekeeper, and her husband, George Hughes Sr., a government laborer, were raising not only Beatrice (age six) but also their son, seven-year-old George Jr.

According to one of Beatrice's daughters, Howard graduate Deborah "Debbie" Jones Taborn, before Clauzelmin passed, Astaire promised to take care of her children. Explained Taborn, "My mother's father was an alcoholic and unfortunately unable to responsibly take care of the children." Beatrice was ten when her father agreed to let her live with Uncle Bill and Aunt Astaire. George Jr. chose to stay with his father. (Bill and Astaire were no doubt doing all they could for the children long before Beatrice moved in with them.)

Speaking of her mom's days with Bill and Astaire, Debbie Taborn declared, "My mother always considered that the turning point of her life and NEVER forgot it." She added: "I think my mother was most grateful for the stability of their home life. Her comfort was in the fact that they would always be there. Things were consistent. . . . There was always a meal, always a comfortable bed, etc." At one point that comfortable bed in which the very "inward" Beatrice slept was in an apartment in Northeast DC's Suburban Gardens complex. Taborn reckoned that during the nine years that Bill and Astaire raised her mom, Beatrice's biological father provided no emotional, physical, or financial child support whatsoever.

Beatrice would always be an integral part of the Bryant family. Always a daughter to Bill and Astaire, she would be "Sistah" to their children and "Sister" to many of the couple's friends. Bill and Astaire raised this Dunbar High graduate until she married at age nineteen in 1944.

By then, with Astaire still working for the Civil Service Commission, Bill Bryant had held down an assortment of jobs. They included working as a laborer, a clerk, and a teacher for the Works Progress Administration, one of President Roosevelt's New Deal agencies. According to one source, Bill even worked on a bookbinding project at Cedar Hill in Anacostia, Frederick Douglass's final home.

Starting in late 1939, for almost a year, Bryant was Ralph Bunche's research assistant on an in-depth study of the Black experience in America, material that would flow into the 1944 two-volume, nearly 1,500-page groundbreaking study of US race relations, *An American Dilemma: The Negro Problem and Modern Democracy* by Swedish economist and sociologist Gunnar Myrdal. The book laid bare the howling contradiction between the nation's image of itself as the world's bastion of democracy and its treatment of its Black citizens. Myrdal's book was not welcomed in some quarters, especially given its release when the nation was in the midst of World War II, fighting for democracy.

Bryant's primary assignment was to research Black resistance, from uprisings led by Nat Turner and other enslaved people to protest groups such as the Urban League, the NAACP, and DC's New Negro Alliance, which waged campaigns against stores in Black neighborhoods that refused to hire Black people. Bryant also sorted through and organized interviews with Black southerners and reports on their lives mailed in by Bunche's field assistants. One was George C. Stoney, a white graduate of the University of North Carolina, Chapel Hill, who would become a legendary documentary filmmaker and the father of public access television. Another was Black communist (and Howard graduate) James E. Jackson, a leader of the Southern Negro Youth Congress, a forerunner of the Student Nonviolent Coordinating Committee (SNCC).

Ralph Bunche himself did fieldwork in the South. But not Bryant.

"I told him, 'Pops, I'm not going down there.'" Bryant still had an intense fear of the Deep South.

While working on the Gunnar Myrdal project, Bryant's admiration for Bunche only grew. In addition to his towering intellect there was Bunche's elegant temperament. In the face of racial insult, Bunche, said Bryant, "seemed to rise above everything"—something he mastered as well, never letting bitterness soil his soul.

After Bill's job with Bunche ended, for about a year he worked for another New Deal agency, the National Youth Administration, as a chauffeur/messenger/clerk, then for about three months as a junior social science analyst for the Department of Agriculture. In June 1942, thanks to Bunche, Bryant landed a job as an assistant analyst with the Office of War Information (OWI), a division of the Office for Emergency Management. The OWI was the government's propaganda agency formed six months after Pearl Harbor and the US entry into World War II. Bryant worked in the OWI's Bureau of Intelligence under Philleo Nash.

Bryant's work for the OWI included attending meetings and conventions of Black protest organizations and reporting on what they were up to. He wasn't a spy. "It wasn't an FBI sort of thing," he explained. The OWI simply "wanted to know what these people's concerns were, to what extent they were organized, and what their plans were." At one point Bryant was attached to the Army's division of information, for which he did research on race relations. It was work that sometimes called for him to go south. And he went, feeling safe because he was traveling with military personnel. Once he arrived at a military installation, Bryant never set foot outside it. Lynchings, especially of Black men, were still commonplace in the Deep South.

In January 1943 Bryant entered the army as a first lieutenant. Initially attached to the army's education branch, he worked mostly with the orientation branch, pushing the "Why We Fight" propaganda to Black troops in camps around the nation, including in the Deep South, and once again he never set foot outside of an army base. He recalled that "as a member of the armed forces I felt some security." (White mobs and lone-wolf racists were known to menace, attack, and even kill Black men in uniform.)

As for the Why-We-Fight propaganda, it "got to be a hard sell from time to time," he said. It was difficult to elicit great patriotic stirrings in the hearts and minds of men limited to doing all the "dirty work" while enduring other humiliations wrought by Jim Crow. At a post in Atterbury, Indiana, Bryant witnessed Italian prisoners of war having access to a "huge" PX, one that was "well stocked with anything you want," but it was off-limits to Black soldiers. The post commander was a short, slight, young white man who, said Bryant, "carried a swagger stick and smoked a cigarette all the time. I think he thought he was MacArthur."

The rank inequality angered Bryant, but it also gave him, he said, "a whole lot of respect for Black people as a group, because the restraint that they obviously displayed in these places was just phenomenal." Bryant often spoke out about the inequities Black soldiers endured. He stressed to the powers that be that if post commanders wanted to really get Black soldiers on board with the Why-We-Fight propaganda, they "ought to make things equal." When one of his superiors asked him what he meant, Bryant gave the following example: "If on a post a white soldier can go into a post exchange and go into a cafeteria and make a choice of three entrees on the menu and choose one of them, I think that Blacks ought to be able to do the same thing somewhere on that post."

When this bigwig uttered some claptrap "about the numbers and the economics of it," Bryant replied, "I don't care if they only have one soldier there, if he was a Black soldier, and he goes into the cafeteria, he ought to be able to choose from three meals; he can't eat all three of them, but he ought to have the same choice the other guy has." This lawyer-in-waiting was learning and testing and using his skills of advocacy.

On May 5, 1947, thirty-five-year-old William B. Bryant was honorably discharged with the rank of lieutenant colonel.

He soon landed another job as a researcher. This time on a project that hit close to home: a study of Jim Crow in the nation's capital, directed by Joseph Lohman, a University of Chicago sociologist. Lohman was secretary of the National Committee on Segregation in the Nation's Capital, of which Charlie Houston was a member.

The scathing ninety-one-page report, *Segregation in the Nation's Capital*, declared Jim Crow in DC "a blot on our Nation." The report detailed the gross inequities segregation spawned. It found, for example, that 30 percent of Black homes compared to 3 percent of white homes lacked central heating and that 23 percent of Black homes compared to 5 percent of white homes lacked flush toilets. Public schools for Black youth were too few (which meant overcrowding) and the facilities were subpar. The report also explored the legacy of Woodrow Wilson's segregation of the federal workforce. Black people were relegated almost exclusively to jobs as laborers, janitors, and elevator operators.

By the time *Segregation in the Nation's Capital* was released in late 1948, Bill Bryant was ready to pursue a life in the law, spurred on, no doubt, by injustices in the army he witnessed and injustices in DC he researched.

Bryant recalled that before he entered the army, DC had perhaps two bar review courses, but for whites only. "Of course, they would sell Black people their notes, the written material, but you couldn't attend the bar review course sessions." After the war a man named Carlton Edwards created a bar review course that did not draw the color line. Bryant enrolled in it on the GI Bill.

While studying for the bar, Bryant was required to have some kind of internship. "When I went down to the GI Bill people, they told me I was eligible for one year of this refresher stuff, and I think they paid you $90 a month, $90 or $92 a month, during that period of time. But they required me to have some sort of structure to my education. You didn't have to go to a school especially, but you had to have some sort of instructional atmosphere. You could intern in an office or anything that would be legitimate for structuring your time, spending some uniform hours on the business."

"Go to a law office, intern in a law office, and we will pay you, and you can study," he was told. "And I said, 'Gee whiz, I'm going to do that.'"

Aware that Houston and Houston had an excellent law library and no doubt thinking that bygones were bygones, Bill went over to their office at 615 F Street, NW, one day and spoke to Charlie Houston about an internship. Houston told him that he would let him know in a couple of days. When Bryant returned—no dice. He learned this from fellow Dunbar High and Howard Law graduate Joseph Cornelius Waddy—"Joe" to Bill—who had joined the Houston firm in the late 1930s. Joe told Bill that Charlie said "that it wouldn't work out."

Bryant shared his deep disappointment with Alfred Scott, a buddy from law school who was clerking for his uncle, Armond Scott, the third Black judge to serve on DC's Municipal Court (appointed by President Roosevelt in 1935). Alfred Scott came to Bryant's rescue by introducing him to attorney Wesley S. Williams, who had not been in practice all that long. Williams welcomed Bryant into his one-man firm in a two-room office at 506 Fifth Street, NW, across the street from the Municipal Court.

Bryant's workspace consisted of a desk and a chair. Unlike the Houstons, Williams didn't have much of a law library. But at the end of the day, an internship with Williams was a whole lot better than no internship at all. Moreover, Williams was more than willing to take Bryant over to the courthouse so that he could get the lay of the land.

That internship with Williams was a blessing as was that bar review course, but the very best day of Bill's post-army life was the day that Astaire told him that she was pregnant.

Bill and Astaire had been married for fourteen years and had long been trying to have a baby. Now that Astaire had conceived, Bill pleaded with his wife to quit her job and focus on the pregnancy. Ninety-eight-pound Astaire was in good health, but Bill did not want to take any chances. Winter was coming and the couple didn't own a car. Bill could not bear the thought of his pregnant wife standing at a bus stop en route to and from work when cold weather hit. Moreover, both were still somewhat haunted by the death of Astaire's sister.

Having raised Beatrice, when Astaire became pregnant she and Bill were not only eager, but also well equipped to raise their own biological child. It just so happened that this child was born while Bill was taking the bar exam. It was held June 16–18, 1948; the baby was born on June 17. (Quite a testament to Bill Bryant's ability to focus).

Bill was not present for the baby's birth, but on that blessed day, during the bar exam lunch break, he hurried to Freedmen's Hospital (now Howard University Hospital) to check on his beloved, finding her in labor. Astaire assured her husband that she was absolutely fine and ordered him to get back to his exam.

The baby was a girl. She was named after her mom and nicknamed Penny because she was copper-colored when she emerged from the womb.

Two months after Penny was born, Bill and Astaire were in the kitchen of their cozy Suburban Gardens apartment just about to bathe their baby in a large pan when the telephone rang. It was Judge Armond Scott's secretary calling to congratulate Bill. She had seen his name among a newspaper's list of people who had passed the bar.

"I almost dropped Penny on the floor," remembered Bill.

Having passed the bar twelve years after graduating from law school, Bill Bryant hung out his shingle at Wesley Williams's office rent-free and with Williams schooling him on how to hustle up some work at the Municipal Court.

"In those days," recalled Bryant, up front in the courtroom where arraignments were held, "there were three rows of seats . . . on the right-hand side and lawyers would sit there. As the people would come up charged with crimes, the court would appoint lawyers to represent these people." Legendary trial lawyer Jacob A. "Jake" Stein called these lawyers, of which he was one, the "Fifth Street Irregulars."

Initially, Bryant did not sit up front with the Fifth Street Irregulars. Instead, he sat in the middle, or even in the back, of the courtroom and watched.

"Get any cases, get any cases?" Williams asked day after day.

Years later, Bryant claimed that he was "too shy" to sit up front with the Fifth Street Irregulars. "I just couldn't do that."

Daughter Penny found this hard to believe. She reckoned that it was not shyness that held her father back. More than likely "he was taking his time to assess the situation, the 'players,' and the dynamics, and then deciding how he would conduct himself in the mix. More times than not, if asked a question, or in serious conversation, my father would hesitate a lot longer than most people to respond. You could almost see his mind working. When he did respond, he was right on the money, to the heart of the matter with little or no further explanation necessary." Penny added: "I don't know if he was ever known to display a timid demeanor. Quiet and reflective, yes. But you could bet that during those moments he was sizing up you or the situation before deciding how to respond. It was just like playing pool, you look at the 'lay of the land' on the pool table, size up all the different angles, then you take your shot."

Even after Bill Bryant began sitting up front with the Fifth Street Irregulars, he still hesitated to truly take his shot. According to a *Howard Law Journal* article, he later spoke "of declining the first court-appointed cases he was offered, from a sense of unreadiness, and of sitting through scores of cases until he felt adequately prepared to serve" clients, so many of whom had such "fear in their eyes." When Bryant did take his shot, his court-appointed cases ranged from assault and theft to traffic violations.

According to Jake Stein, the Fifth Street Irregulars assigned to cases (or not) were usually done by early afternoon. "The rest of the day" was "given over to card games or an occasional trip to the racetrack." Bryant spent his afternoons "reading law in a friend's office." When "a distraction was needed," he headed to "a poolroom up the street."

While Bryant was gaining experience, he wasn't earning much money. Getting paid for his services was "catch-as-catch-can." Sometimes a numbers runner or a person with a traffic violation—one who had a job—paid him ten or more bucks. From most clients, all he probably received was something like, "Thanks, man." It simply was not in Bryant's nature to browbeat people for fees.[8]

Fee or no fee, Bryant did his level best—and kept many clients out of jail. "The pay was unimportant," explained Stein. "What was important was the hope that we could demonstrate some ability in the courtroom, win a few cases, and wait for established lawyers and bail bondsmen to refer paying cases to us."

As a Fifth Street Irregular, Bryant became utterly fascinated with the law—got "sucked into" it. He especially loved the preparation and the research. "You could feel yourself grow when you got in the books." The long hours he put in never bothered him, "because I learned so much." Bryant was so consumed by the law that pastimes

8. Indigent criminal defendants weren't entitled to public defenders at the government's expense until 1963.

such as shooting pool and playing poker, "all of that kind of went by the board," for a time.

"Bill quickly became a winner," remembered Stein. "In those days the art of cross-examination was a thinking-on-your-feet, spontaneous art. There were few documents and no discovery." Along with a keen intellect, Bryant had excellent instincts. "Bill sensed when a witness was not telling the truth," said Stein. "He exposed the lie and then stopped when he made his point."

Some successes were the result of simple legwork, as happened in the case of Hilda Stroup's $225 fur coat. Shortly before Christmas 1949, this white woman's fur coat was stolen from a church's cloak room. The accused was a Black laborer in his early twenties. Charges were dropped because Bryant proved that his client was in Gallinger Hospital when the theft occurred.

Bryant simply used common sense and the letter of the law to find justice for Julius Hopkins and Jozell Moon. In October 1950 these two Black men were passengers in a speeding car that struck and killed a city worker. An off-duty police officer who happened to be on the scene immediately arrested the driver, Hilliard Johnson, while Hopkins and Moon fled.

Picked up the next day, the two were charged with compounding a felony per a statute that had not been used in fifteen years. Bryant pointed out that the charge applied only to instances where someone "failed to notify officers of the court or of the law of a felony in cases where said officers are not cognizant of how the felony happened." How could that possibly apply to his clients? That off-duty cop's immediate arrest of the driver made officials fully aware of how the felony happened. The charges against Bryant's clients were dismissed.

Prosecutors, including ones who lost to Bryant, truly came to respect and admire him. One day Assistant US Attorney (AUSA) Robert Scott (a future DC Superior Court judge) urged him to switch sides. "You really ought to apply" for an AUSA position, said Scott. "You're a great lawyer. We all like you. We'd love to have you."

For as long as Bryant could remember, there had always been only one Black person in the US Attorney's Office: "One man who would take oaths on warrants and never go to court. He didn't perform as a lawyer. He was more a warrant clerk." Still, Bryant was intrigued by the prospect of becoming an AUSA. He could build on his skills, become more expert in the law. And a steady paycheck wouldn't hurt. Astaire had never returned to the workforce, and by then the couple had another child. William Benson Bryant Jr., nicknamed Chip, had been born on December 9, 1949.

Bryant knew that if hired as an AUSA, he would start in the Municipal Court, but he did not want to remain there. When he met with US Attorney George Morris Fay, he asked point-blank, "If I can cut the mustard can I go to the big court?" The "big court" was the US District Court for the District of Columbia (hereafter, "the District Court"), then housed in City Hall. No Black prosecutor had ever tried a single case in this federal court.

"Yeah, you can do it," Fay replied. But first things first. Before Fay could hire him as an AUSA, Bryant had to get "political clearance," said Fay.

Bryant had absolutely no idea what Fay was talking about.

Back at 506 Fifth Street, Bryant telephoned his former OWI colleague and good friend Philleo Nash, President Truman's special assistant on minority affairs since 1946. Thanks to Nash, Bryant soon had a meeting with Chicago congressman William Levi Dawson, one of the most powerful Black politicians of the day and one of only two Black members of Congress.[9] On the appointed day, it was a few minutes before 1 p.m. when Bryant arrived at the congressman's fifth-floor office in the Longworth House Office Building. After he introduced himself to Dawson's secretary, Christine Davis, she called out, "Congressman, Mr. Bryant is here."

"I am standing out there," Bill recalled, "and Bill Dawson is at his desk, and apparently, she didn't get any response. I didn't hear anything. She said again, 'Congressman, Mr. Bryant is here.'"

Bryant stepped toward Dawson's door.

"Oh yeah, yeah, Philleo said you are all right, so okay." Dawson never even looked up.

Two weeks later, Bryant got a call.

"How soon can you go to work?"

---

9. The other Black member of Congress was New York City firebrand Adam Clayton Powell Jr.

It was George Morris Fay.

"Yesterday," replied Bryant.

The Baltimore *Afro-American* (the *Afro*) reported that "at least 11 local lawyers" had applied for the position.

Bill Bryant was sworn in as an AUSA on February 12, 1951. "Mr. Bryant's appointment brings the number of assistant United States attorneys to 38," reported the *Evening Star*.

Chapter 5

REPRESENTING THE GOVERNMENT, YOUR HONOR

A late December 1951 *Washington Post* piece on AUSAs at DC's Municipal Court began with this: "A pathetic little woman sat at a table near the 'front counter' of the United States Attorney's office and wrote out an assault complaint against her husband."

The woman's face "was a mass of bruises and her eyes were red from weeping. On her arm was an infant screaming away. The story she wrote down about a night of terror at the hands of her husband is an old one to the prosecutors in Municipal Court." The *Post* reporter stated that "until they reach the 'front counter,' many of the prosecutors have known only the law book side of the courts. Now, they must deal with human nature."

Of course, this did not apply to Bill Bryant. He had several years of lawyering under his belt. He also had the advantage of being both book-smart and streetwise.

By the time that *Post* piece appeared, Bryant was head of the Municipal Court division of the US Attorney's Office. Two months earlier the prior division head, J. Warren Wilson, handed him his keys after returning from his favorite lunch spot, Squire's Grill, one of the many restaurants in downtown DC that still refused to serve Black people. "It's all yours," said Wilson when he handed Bryant his keys. Wilson was taking a job in the Justice Department's tax division.

There were twelve AUSAs assigned to the Municipal Court, ten of them white. Bill Bryant's skill, his judgment, his character—his very being—convinced the powers that be that he deserved to head the division. In taking those keys from J. Warren Wilson, Bryant was blazing a trail for other Black lawyers. But this was probably not uppermost on his mind. As he readily told a reporter years later, "I was scared to death."

The cases Bryant personally handled included one in which a Mr. Jansson, a small man, claimed that a Mr. Beck, a former homicide squad detective—and a much larger man—had punched him in the face and broken his glasses during an argument following a fender bender. Mr. Beck claimed that Jansson had emerged from his car "flailing" and that he had merely given the man a shove.

Mr. Jansson was apparently not suffering serious bodily harm. In deciding not to pursue charges in the case, Bryant lamented that "otherwise sensible, congenial people get behind a steering wheel and become near-beasts." He also offered Mr. Jansson some advice. "He told Mr. Jansson he nearly committed suicide in arguing with a man as big as Mr. Beck," reported the *Evening Star*.

In the spring of 1952, Bryant recommended that charges be dropped against a woman who had been picked up in a raid on a numbers joint because she had been in the business for only a month, had left it behind, and was gainfully employed at a hospital as a laundry worker.

In the way he handled case after case and in the way he comported himself in the office and in a courtroom, Bill Bryant was developing a solid reputation, gaining the respect of his peers and the judges. He definitely cut the mustard, and then some! In September 1952, about a year and a half after he became an AUSA, he got his wish: He was transferred to the "big court," assigned to its grand jury section.

The person who transferred Bryant to practice before the US District Court for the District of Columbia wasn't George Morris Fay but Charles Irelan, whom President Truman had appointed to replace Fay after he decided to return to private practice. Irelan was formerly the principal trial attorney in the Justice Department's Lands Division, then a legal advisor to Truman. A colleague remembered Irelan as someone who "felt that the legal profession was of the highest calling and took pains to assure everyone with whom he worked and came in contact that the dignity of the Court was above reproach, and that at all costs, that solemn dignity must be preserved." A man after Bill Bryant's own heart.

Shortly after his promotion, Bryant did something he had never done before. He took his family on vacation, going to Detroit to visit with Aunt Josephine and her boyfriend-turned-husband, the Howard Med graduate John W. Edwards. He was operating his own medical clinic out on Eight Mile Road, the dividing line between the predominantly Black inner city and the predominantly white suburbs.

A few days into that vacation, Bryant received an urgent telephone call from his boss. Irelan wanted him back in DC pronto so that he could transfer him from the grand jury section to the trial section. "He wanted to do it quickly," Bryant explained, "because he didn't know how long he would be in office."

In the 1952 presidential election, General Dwight D. Eisenhower, Republican, defeated Democrat Adlai Stevenson in a landslide, and Irelan's days were, indeed, numbered. Several weeks after Eisenhower took the oath of office, he replaced Irelan with Leo Rover, who had served as DC's US Attorney from 1929 to 1933. Bryant remembered this Republican as "a little, short man with a foghorn voice" who was "a hell of a lawyer."

Immediately after he became US Attorney for the second time, Rover fired AUSAs who were Democrats. Bryant, a Democrat, believed that was probably the first time in his life that his race was an asset. It wouldn't look good to fire him and not replace him with another Black person. And Rover, said Bryant, "had not associated himself with any Black lawyers who you would think about putting in the US Attorney's Office. He didn't know any." Bryant later learned that Rover "went around to a few Republican judges, and people he knew in the courthouse, inquiring about me. Apparently he got some good vibes about me."

By then the District Court was in a new granite modernist building at Third Street and Constitution Avenue, NW. There the District Court's first Black prosecutor tried cases before legendary white judges. One was John Sirica, whom Bryant remembered as "straightforward, fair, and courteous"—and who would become a household name in 1973 when he presided over the Watergate trials that dealt with the 1972 break-in at the Democratic National Committee headquarters in the Watergate Office Building on behalf of President Richard Nixon's reelection campaign.

When prosecuting two men for robbery, Bryant had a rather amusing and revealing memory of Judge Thomas J. Bailey—"Old Bailey." After the elderly Tennessean took his seat on the bench and the clerk called the case, Bryant declared himself "Ready for the Government," and the defense attorneys declared themselves, "Ready for the defense." Only then did Old Bailey, who had apparently been distracted, look up. When his eyes landed on Bryant, he snapped, "What are you doing here?"

"Representing the government, Your Honor," Bryant respectfully replied, rising above the insult. He let it slide because, he said, "I guess I was much more mature in this business of race relations than the average person." He understood that a Black prosecutor was a foreign concept for the judge, a man born in 1867. "So I didn't react to this old man in a bitter fashion. He didn't know any better."

After Bryant succeeded in getting convictions, the judge sent him a note. "Tried like a seasoned lawyer." That was Bryant's one-and-only—and never-to-be-forgotten—appearance before Old Bailey.

On one occasion, Bryant had four cases, back-to-back, before Alexander Holtzoff, one of the most brilliant legal minds of the day—and a man who did not suffer fools gladly. "The court appreciates the manner in which you handle your business," Judge Holtzoff told Bryant. This was high praise.

One of the secrets of Bryant's success was his efficiency. "I didn't waste any time with a case," he recalled. "I knew I had a case, and I knew what the elements were. I knew what horses I had to pull the wagon. I knew what witnesses would do it."

Bryant rarely challenged jurors during voir dire. He believed that challenging just to challenge was a waste of everybody's time. "The government is satisfied, [Your Honor,] any twelve," he often said. As he saw it, trying to predict what jurors would do once they were actually on a case was like "trying to tell the price of pork chops in the marketplace by looking at the hog's feet on the farm."

Bryant had tremendous faith in the jury system. "I think when you get twelve people in a jury box that you have got a whole lot of human experience that the average judge doesn't have." He knew judges who could not imagine that a police officer would lie on the witness stand, who could not fathom why anyone would not believe a cop, whereas many jurors were not so naive. "They have been around, and they have seen what happens in the streets and some of them have been exposed to some things, you know, that are not too pleasant." In contrast, a lot of judges had been "raised like chickens on wire . . . their feet have never hit the ground, they haven't had any real experience in adversity."

According to Richard Kirkland "Kirk" Bowden, a distinguished Black Metropolitan Police officer who became a distinguished deputy US marshal, there was more to the way Bryant handled voir dire than his belief that it made no sense to try to predict what a juror would do. "Body language from a trial attorney is in some cases more important than verbal language," said Bowden. "When Bill Bryant was the prosecutor, sitting at the table nearest the jury box, he never would look up at the jury. They would put twelve people in the jury box. The court would say, 'Mr. Bryant.' He would be busy writing, taking notes, scribbling something on a pad. The court would oftentimes have to call him twice. 'Mr. Bryant.' 'Yes, Your Honor?' 'You have any strikes?' 'No, Your Honor, the Government's satisfied.' And this would go on throughout the selection. . . . And what this told the jury is, 'I don't care who you put in the jury box, my case is strong enough for a conviction. I don't have to pick over whether you look like you like me or you don't like me.' He had done his voir dire."

Bowden remembered that if Bryant caught a witness "in what he called an untruth, he would feed him enough concrete around his feet until he would sink himself." This ace prosecutor also had a way of turning his back on a witness, signaling to the jury, said Bowden, "I don't believe a word and you shouldn't believe a word this person is saying."

As a young man, the distinguished, long-serving Senator John W. Warner of Virginia was also captivated by AUSA Bill Bryant. Warner first met him in 1953 when, straight out of the University of Virginia School of Law, he clerked for Judge E. Barrett Prettyman on the US Court of Appeals for the DC Circuit. Warner remembered that he and other law clerks "were anxious to learn all aspects of the law that wasn't in the books" and "gravitated to" certain AUSAs. Bill was "a magnet."

Bryant's workload was intense. He remembered trying cases "every day, every day, every day." He estimated that during any given month there were only three days when he was not in trial. It was tremendous experience, sharpening his skills, keeping him on his toes.

While trying cases every day, every day, every day, Bryant definitely had to be twice as good, for he was working at a distinct disadvantage. He did not have free and easy access to the magnificent library in the federal court building, a library with all manner of reference material from books containing court opinions and treatises on fields of law to law journals commenting on case decisions and encyclopedias such as *American Jurisprudence* and *Corpus Juris Secundum*. This library belonged to the Bar Association of the District of Columbia (BADC). This voluntary association, founded in 1871, began admitting white women attorneys in 1941 but would not admit Black attorneys until 1959.

As Howard Law professor J. Clay Smith Jr. explained, BADC's library in the courthouse—for which the organization paid no rent—"provided white lawyers with a convenience that gave them a significant edge in trying cases. During court recesses, or at critical moments during a trial, white lawyers could run to the library in the courthouse to find precedents to support a point of law; black lawyers could not"—that is, unless they paid an annual fee of eight dollars. (At the time BADC's annual membership was twelve dollars.) Bryant refused to pay a fee as a matter of principle and availed himself of a workaround: Warren T. Juggins, a Black librarian, let him slip into the library after closing time.

In his quest to be a first-rate prosecutor, Bryant, already possessed of an intact moral compass, took as his guiding light words of US Supreme Court Associate Justice George Sutherland, whom Bill the elevator operator had occasionally observed enjoying an after-dinner cigar and stroll. Justice Sutherland had written the opinion in *Berger v. United States* (1935), in which the high court ordered a new trial for Harry Berger, a Brooklyn man who had been sentenced to a prison term of a year and a day for counterfeiting. The Court threw out Berger's conviction because during the trial AUSA Henry Singer had engaged in misconduct. This included carrying out a character assassination when he cross-examined Berger.

"The United States Attorney," stated Justice Sutherland, "is the representative not of an ordinary party to a controversy, but of a sovereignty whose obligation to govern impartially is as compelling as its obligation to govern at all, and whose interest, therefore, in a criminal prosecution is not that it shall win a case, but that justice shall be done. As such, he is in a peculiar and very definite sense the servant of the law, the two-fold aim of which is that guilt shall not escape or innocence suffer." Sutherland applauded a vigorous prosecution but condemned dirty tactics. While a prosecutor was free to "strike hard blows, he is not at liberty to strike foul ones."

By all accounts, AUSA Bill Bryant struck no foul blows. Whether prosecuting a case of police brutality or of influence peddling, his commitment to seeing "that justice shall be done" was evidenced in the case of Donald Morey, charged with starting a fire in the warehouse where he worked, a fire that caused more than $60,000 worth of damage. At one point during the trial, Bryant told Judge James R. Kirkland that he had doubts about the defendant's mental competency. The judge declared a mistrial and ordered Morey to be given a psychological evaluation. Initially, Morey was found to be of unsound mind, but later to be competent to stand trial. He was convicted of arson and sentenced to sixteen months to five years in prison.

Bryant could be as tough as he could be tender, and in one case he realized at the eleventh hour that he had been too tough. He was prosecuting a man charged with raping a fifteen-year-old girl. Usually, Bryant did not get emotionally involved when trying a case, "but what this guy did to this little girl kind of got to me. I didn't like it. I thought it was the kind of thing that he should be put to death for." At the time, a person convicted in DC of rape or first-degree murder could be sentenced to the electric chair.

"I went to trial, and I put it to the jury that it would be a good idea to make it safer for society to get rid of him." Bryant had no doubt whatsoever of the man's guilt. The evidence was overwhelming.

After closing arguments, Bryant was in good spirits—"feeling pretty good about my case." He continued to feel good about it down in his office where he awaited the jury's verdict. But then, when a marshal informed him that the jury had reached a verdict—

"I broke out in a sweat. I got so scared. I got scared to death. I realized what might happen and I lost my nerve." It suddenly dawned on him that he had issues with the death penalty. "I just didn't want to be the catalyst in any situation where somebody was killed." All in knots, Bryant asked AUSA Vic Caputy to take the verdict. After Caputy went upstairs, Bryant followed. He did not step foot inside the courtroom; he only peered in. "I saw the jury come back in and the foreman stand up. And I saw the clerk read, and I couldn't hear anything, but I saw the jury foreman move his mouth once and he said guilty and nothing else."

No death penalty.

"I don't ever remember being so relieved in all of my life."

"I don't like sending anybody to jail," said Bryant in an article that appeared in a January 1954 issue of the *Afro*. That said, he added that he had a particular disdain for "narcotics violators and sex offenders. They are the kind of individuals I try extra hard to convict."

At the time of the interview, Bryant was presenting a grand jury with the case of two suspended Metropolitan Police officers: Lieutenant H. H. Carper, former chief of the narcotics squad, and Sergeant William Taylor, his second-in-command. They were charged with taking several thousand dollars in protection money from drug kingpin James "Jim Yellow" Roberts, and other drug dealers.

"Mr. Bryant," said the *Afro*, "is the kind of prosecuting attorney one reads about or sees in the movies—a fiery tireless person who won't rest until a criminal has been convicted."

Bryant told the paper that he had no patience with people who blamed their criminal actions on booze. "Most drunkenness is voluntary. It is hard to feel sympathetic toward a criminal who comes before me on a 'cheap' murder charge after he has gotten drunk and slapped or beaten his wife, or anybody for that matter, to death." He added that when "drunkenness is being used as a defense, I generally consider the whiskey or wine which they say they were drinking as an aggravation rather than a mitigation of the offense."

Bryant's boss, Leo Rover, told the *Afro* that he regarded Bryant "as a highly competent prosecutor." Rover found him "at all times most loyal," and he had his "complete respect and confidence, also that of every judge before whom he has appeared. I am sure everyone with whom he works shares the same feeling."

At the end of the article, the *Afro* told its readers that Bryant did not like radio or television and spent his free time "reading news magazines or detective stories, and doing chores about his home." That home was a two-story, three-bedroom detached brick Cape Cod at what was then 1903 Kenilworth Avenue in Beaver Heights, a small community in Prince George's County, Maryland. Penny and Chip enjoyed a large backyard with a huge oak tree and delighted in living just down the road from a farm.

Trying cases every day, every day, every day and all the preparation that entailed—from interviewing witnesses to research and writing briefs—did not leave Bryant with a whole lot of time to spend with his family, but his love was never lacking—and he devised ways to make that apparent. Typically, he went home about 5 p.m. to have dinner with his family and to put Penny and Chip to bed, a ritual that included prayer. Bryant then headed back to the office, returning home around 10 p.m. On Sundays, he often cooked breakfast for Astaire and the kids and stayed home all day.

Bryant was in his third year as an AUSA when Joe Waddy approached him about joining the Houstons' firm. Charlie had died of a heart attack back in 1950 at age fifty-four. His father passed in the fall of 1953 at age eighty-three.

When Waddy reached out to Bryant, the Houstons' firm was a two-man firm. Waddy's partner was Springfield, Ohio, native William Courtleigh Gardner, a graduate of Howard and Harvard Law. Gardner—"Bill" to Bryant—who worked nights at the post office, had joined the firm after old man Houston passed.

When Bill Bryant first met Bill Gardner, he "instinctively" liked him. Gardner, he said, possessed "the best legal mind" he had ever encountered. Another admirer of Gardner called him "judicious, sound, common-sensical, and warm." He was someone who brought to all of his dealings "a delightful sense of humor and a very human touch."

Bryant also really liked Joe Waddy, a remarkable practitioner of labor law. Bryant could see himself working very well with both men. And there was the added draw of the firm's fantastic library with up-to-date copies of vital reference books such as *American Jurisprudence*, *Federal Reporter*, and the *United States Supreme Court Reports, Lawyers' Edition*.

No doubt about it, given Bryant's history with Charlie Houston, joining the firm would be something of a coup.

When Bill told Astaire about the offer, she was not thrilled. "Well, you have got a job," she said.

"Well, you know those jobs are not really secure," he responded. "You get fired in those jobs."

If Bryant joined Waddy and Gardner, he would definitely be taking a gamble. After old man Houston died, many clients left the firm. Still, Bryant could not resist, not even when he told Rover about the offer and, much to his surprise, learned that he was in line for a pay raise.

His last day as an AUSA was on February 26, 1954. Just like all those years ago when he could have played it safe and become a postal worker, Bill Bryant, ever craving independence, took a risk. With Astaire's support, he left a job that paid a little under four thousand dollars a year (about $45,000 in today's dollars) and returned to catch-as-catch-can.

Chapter 6

RAW JUSTICE

Bryant returned to private practice a few months before May 17, 1954, the day the US Supreme Court handed down its unanimous decisions in five school desegregation cases, cases for which Charlie Houston had laid the groundwork in the 1930s and 1940s. The lead case was *Brown v. Board of Education of Topeka*, which Thurgood Marshall, still director of the NAACP LDF, argued.

Like the Brown case, the other four desegregation cases had been separately filed against school boards in Delaware, South Carolina, Virginia, and in Bryant's DC. In the cases challenging the states' segregated school systems, the Court found that segregated schools violated the Fourteenth Amendment's promise of equal protection of the laws. In Washington, DC, it violated the Fifth Amendment's "due process of law." When the cases came before the Supreme Court, the four state court cases were consolidated under one name: *Brown v. Board of Education*. The fifth case, challenging school segregation in DC, carried a separate name, *Bolling v. Sharpe*.

Chief Justice Earl Warren delivered the opinion. "Today, education is perhaps the most important function of state and local governments. Compulsory school attendance laws and the great expenditures for education both demonstrate our recognition of the importance of education to our democratic society. It is required in the performance of our most basic public responsibilities, even service in the armed forces. It is the very foundation of good citizenship." Education, Warren declared, "is a right which must be made available to all on equal terms." In public schools "the doctrine of 'separate but equal' has no place. Separate educational facilities are inherently unequal."

Bill Bryant remembered that there was "a lot of rejoicing" in his F Street office when the decision was handed down. "We had the feeling that, well, the walls are crumbling now." He also remembered his former law professor George E. C. Hayes saying, "Well, I can finally get my breath a little bit." With Howard Law professor Dr. James M. Nabrit Jr., Hayes had argued *Bolling v. Sharpe*. And his firm, Cobb, Howard, Hayes, and Windsor, was still at 613 F Street, NW, next door to Houston, Waddy, Bryant, and Gardner.

Although the NAACP LDF's victory certainly did not result in an immediate end to segregation in public schools, it was nevertheless a watershed moment. It sent a signal that Jim Crow had no place in other public spaces. It spurred civil rights activists to step up the crusade—in the courts and in the streets—for an end to Jim Crow in housing, transportation, restaurants, hotels. Everywhere. Fisk University's president, Charles Johnson, said this: "If segregation is unconstitutional in educational institutions, it is no less so unconstitutional in other aspects of our national life."

Jim Crow's grip on Bill Bryant's DC had already begun to loosen.

In 1948, when the Department of the Interior was the only integrated government agency, President Truman issued an executive order aimed at ending job discrimination in the federal workforce and ending segregation in government buildings where it still existed.

In 1953, in *DC v. John R. Thompson Co., Inc.*, the high court ruled that Jim Crow in DC eateries had to go, finding that two "lost laws" from 1872 and 1873 were still valid: They banned discrimination against people in a range of places of public accommodation, from restaurants and hotels to barbershops—so long as those people were "well-behaved."[10] These civil rights laws had never been repealed.

The decision in *DC v. John R. Thompson Co., Inc.* was the culmination of a three-year campaign led by the eminent feminist and civil rights leader Mary Church Terrell, an octogenarian who, along with some other Black warriors for justice, had been refused service—just

10. Pauli Murray discovered the "lost laws." This poet, author, civil rights activist, women's rights activist, and first Black female Episcopal priest made the discovery in 1944 while a student at Howard Law, researching DC Reconstruction laws. After earning an LLB from Howard, Murray earned an LLM from UC Berkeley School of Law and a JSD from Yale (a first for a Black person).

as they expected—at Thompson's Restaurant, a cafeteria on Fourteenth Street, NW.[11]

The case against Thompson's had the backing of President Eisenhower. Shortly after his inauguration, in his February 2, 1953, State of Union address, the president announced, "I propose to use whatever authority exists in the office of the President to end segregation in the District of Columbia, including the Federal Government, and any segregation in the Armed Forces."[12]

As for DC's places of public accommodations other than restaurants, historian David A. Nichols stated that Eisenhower "enlisted Hollywood moguls to pressure movie theaters to desegregate, and he and the first lady refused to attend segregated activities in the city. By the end of his first year, segregation of public facilities had virtually ended."

Ever since Black people were trafficked to the United States and forced into slavery, they have fought for fair treatment and civil rights, but in the 1950s the nation's civil rights record came under increasing scrutiny and assault from without—especially from the Soviet Union. Jim Crow in the nation's capital was particularly embarrassing and made things more than a little awkward for nonwhite foreign dignitaries visiting the city.

Meanwhile, business at Houston, Waddy, Bryant and Gardner was not bustling. The firm did mostly probate work and handled cases involving negligence, traffic accidents, and product liability. There were weeks when, after paying their secretary, the partners had about $150 to split three ways. "We had some lean days, really lean days," said Bryant.

While money was tight, Bryant's family never went without the basics. One of the many things Bill and Astaire had in common was

---

11. Mary Church Terrell was the widow of Robert H. Terrell, a cum laude graduate of Harvard (1884), who earned an LLB, then an LLM from Howard. He was DC's second Black justice of the peace (1901–1910) and the first Black judge on its Municipal Court (1910–1925). When Bill Bryant was a boy, he was very much aware of Judge Terrell.

12. In 1948 President Truman issued Executive Order 9981 banning segregation in the US military, but there had been much foot-dragging. Not on Eisenhower's watch. By the end of 1954, segregated units were a thing of the past.

frugality. Bill was content to have just a couple of suits at one time—suits of quality, however. (Hickey Freeman became one of his favorite brands.) What's more, during his long life, he owned only a few cars.

Astaire, a wizard at the sewing machine, made most of her and Penny's clothing, along with home furnishings, from slip covers to draperies. Astaire was a bargain hunter and haggler extraordinaire. As the family's money manager, she was adept at robbing Peter to pay Paul. Over the years, Bill had nothing but absolute trust in her handling of their finances.

Running her house like clockwork, Astaire's pleasure was to make home an oasis. Thanks to her green thumb, the family enjoyed beautiful house plants and backyard flower beds. And because Astaire was a pet person since childhood, there was a variety of pets over the years—dogs, tropical fish, a frog, a turtle, hamsters, and the parakeets, Petey (pale yellow) and Pop (blue and green). But no cats! Astaire and Chip were allergic.

Bill Gardner said that he was "convinced, early on," that Astaire and Bill's "companionship with her were the chief sources of his good spirits and sparkle."

The couple lived a low-key life. They did not crave to be out and about on the town a lot. Every now and then they went to a dance at Murray's Casino or at the Masonic Temple, both on U Street, NW. By and large, casual affairs such as card parties with friends were sufficient for them. "They didn't seem to make a big deal about their birthdays or anniversary," remembered Penny, though "cards and gifts were always exchanged."

In training up their children in the way that they should go, Astaire and Bill often used proverbs. "Love many and trust few, but always paddle your own canoe," was one of Astaire's favorites. Another was "Neither a borrower nor a lender be."

"Some folks grow up, while others just grow," Bill often said after witnessing (or hearing about) some adult behaving immaturely.

More by example than word, the couple taught their children not to be swayed by crowds and fads and not to be snobs. They instilled in Penny and Chip the reality that they were no better than anybody else and that nobody was better than them. Chip remembered that his dad taught him and Penny "to deal with people as individuals, and he practiced what he preached. He always sought to look past people's differences to find common ground because he truly believed that given the same set of circumstances, folks were folks, pretty much the same. So he taught us by example to assume everyone was innocent until proven guilty and to treat everyone with dignity and respect."

Penny recalled that she and Chip were not allowed to use the word "hate." She never heard her parents use putdowns such as "stupid," "dumb," or "lazy." They hardly ever cursed in front of the children. If Astaire said, "Damn," they knew that she was "spitting mad." If Bill was frustrated, annoyed, or angry with, say, a slow driver up ahead of him on a road, his term for that person was "Maryland Farmer." Said Penny: "It took me years to realize the initials were MF. I was grown."

Astaire and Bill never told Penny and Chip about any negative experiences in their pasts. Bill, for example, never spoke about Red Summer. Not until Penny and Chip were grown did they learn that their great-grandfather had barely escaped a lynch mob in Wetumpka. When Penny and Chip were growing up, Bill and Astaire focused on whatever was positive in the present. "As a young boy," said Chip, "whenever I expressed any serious concerns about life in general or our family in particular, my father always reassured me that he was on it and not to worry. He'd tell me time and again, 'Don't worry 'bout the mule (him), just drive the wagon' (live your life)."

One major aspect of life where Bill and Astaire did not see eye-to-eye was religion. Although Bill was deeply spiritual, a man who prayed regularly, he had no truck with organized religion. Astaire, however, was a practicing Catholic, and, said Chip, "she wanted us to be spiritually grounded in some form of religion." And so, he and Penny were raised Catholic. They not only attended a Catholic church but also went to Catholic schools for most of their youth, Penny starting in the fifth grade, Chip in the fourth grade. This was all done, said Chip, "with our father's blessing."

At Houston, Waddy, Bryant and Gardner, Saturday morning was usually the partners' "sitting-down day," remembered Bryant. "We [read] the slip opinions coming in from [federal courts of appeals], and the Supreme Court, and from the District of Columbia Municipal

Court of Appeals." He gained invaluable insights into the mindsets of various judges.

If the partners had no pressing work, after they read the slip opinions, they went out to lunch. After that Bryant often went over to Seventh Street to shoot a little pool before heading home. By then his favorite pool hall was Stage Door on Seventh and T Streets, NW, a place that doubled as something of a second office; he often met with clients there. For many of these clients, Bryant was a court-appointed attorney. He recalled that "every Monday morning there would be a letter in the mail appointing me to represent somebody who had been arraigned in the US District Court on a previous Friday."

At trial simplicity was Bryant's M.O. He refrained from raising objection, after objection, after objection. He observed that so often objections were frivolous and a waste of time. He also knew that a barrage of objections could easily make jurors suspicious. He came to this realization while sitting in George E. C. Hayes' office waiting to meet with him. A woman who was on jury duty came into the office to chat with Hayes' secretary. At one point the woman complained about the defense attorney in the case she was hearing. "He didn't want us to hear anything," Bryant recalled the woman saying. "He didn't want us to find out nothing, every time all he would say was 'object, object;' he said 'objection' all day long." After hearing that, Bryant made up his mind to keep his objections to a minimum "unless I had a record to protect, unless I was getting hurt very badly and had some reason."

Bryant also did not believe in excessive witness prep. When a witness testified, he wanted the real deal, not a performance. As for cross-examining witnesses, he maintained that often the best cross was, "Your Honor, no questions," although he was brilliant at cross-examination when necessary.

More so than Joe Waddy, Bill Gardner was Bryant's sounding board. Gardner was a fount of wisdom and common sense. "He had an extraordinary sense of the relevant," said Bryant. "With any problem he would get to the core of it and isolate the real issue right quick."

Bryant was a truly "gifted advocate," declared Bill Gardner. "How he could seduce and beguile a jury with an electrifying argument or dazzling phrase. There was none better. But yet he had the understanding to know that there was a greater aim of the advocate, greater than just seducing a jury. He knew that at the end of the road there was the doing of justice."

Bryant had his quirks. During trials he had a habit of fiddling with paper clips, breaking them up while he listened and observed. And he was famous for sitting at the defense table with a blank yellow pad before him. He hardly ever took notes. ("I can't listen and write at the same time," he said.) He often had total recall of a witness's testimony.

As business picked up and Bryant had more paying clients, he worked very long hours, sometimes until after midnight—at times only after he had been home to have dinner with his family. One of Bryant's paying clients was John "Lefty" Winston, with whom he had gone to grade school. Winston was a major player in the numbers game, which Bryant regarded as nothing more than "a poor man's stock market."

Along with seven other men in the same business, Winston faced a series of charges related to bribing—to the tune of a thousand dollars a week—a police captain and a sergeant to look the other way when it came to their enterprise. Lefty Winston's codefendants included a white guy, whose street name was "White Smittey." The other codefendants included Charles "Geechie" Anderson, Curtis "Bozo" Taylor, and Roger "Whitetop" Simkins. Their trial started in the spring of 1955, in the courtroom of Burnita Shelton Matthews, the first woman to serve as a federal trial judge. She had been on the bench since 1949.

Bryant's defense was entrapment by the police. He got across to the jury that his client had been repeatedly approached about paying a bribe, that Winston was basically harassed into doing so. He also got before the jury the fact that Metropolitan Police Department's gambling squad had repeatedly tried and failed to get a gambling charge on Winston to stick. As Bryant later put it, the gambling squad "decided to make another kind of criminal out of him. They decided to make a real criminal out of him. They decided to make him a briber, a man who corrupts the institution."

Bryant was honest with the jury. "I'm levelin' with you," he said in his closing argument. "We're not saying our clients are as pure as the driven snow." According to the *Evening Star*, Bryant was "peering intently at each juror in turn."

"Anyone with any common sense at all can see that they're not," Bryant continued. "We're not asking for justice all dressed up in a mink coat. All we want is raw justice." At the end of this twenty-two-day, high-profile trial, Lefty Winston was the only man acquitted. When Bryant left the courtroom that day, he recalled, "My feet didn't hit the ground." It was one of his favorite cases.

Ironically, Winston's codefendants all had high-priced lawyers. Whitetop Simkins had two, one of whom was George E. C. Hayes. They each charged Simkins $7,500, according to Bryant. In contrast, he charged Winston $2,500. Surely, Winston could have afforded to pay more, and surely had Bryant charged him more, Winston would have paid it.

Several days after the trial, a guy from the high-end menswear store Lewis & Thomas Saltz delivered a package to Bryant's home. Inside was a suit that cost, Bryant reckoned, three or maybe four hundred dollars—definitely a lot of money for a suit in 1955. "It was a beautiful suit, Oxford gray, exquisite tailoring," he remembered. And he knew that it was a gift from Lefty.

Bryant's absolute favorite case was that of Matthew Harrison, a Black US Park Police officer charged with two counts of first-degree murder. The victims were his wife of sixteen years, Lenore (Lenora in some sources), and her boyfriend, Billy Johnson.

Bryant learned about the case from another Black attorney, Barrington D. Parker Sr.[13] Matthew Harrison had reached out to Parker because Parker's father had once handled a legal matter for him. Parker, who did not take criminal cases, in turn reached out to Bryant.

"I'm in my office one day and Barrington Parker called me up and asked me if I could come up to his office." When Bryant arrived at Parker's office, he was introduced to a high-ranking white US Park Police officer. Along with others on the force, this officer thought very highly of Matthew Harrison and, said Bryant, they "were anxious to

13. In 1969 President Nixon nominated Parker to a seat on the District Court. Parker was best known for presiding over the 1982 trial of President Ronald Reagan's would-be assassin, John Hinckley Jr. Parker's son Barrington D. Parker Jr. became a judge on the US District Court for the Southern District of New York, then on the US Court of Appeals for the Second Circuit.

have him defended and defended well." He was more than eager to do precisely that after learning of Harrison's heartbreaking story in Barrington Parker's office.

On May 21, 1955, Matthew came home from work around midnight to find his place in disarray and filthy and his six children alone. The oldest was fifteen; the youngest, six.

Around 4 a.m., he left his home on Fifth Street, NE, and went looking for his wife, a part-time cab driver. As required when off-duty, he carried his service revolver. Bryant recalled being told that Matthew knew about his wife's hangout: "a little card-playing joint in a little street off of North Capitol Street. So he went out and got in his car and drove up to this place and knocked on the door." When he asked for his wife, he was told that she wasn't there, but he knew better. He had seen her cab parked nearby. So he waited outside the joint, and, sure enough, Lenore soon emerged with boyfriend Billy. After they got into her cab and started off, Matthew drove up beside them. He urged his wife to pull over, but she gave him the brush-off. He pleaded with her again to pull over.

Billy told Lenore to tell her husband to go eff himself.

Bryant was told that the next thing Matthew knew, he was in his mother's house "with his head in her lap and she's asking him, 'What happened, what happened, what happened?' And he couldn't tell her. He was just out of his damn mind."

Matthew had managed to stop his wife's car, then jumped out of his and started firing. One bullet penetrated Lenore's left breast. Another pierced her left arm. The bullets passed through her body and struck her boyfriend in the arm and in the chest. When Billy jumped out of the car to flee, Matthew shot him in the back. Twice. Billy died in the hospital. Lenore had been pronounced dead on the scene.

At his mother's house, Matthew eventually came to his senses. He called the police and turned himself in.

After Bryant agreed to take the case, there was a very awkward moment in Barrington Parker's office. That high-ranking Park policeman asked him if he thought he should have an additional lawyer on the case.

"And I knew what he meant, but I acted like I didn't quite understand him."

Finally that officer came out with it: "Do you think you ought to have a white lawyer in the case too?"

Bryant kept his cool. "Well, who do you have in mind?"

The lawyer the officer wanted to bring in was, said Bryant, "a charlatan and a fraud." He agreed to have a white lawyer on the case but told the officer, "I will choose him." His choice was fifty-something T. Emmett McKenzie, a graduate of Georgetown Law.

When Bryant telephoned him—"Emmett, do you want to try a murder case with me?"—McKenzie was baffled.

"What are you talking about?"

"Do you want to try a murder case with me?"

"You don't need no help trying a murder case," responded McKenzie, who in the end agreed to serve as co-counsel.

Their defense was temporary insanity in a trial that began in late October 1955. The presiding judge was Richmond B. Keech, whom Bryant viewed as a "good judge." The prosecutor was Arthur McLaughlin, with whom Bryant had worked when he was an AUSA. McLaughlin, described by one reporter as a "diminutive but fiery attorney" and someone Bryant regarded as "an ace prosecutor," was out to convince the jury that Matthew Harrison had committed cold-blooded murder, that his wife and her boyfriend had been "shot down in the street like dogs."

One of McLaughlin's witnesses, psychiatrist William C. Cusher, who examined Harrison a few days after the murders, testified that he believed the man was perfectly sane at the time of the shootings. Defense witness Dr. Amino Perretti, a psychiatrist at General Hospital, disagreed. He testified that after meeting with Harrison several times and speaking with family members, he concluded that Harrison was not in his right mind when he committed the crimes. Under cross-examination, Dr. Perretti was asked if he judged Harrison to be of sound mind when he examined him. Yes, the doctor did. Another defense witness was Park Police chief Harold Stewart. He testified to Harrison's exemplary record and excellent character.

Defying conventional wisdom that a defendant should not testify, Bryant put his client on the stand. Matthew Harrison testified to his wife's habitual neglect of their children. He also testified that he had repeatedly asked Billy Johnson to stay away from his wife and had repeatedly pleaded with his wife to break it off with Billy.

Bryant also put Harrison's oldest child, Barbara Jean, on the stand. She testified that because of her mother's absences she had often stayed home from school to care for her siblings. Also, that she had done most of the cooking for the family.

On the afternoon of October 21, the case was in the hands of the jury. The possible verdicts: guilty of first-degree murder, guilty of second-degree murder, not guilty by reason of insanity, and simply not guilty.

During deliberations, the jury had a question for Judge Keech.

What would happen to someone found not guilty by reason of insanity?

Judge Keech replied, "That's none of your business."

"Your Honor," said Bryant, "you have got to tell them."

He had in mind a recent Court of Appeals opinion in *Durham v. United States* that gave rise to the rule that juries *had* to be told that if they found someone not guilty by reason of insanity, that person would be committed to a mental institution until deemed no longer insane and of no danger to themselves or others. Bryant had read about this during one of those sitting-down Saturdays at his law firm.

Judge Keech was not aware of the *Durham* opinion.

"I didn't want to tell Keech that he didn't know what the hell he was doing." Bryant persisted as politely as he could, "Your Honor, I know as a matter of fact that I am right."

Judge Keech recessed the trial for the dinner break shortly before 6 p.m. During that time he did his research. When jurors returned to his courtroom, the judge told them what would happen to Harrison if found not guilty by reason of insanity.

Back to the jury room they went. About fifteen minutes later, they were ready to render a verdict.

Count one: Not guilty.

Count two: Not guilty.

The *Washington Post* reported, "Harrison sagged as the jury returned the verdict to Judge Richmond B. Keech. 'Thank you, thank you very much,' he said, his voice charged with emotion." His parents "sobbed when the verdict was announced."

Bryant recalled that "a couple of the [jurors] broke out and cried. That's the most dramatic moment I have ever had in the courtroom. That was really full of pathos, and just drama. Not guilty, not guilty."

As far as Bryant knew, Harrison never got into a lick of trouble after his acquittal.

Harrison's acquittal came three months after Bill Bryant met with defeat—at least initially—in what was undoubtedly his most noteworthy case: the defense of Andrew Roosevelt Mallory.

Chapter 7

NO COOPERATION

Andrew Roosevelt Mallory was nineteen when he arrived in DC from Greenville, South Carolina, in late winter 1954. He apparently had few possessions, little money, and no job prospects.

He did, however, have a place to stay. He could bunk with his half-brother Luther Mallory Sr., the janitor of an apartment building at 1223 Twelfth Street, NW. Luther lived in the building's basement apartment with his wife, Metzie (or Meltzie), two grown sons, Luther Jr. and Milton, and teenage son, James.

It was in the basement of 1223 Twelfth Street, on the evening of April 7, 1954, that a white tenant was raped: thirty-eight-year-old Stella O'Keane, a department store clerk.

Around 2:30 p.m. the following day, Andrew Mallory was arrested on Owens Place, NE, and hauled to police headquarters. There he encountered Luther Sr., Luther Jr., and Milton. Luther Sr. was not a suspect, but, along with Andrew, those two sons were, and the police asked these three young men if they would take a lie detector test. This was a little after 4 p.m. They agreed, but then came a wait because the officer who administered polygraphs was not at the police station. After he arrived at about 6 p.m., he administered the test to Andrew's nephews first.

Andrew was taken into the polygraph room around 8 p.m., and by about 9:30 p.m., he had allegedly confessed to several officers. After the police telephoned the home of US Commissioner Cyril S. Lawrence and learned that he was not available to arraign him, the confession was reduced to writing.

Andrew Mallory was arraigned the next morning, then hustled off to the DC Jail.

From December 9, 1954, to March 2, 1955, Mallory was held at Saint Elizabeths for a psychological evaluation. When he was returned to the DC Jail, he had been found fit to stand trial.

The presiding judge would be the diminutive Alexander Holtzoff, once described as having "the demeanor of a happy leprechaun, the firm, disciplinarian authority of a Victorian school-master—and a mind like a steel trap." This very tough judge who had appointed Bryant to represent Mallory—and who had given Bryant high praise when he was a prosecutor—was, Bryant remembered, very much a prosecution-oriented judge—"notoriously one-sided." (Bryant also recalled that Holtzoff tapped his foot when excited.)

The prosecutor would be Bryant's former colleague Arthur McLaughlin.

Bryant's defense would be not guilty by reason of insanity. And defending Mallory was difficult. He did not like Bryant, did not trust him, hardly spoke to him at all.

Mallory's trial began more than a year after the assault, on Tuesday, June 21, 1955. All we know about the jury is that it was composed of Blacks and whites and had six women and six men. (The two alternate jurors were both men.)

Following McLaughlin's long, winding opening statement in which he outlined all that he would prove, Bryant reserved his opening statement, and McLaughlin soon called his first witness, Stella O'Keane.

She testified that on the evening of April 7, 1954, at about 5:50 p.m. she and her husband left their second-floor apartment for the basement, with her husband carrying the basket of laundry for her. After he pulled their washing machine out of the locker, he headed back to their apartment, and she knocked on the janitor's door seeking help with a washing machine hose.

When McLaughlin asked if she could identify the person who helped her, Stella O'Keane pointed to Andrew Mallory. When McLaughlin asked where the defendant went after helping her, O'Keane replied that he returned to the janitor's apartment.

After O'Keane got her first load of laundry going, she went into the "drying room," where she began to remove another tenant's laundry from the clothesline. When she happened to "glance around," she saw a Black man with a handkerchief over his face. She screamed and the man told her "in a very quiet voice to be quiet, two times."

McLaughlin: And then what happened?

O'Keane: Then he run over to me and he choked me. The next thing I knew I was picking myself off the floor, and then he got ahold of me and started to drag me toward the furnace room.

Once there, her attacker pulled off her shorts and her panties.

McLaughlin: At that time, can you tell us whether or not he had sexual relations with you?

O'Keane: Pardon?

McLaughlin: Can you tell us whether or not he had sexual relations with you?

O'Keane: Yes, he did.

McLaughlin: In other words, he penetrated you? You felt his privates in your private parts?

O'Keane: Yes, sir, I did.

When the ordeal was over, Stella O'Keane put on her husband's bathrobe, ran upstairs to her apartment, told her husband that she had been raped, then ran down to the first-floor apartment of Mrs. Poropat.

O'Keane could not describe her attacker. All she remembered was the handkerchief over his face, that his eyes were "very, very, very bright," and that he wore something "like a high slouch hat."

When McLaughlin showed O'Keane a pair of navy blue shorts, a pair of panties, and a pink blouse, she identified them as clothing she had on when attacked.

McLaughlin soon asked a question clearly intended to convey to the jury that her attacker had to have come from the janitor's apartment.

McLaughlin: While you were in the basement, in the position you were prior to the time you were grabbed, were you in a position to hear anyone who might come down those stairs [that led to the basement].

O'Keane: Yes, sir, because you would have to hear anybody coming down those steps because it was a very heavy door, and the steps were wooden, and they made quite a lot of noise as people walked down them.

When asked if she had heard anyone come down this wooden staircase, the witness replied, "No, sir."

Throughout the trial, Bryant frequently chose not to cross-examine witnesses. When he did, his cross was often brief. That was the case with Stella O'Keane. He was not only brief but also gentle and respectful.

When Andrew Mallory helped her with the hose, had she noticed "anything distinctive" about him?

She hadn't.

Could she say that the person who helped her with the hose was the same person who assaulted her?

She couldn't.

In redirect, McLaughlin asked if Mallory "fit the same general description" of her attacker.

He did.

In recross Bryant asked, "Mrs. O'Keane, when you say the same general description, can you be a little more specific? Was it in the matter of clothing or general build, or what was it?"

"He was tall. The height."

Next, the jury heard from several people who corroborated much of Stella O'Keane's testimony. The victim's husband, William, for example, testified that when his wife returned to the apartment, she shouted, "Call a doctor. I have been raped," and that he followed her down to Mrs. Poropat's apartment, where that neighbor began cleaning up his wife. He also testified to seeing bruises and scratches on his wife's body.

The jury also heard from Milton Mallory. He testified that on the day of the assault when he arrived home from work between 5:30 p.m. and 6 p.m., Andrew was the only person in the apartment. Milton stated, as well, that he himself was there for only a few minutes, just long enough to gather up some clothes to take to the dry cleaners.

Detective Charles Mackie with the sex squad was among the police officers McLaughlin put on the stand that day. He testified that it was around 9:30 p.m.—after Andrew Mallory had taken the lie detector test—that he confessed to him and Detective Vernie Tate and then later, in the presence of others, admitted to Stella O'Keane that he had raped her. When McLaughlin asked what happened next, Mackie replied, "After that he was asked if he wanted to put his statement into writing. He agreed to do so." When McLaughlin asked what happened after Mallory's statement was taken, Mackie replied that the defendant was asked about "the clothing."

McLaughlin: What clothing?

Mackie: The clothing that was worn by him at the time of the attack. He said the clothing was in the apartment where he lived, and he gave us a written statement giving us permission to go to the apartment.

Bill Bryant raised an objection. He and McLaughlin were soon at the bench.

Holtzoff: What is your objection?

Bryant: At this point I raise my objection to any so-called permission to go to the premises and take anything that belonged to him, and also to the admission of any written statements made by this man, on the theory that he was not in such shape as to consent to anything. I think this is a seasonable time. Maybe I am late.

Holtzoff: No, this is a seasonable time.

However, Judge Holtzoff did not deal with the matter then and there.

McLaughlin resumed his direct examination of Detective Mackie, eliciting testimony to the effect that Mallory had not been pressured into giving the police permission to search for that clothing. Mackie also testified that when he was in Mallory's presence, he seemed to be in his right mind.

The trial was adjourned at 3:30 p.m., and when it resumed the next day, Judge Holtzoff called counsel to the bench to deal with Bryant's objection regarding the admissibility of Mallory's written confession and permission to search for his clothing.

The judge asked Bryant if he had filed a motion to suppress the clothing.

He had not. "I didn't know about the circumstances surrounding anything. I have had no cooperation from the defendant." McLaughlin could not say definitively that Bryant had been informed that the clothing had been obtained by search and seizure. Judge Holtzoff decided that before he ruled on whether the consent to search was voluntary, he first wanted to hear testimony on the voluntariness of the written confession. The jurors, no doubt restless, were escorted from the courtroom.

In this hearing, Detective Mackie testified that when Mallory was asked if he wished to reduce his confession to writing, he was advised of his rights. "We told him that the statement would have to be voluntary" and that "his statement could be used for or against him in court, and he agreed to give the statement." Mackie also testified that when asked about the clothing he had on at the time of the assault, Mallory volunteered to go with the police to the apartment to retrieve the items. He then signed a statement giving permission for the search. At no time had Mallory been coerced or threatened, said Mackie, who repeated that, all along, the defendant seemed to be in his right mind.

Deputy Coroner Richard M. Rosenberg, who examined Mallory after he confessed, testified that Mallory told him that he had not been roughed up, that earlier in the evening he had been given "some soup, bread, a couple of cokes and chewing gum, that he had been given plenty of cigarettes," and that he had been taken to the bathroom "whenever he wished." When McLaughlin inquired about Mallory's mental state, Dr. Rosenberg said that he had found him to be "of sound mind."

In his cross Bryant zeroed in on the fact that the doctor had been called in to examine the defendant for signs of physical violence and to collect any physical evidence that might connect him to the rape. "As a matter of fact, Doctor, you are not a psychiatrist are you?"

Rosenberg: No, sir.

Holtzoff: But you are a physician of many years standing, are you not?

Rosenberg: Thirty years, sir.

Holtzoff soon asked, "Isn't an experienced physician who is not a psychiatrist capable of diagnosing or determining whether a patient, or prospective patient, is mentally ill?"

"Yes," the doctor replied, noting that "people who are mentally ill do not reveal their illness at all times. There are intervals when they are just as normal appearing as anyone, and other times when anyone, a layman, knows that there is something wrong with the individual's mind."

The judge also heard from Irma Smith, who typed up Mallory's confession and permission to search the Mallory apartment for clothing. She was followed by Detective Tate. The upshot of their testimony was that from the time of his oral confession through the signing of the written statement and the permission to search, Mallory seemed fine to them and that he had not been coerced.

Bill Bryant could not have been surprised by the judge's ruling: "The Court finds that the oral and written statements of the defendant were made voluntarily and are therefore admissible, and that the consent to the search of the apartment was also executed voluntarily and is therefore valid and binding."

That afternoon, from Dr. Rosenberg and others, the jurors heard for themselves testimony to the effect that Mallory had never been abused and that he had confessed voluntarily.

From DC General's Dr. Emanuel Stadlan they learned details about Stella O'Keane's emotional and physical condition on the night of the rape. Dr. Stadlan read from the records of her examination: "Patient appeared nervous and distraught. Abrasions of the left knee, back, left temple and neck. Small lump in back of head. General physical examination was essentially normal." He then asked McLaughlin, "Do you want me to continue with the examination of the genitalia?"

McLaughlin: Yes.

No doubt some in the courtroom squirmed.

Stadlan: Labia minora swollen and tender. Vaginal walls hyperemic. Seropurulent discharge in vaginal vault.

Holtzoff: Suppose you translate that into nontechnical terminology.

Stadlan: The examiner found evidence of injury to the left knee, back, left temple and neck, and also to the back of the head, a lump in the back of the head. As regards the genital examination he found that the genital organs, the external organs, revealed evidence of irritation, of trauma, and that there was present a discharge in the passageway, the genital passageway.

McLaughlin: Is that what they call the vagina?

Stadlan: Yes, sir.

McLaughlin: Why didn't you say it? That's all.

On the following day, under direct examination, Officer James McCarty testified that right before he administered the polygraph,

Mallory stated that he had nothing to do with the rape but that about an hour and a half later, he stated "that he could have done this crime, or that he might have done it. He finally stated that he was responsible and went into some detail as to what actually did occur."

The jury sat through another account of the rape of Stella O'Keane as McCarty himself went into some detail about what Mallory allegedly told him.

McLaughlin: Was it after that conversation [with] you that you called Officers Mackie and Tate?

McCarty: Yes, sir.

Bryant used his cross-examination to paint a picture of the polygraph as a stressful experience, a form of psychological pressure. McCarty's answers to Bryant's questions put Mallory in a small, closed-door room confronted by a machine embedded in a desk, a machine, said McCarty, that "is 11–1/2 by 12–3/4 by about 18 or 19 inches in length, and weighs 61 pounds" and with a series of controls and "recording pins which record on a continuing moving graph."

When Bryant asked how a subject is connected to this machine, McCarty replied, "The pneumograph[y] component requires a hose connection from the instrument to a convoluted tube. That tube is held in place by a little chain reaching around the chest. That is fastened in the visceral section of the body."

Bryant: You put that around the subject?

McCarty: Yes, sir, to record the breathing. From the cardial section of the machine, the second component, there is a hose leading to a little wrist cuff that fastens around the wrist the same as a physician would use to check blood pressure. The third component of the instrument is a psychogalvanometer.

Bryant: Tell us about that.

McCarty: From the instrument there is a little wire running out to two metal clips of German silver, and those two clips are placed on the fingers with tape around those two to hold them together. That is the connection between the person and the instrument.

No information about the actual lie detector test was ever discussed or entered into evidence.

That day's most dramatic moment was not anything uttered on the witness stand. It was when McLaughlin—over Bryant's objection—entered into evidence Mallory's alleged confession and read it to the jury.

If any jurors, spectators, or reporters, had been daydreaming, fidgeting, or wondering what might be going on in the mind of Andrew Roosevelt Mallory as he sat through day three of his trial, McLaughlin no doubt had their undivided attention now.

Chapter 8

NEVER BEEN IN THIS POSITION

Andrew Mallory's alleged confession told of him lounging around in the basement apartment on April 7, 1954, when sometime after 5 p.m. a woman knocked on the door needing help with a hose. It told of Mallory helping the lady, then returning to the apartment and making a pitcher of ice water. Milton soon arrived, asked to borrow a suit, then headed out.

"I went back and laid down. Then that's when the idea came into my head. I had been drinking but I don't know if that was the cause of it or not. The idea I had in my mind was that I wanted the woman I had seen out at the washing machine."

The statement told of Mallory approaching the woman with a handkerchief around his face. "When she saw me, I was in the drying room and she said, 'What do you want?' I told her to be quiet. She screamed and I put my hand over her mouth and threw her down." Next, he ran up the stairs to lock the door that led to the first floor, then ran back down and half-carried, half-dragged the woman into the boiler room.

"She said, 'What do you want, money?' I said, 'No, I don't want money.' She said, 'What do you want?' And I said, 'I want you.'

"By this time, I had done threw her down. I began to rip off her clothes—her shorts and pant[ies]. They came off together. She repeated, 'How much money do you want? I'll get you all the money you want.' I repeated, 'I don't want any money.'

"Then I opened my pants and I stuck my penis in her. Then I told her to work with me and she started working. She asked me, 'Is this good enough?' And she kept repeating this. She asked me again how much money did I want and I didn't say anything.

"I think it was about ten minutes before I come in her. She said, 'Take it out,' and I did."

The statement, witnessed by Detectives Mackie and Tate, was completed at 12:25 a.m.

After reading the confession, McLaughlin called to the stand FBI Special Agent Peter G. Duncan. His expertise included analysis of bodily fluids. McLaughlin showed him clothing the police had retrieved from the Mallory apartment: a pair of men's shorts, a coat, a shirt, and pair of trousers. Agent Duncan identified them as the items he had received from Detective Mackie in April of the previous year. He then testified to finding semen stains on the clothing.

Bryant had no cross.

After McLaughlin entered into evidence that clothing and some other items, he rested the government's case.

Bill Bryant's first witness was Lucy Mallory, Andrew's fifty-six-year-old widowed mother. She had arrived in DC from Greenville, South Carolina, two days before the trial began. Lucy Mallory testified that Andrew, the youngest of her seven children, had "always acted different from the other children." Moreover, young Andrew had apparently gotten into some trouble when the family lived in Spartanburg, South Carolina, trouble that had a Mrs. Greer calling on his mother.

Bryant kept his language as plain and simple as he could with Mrs. Mallory. She was a willing witness, but, unfortunately, she had difficulty understanding and responding to some questions. When he asked if Mrs. Greer worked "for the juvenile people," Mrs. Mallory replied, "That's right."

Bryant: How did you come to know her?

Mallory: Well, that was in juvenile at Spartanburg.

Bryant: Yes, ma'am. I mean how did you come to know her?

Mallory: Mrs. Greer?

Though Bryant tried mightily, he was never able to get a cogent answer from Mrs. Mallory as to why Mrs. Greer came to see her about Andrew. Bryant did, however, succeed in getting before the jury some other information about young Andrew, including that, when he was about nine, he fractured a jawbone when he fell off the milk truck on which he was working. Jurors also heard Mrs. Mallory's admission that when people began telling her that Andrew was "acting queer and funny," she should have had him examined. "Well, I guess it was too late then, and see I didn't have nobody to help me."

While examining Mrs. Mallory, Bryant saw psychiatrist Joseph M. Rom enter the courtroom. He was a witness he had been waiting for and someone whose time was tight. Dr. Rom had examined Mallory three months after O'Keane was assaulted, by order of the court. With Judge Holtzoff's permission, Bryant interrupted Lucy Mallory's testimony and called Dr. Rom to the stand.

He testified that, after examining Mallory in early July 1954, he diagnosed his condition "as being that of a psychosis with mental deficiency."

Bryant: And as to whether or not he was of sound or unsound mind, what conclusion did you reach?

Rom: That at that time he was of unsound mind.

When Bryant asked Dr. Rom if he had reached a conclusion as to how long Mallory had been of unsound mind, the doctor replied that in his opinion "it was of long duration." He believed that Mallory had been ill for "almost a year, at least."

In cross-examination McLaughlin asked Dr. Rom his opinion as to Mallory's mental condition on April 7, 1954, the day of the assault.

Rom: In light of the condition that I saw him in July, I feel very strongly that the same condition was in operation in April.

McLaughlin: Would you say definitely as to his mental condition on April 7th of 1954?

Rom: Not having examined the man I cannot state what his condition was on that specified date.

The jury learned that in examining Mallory, the doctor observed that the "man was dull. He was retarded. He was confused, and apparently had no appreciation of the situation he was in."

When McLaughlin asked if Mallory was "suffering from delusions," the jury learned that he was not but that he was hearing voices, "voices relating to the theme of rape." Those voices, said Dr. Rom, were "unknown voices." Also, the speech was "garbled."

McLaughlin peppered the doctor with questions designed to shake his belief that Mallory's mental illness was long-standing. It didn't work, but it may very well have made jurors doubt that Mallory was mentally ill at the time of the crime.

When McLaughlin asked Dr. Rom if he would say that when he examined Mallory he was "stupid," the doctor seemed a bit rattled. He first said that he deemed Mallory to be a "low-grade moron," then a "high-grade moron" with an IQ of a six-year-old. When McLaughlin pressed him on Mallory's IQ, the jury learned that the doctor never actually administered an IQ test.

After McLaughlin finished questioning the doctor, Judge Holtzoff, perhaps tapping a foot, returned to Mallory's auditory hallucinations. "Isn't it possible for a person to sham the hearing of voices?"

Dr. Rom did not think Mallory had the wits to fake it, and the judge was like a dog with a bone. "Well, isn't it possible for some of the other prisoners in jail to plant that suggestion in his mind, that he should pretend that he heard voices. Did you consider the possibility?"

Rom: Yes, I did consider that possibility.

Holtzoff: That is possible?

Dr. Rom said that it was but added that in Mallory's case he had concluded that the "auditory hallucinations should be considered as real, as valid."

Following the luncheon recess, Bryant recalled Lucy Mallory to the stand.

One of the first things he wanted to know was if Mrs. Mallory allowed Andrew to play with the rest of her children between the time that he was eight or so and the time that he left home.

No. She repeated that Andrew "was always different from the other children," adding that he "didn't understand how to play with the other children." When Bryant asked her to be more specific, she replied, "Well, sir, to just make it plain to you, I always said he didn't have a good mind—that's what I said about him—because I never did have his mind checked, but you know how one is different from the rest, you know it, you can tell it, anyone that's had children."

In his cross-examination McLaughlin suggested to Mrs. Mallory that her family was just like most other families, that it was not uncommon for siblings to get into scrapes. No matter how many ways he pitched that idea, she never conceded that Andrew had been a normal child.

After Mrs. Mallory left the stand, Bill Bryant faced perhaps the most harrowing moment of the trial. His client insisted on testifying. At the bench, Bryant told Judge Holtzoff, "I have asked him what he wanted to say, in order to get some basis for at least presenting him to the Court. He won't tell me what he wants to say. I have never been in this position." In the end, the judge advised, "You just question him the best you can."

With Mallory on the stand, Bryant advised him to speak up, asked him to state his full name, then asked, "And you are the defendant in this case, and you are charged with committing a crime?"

Mallory: That is correct.

Bryant: Now, you have been here since Tuesday.

Mallory: That is correct.

Bryant: Right?

Mallory: Yes.

Bryant: And you have heard all the people who have been where you are now and heard what they said, is that right?

Mallory: That's correct.

When Bryant asked if he had heard what Stella O'Keane said happened to her, Mallory replied, "Yes."

Bryant: Did you do that?

Mallory: No.

Bryant: Do you remember being arrested?

Mallory: Yes.

Bryant: Do you remember going down to headquarters?

Mallory: Yes, sir.

Bryant: Do you remember some policemen talking to you for a while?

Mallory: Yes.

Bryant: Do you remember sitting down at a typewriter or close to a typewriter and telling some lady what to type?

Mallory: No.

Bryant: Would you say that you did that or you didn't do that?

Mallory: I say I don't remember doing it.

Bryant: Your Honor, I have no further questions.

Under cross-examination, Mallory remembered a great deal about the day Stella O'Keane was assaulted.

He remembered heading to Maryland early that morning with the two Luthers in search of a job in construction, returning home that afternoon, going to a corner store for a Pepsi-Cola at about 3 p.m., then, at about 5:30 p.m., heading over to Tenth Street to see his friend Evelyn, who wasn't home, and so he was soon back at 1223 Twelfth Street, NW.

McLaughlin: And when you came back at that time, did you see anybody in the apartment?

Mallory: No.

He testified to helping Stella O'Keane with a hose and stated that after he did he returned to the apartment, had a little whiskey with a guy looking for one of his nephews, and after the guy left, he listened to the radio, drank a little more soda, then left the building. When he returned he saw cop cars. Inside the apartment one of his relatives told him that a woman had been attacked and that her attacker wore a white hat.

"So I said, 'I have on a white hat.' So I said, 'I had better go up and show them my hat.'" He remembered Luther Sr. telling him not to do that, and he reckoned that he left the building again around 8:30 p.m. When McLaughlin asked him where he went, Mallory refused to tell him. "That's something that I must keep to myself." But he did say that he never returned to the apartment that night.

Mallory remembered being arrested the following day, being taken to police headquarters, being photographed, being fingerprinted, being taken into a room with benches, where he saw Luther Sr., Luther Jr., and Milton. He remembered being questioned by a police officer for about thirty or forty-five minutes. "Before they questioned me they told me that my brother said that I was the man. And they asked me, Wasn't I. And I told them, No. And they would [have to] kill me before they got any statement concerning that as far as my guilt was concerned."

Mallory remembered agreeing to take a lie detector test, but he did not remember taking it—did not remember anything from about 6:30 p.m. until the following morning when he woke up in a jail cell.

Mallory: Let me tell you this, then you take it from there: They brought us something in. I don't know what it were. But anyway, I ate part of it and drank some of the coffee. And so help me God, that's the last thing I remember until the next morning.

McLaughlin: You are telling us they put a Mickey in that?

Mallory: I don't know what it were.

When McLaughlin asked if, up until the time that he was given food and drink, any cops laid a hand on him, Mallory replied, "No." When asked if he had been treated kindly, Mallory replied, "That's right."

McLaughlin: And there's no one that tried to force you to do anything, did they?

Mallory: Well, I have to answer that question this way: During the time that they was questioning me that afternoon, they made some promises, but I still said I didn't do anything whatsoever about what they were talking about.

McLaughlin: All right. Now, let's hear the promises they made to you, Andrew.

Mallory: They said it would go as light—they said they would talk for me and it would go as light as possible on me. But I said that I didn't know what they were talking about.

When McLaughlin showed him the confession, Mallory denied that the signature was his. As the questioning continued, he went from denying that the signature was his to saying that he didn't remember signing the confession.

Near the end of his cross-examination, McLaughlin returned to the day O'Keane was assaulted. "Well, outside of that little whiskey you had up in the apartment—I mean there was nothing the matter with you mentally? That you couldn't remember?"

Mallory: Well, what I say on that wouldn't make any difference because I had a psychiatrist—there is no need to tell me this—that every man thinks the other person is crazy but himself. Therefore, I wouldn't say either way. But I don't think I were.

When McLaughlin finished with Mallory, Bryant had no redirect. After a brief recess, he rested his case.

Closing arguments were set for the following morning.

Chapter 9

HEART WAS JUST POUNDING

The trial transcript states that when the trial resumed at 10 a.m. on Friday, June 24, McLaughlin and Bryant delivered their closing arguments (not included in the transcript), and the judge soon charged the jury.

Judge Holtzoff reminded the jurors that being charged with a crime is no indication of guilt, that the defendant is presumed innocent, and that it was up to the prosecutor to prove guilt beyond a reasonable doubt. Judge Holtzoff informed the jurors that he had the authority "to summarize and discuss the evidence" but that whatever he said was "not binding" on them. In the end, it was their recollection, their understanding "that must prevail."

As Bryant said years later, Judge Holtzoff was "very, very one-sided when he gave the summary of evidence."

Judge Holtzoff told the jury that Stella O'Keane had given detailed testimony about the sexual assault, including that when she returned to her apartment, she shouted to her husband, "Call the doctor. I have been raped." The judge mentioned the testimony of the DC General physician. He testified, said Holtzoff, "that her genital organs were irritated, had been subjected to trauma, which is a medical term for physical violence, and that she had a discharge from her private organs." Holtzoff also made a statement that was flat-out wrong: "Mrs. O'Keane identified on the witness stand the defendant as the person who raped her."

O'Keane had, in fact, only identified Mallory as the person who helped her with the washing machine hose.

The judge then referred to testimony that Mallory confessed to several police officers and to the victim. He reminded the jury of the confession that had been read in open court. Holtzoff conceded that Mallory said that he did not remember dictating the statement or signing it. "It is for you, ladies and gentlemen of the jury to determine what the facts are, and where the truth lies." The judge stressed that "there is no contention here of any physical coercion of any kind."

He explained that if the jury believed the defendant guilty but also believed he was insane at the time of the assault, the verdict was to be not guilty by reason of insanity. If, however, they believed the defendant guilty but not insane at the time of the crime, they were to return a verdict of guilty. He reminded the jury that Dr. Rom had testified that he believed the defendant was mentally ill before the date of the crime, then added that the jury had "a right to consider," for example, Dr. Rosenberg's testimony that on the day of his arrest Mallory was suffering no mental illness.

If the jury found Mallory guilty, it still had "one more problem," said Judge Holtzoff. "The punishment provided by law for the crime of rape is either a death penalty or imprisonment for a term of years. The decision whether the death penalty should be inflicted is made by the jury."

In closing he told the jurors that there were four possible verdicts: "Either guilty as charged with the death penalty, or guilty as charged, or not guilty on the ground of insanity, or not guilty." He reminded them that the verdict had to be unanimous.

Then to Bryant and McLaughlin, "Are there any objections or requests?"

McLaughlin had none and Bryant said nothing about the judge's inaccurate statement that on the witness stand Stella O'Keane had identified Mallory as the man who raped her. Bryant had to make a strategic decision. Was it better to just let it go, since you can't unring a bell in front of a jury? Or, was it better to object and risk Judge Holtzoff saying something more prejudicial in response?

It was around noon when the marshal escorted the twelve main jurors to the jury room to choose a foreperson and begin deliberations.

About five hours later the jurors returned to the jury box. Bryant assumed they had reached a verdict—"and my heart was just pounding."

Judge Holtzoff called counsel to the bench and showed them a note with three questions from the jury. "I think as to the question they ask on No. 2 I shall have to say that I cannot give them any such assurance."

"That is right," responded McLaughlin. Bryant made no comment, and the judge proceeded to answer the questions in open court, addressing himself to the foreperson, Julian Gensheimer.

First, the jurors wanted to know, "Have we other choice of verdicts" other than the four he had given them.

"Now, those four are the only possible verdicts," said the judge. "No other verdict is possible."

The second question: "Can we the jury be assured that the defendant [will] legally be imprisoned for the remainder of his natural life? No possibility of release."

"I can give you no such assurance," Judge Holtzoff replied. He explained that the maximum sentence that he could impose was thirty years, and the minimum ten years. After Mallory served ten years, "the Parole Board would have to decide whether the maximum should be served, or anything less than the maximum. So that I can give you no assurance that the defendant would legally be imprisoned for the remainder of his natural life if he is found guilty as charged."

The jury's third question: "May the jury have a reading of the DC Code re: rape?"

Holtzoff read the code: "Whoever has carnal knowledge of a female [forcibly] and against her will shall be imprisoned for not more than 30 years provided that in any case of rape the jury may add to their verdict if it be guilty the words 'with the death penalty,' in which case the punishment shall be death by electrocution. Provided further that the jury fails to agree as to the punishment, the verdict shall be received, and the punishment shall be imprisonment as provided in this section."

Having returned to the jury room at 4:55 p.m., the jury was back in the courtroom at 5:15 p.m. with a verdict: Guilty with the death penalty.

The following day the *Washington Post* reported that this was the first time in five years that someone convicted of rape in DC received the death penalty.

Four days after the verdict, Judge Holtzoff was ready to pronounce sentence. Before he did, Bryant was at the bench. Over the weekend he had worked feverishly on grounds for a motion for a new trial.

He had already given McLaughlin a copy of his motion and now presented the judge with a copy, then made his case for a new trial.

Bryant maintained that Judge Holtzoff's "no such assurance" response to the jury's second question was in error. He based this on *Lovely v. United States* (1948), in which the trial judge told the jury that if the defendant, William Lovely, charged with rape, was found guilty without the death penalty, the court could sentence him to life in prison, but that the man would be eligible for parole after fifteen years. The US Court of Appeals for the Fourth Circuit granted a new trial to Lovely in part because the jury, which had to decide on life in prison or capital punishment for the defendant, had been instructed that a person sentenced to life imprisonment was eligible for parole after fifteen years.

Bryant argued that Holtzoff's response to the jury's question asking for an assurance that if found guilty, Mallory would spend the rest of his life in prison was "more prejudicial" than if it had been part of his charge to the jury. He read aloud a particular passage from Judge John J. Parker's opinion in *Lovely*: "Whether he should be paroled after fifteen years, if not given capital punishment, was a matter which they could not decide and which should not have been called to their attention, even though they were told at the same time that they had nothing to do with it."

"That 'nothing to do with it' seems to be rather definitive language," said Bryant, "and on the basis of this particular authority, I most sincerely urge upon the Court that the motion for a new trial be granted."

Motion denied.

Judge Holtzoff asserted that the jury was "properly entitled to an answer to that question, and the Court answered it." He then summoned Mallory to the bench.

The *Washington Post* reported that the defendant had been brought into the courtroom "with his arms shackled and heavily guarded by deputy US marshals." Mallory's left wrist and forehead were "heavily bandaged." He had cut himself with a tobacco can.

As Mallory stood before the bar, Judge Holtzoff asked, "Andrew Mallory, have you anything to say why sentence should not be pronounced according to law?"

A silent Andrew Roosevelt Mallory was sentenced to die in the DC Jail's electric chair in four months, on November 11, 1955. According to the *Evening Star*, he "took the sentence calmly."

Mallory had been uncooperative and downright hostile. He could not pay Bryant a dime. He was someone many people probably wrote off as a waste of space. "He was sick," Bryant told a reporter. "He was difficult to work with—not the sort of person you warm up to. But when he got the death penalty, I knew I had to appeal for him." He added, "You know, I'm not solely working for the protection of the defendant. I'm working for the protection of the system of law."

For that cause, eight months after Mallory was sentenced to death, on March 26, 1956, Bryant was before the US Court of Appeals for the DC Circuit, heard by Chief Judge E. Barrett Prettyman Sr. and Associate Judges Walter M. Bastian and David L. Bazelon.

Bryant maintained that Mallory's clothing with seminal stains should not have been entered into evidence, challenging the claim that his client's consent to search was voluntary. He contended that Judge Holtzoff's "no such assurance" comment to the jury was prejudicial. Bryant also argued that Mallory's confession was inadmissible under the McNabb Rule.

In *McNabb v. United States* (1943), the US Supreme Court voided the second-degree-murder convictions of three Tennessee moonshiners charged with killing a federal agent. The convictions rested primarily on confessions made after more than thirty hours of detention. Only after they confessed were the men arraigned. This was in violation of Rule 5(a) of the Federal Rules of Criminal Procedure, which mandated that arrestees be arraigned "without unnecessary delay." In *McNabb*, the high court ruled that the confessions were inadmissible because the men had not been promptly arraigned, and so had been illegally detained.

On June 28, 1956, in a 2–1 decision, the Court of Appeals upheld Mallory's conviction with Chief Judge Prettyman having penned the opinion. On the clothing, he maintained that "since Mallory had already confessed to the crime itself, in the absence of evidence to the contrary his express consent to the taking of specific property involved in the crime must be treated as being of the same voluntary nature." On Holtzoff's response to the jury: "Unlike the situation in the ordinary case, the jury had a serious responsibility in respect to punishment for this crime." The jurors "had a right to know what the law is upon that punishment. Thus, clearly, they had a right to know that the punishment other than death is imprisonment for not more than thirty years." Judge Prettyman asserted that Holtzoff "did no more than state accurately the whole law in respect to punishment for this crime."

Judge Prettyman declared that the delay between Mallory's arrest and arraignment was not unreasonable. "The police had three suspects and it is inconceivable that they should be required to lodge charges against any suspect until their investigation has developed with some certainty a justification for charges; provided always that the investigation is not unduly prolonged. Moreover, there is no evidence that the confession was due to the delay, such as it was."

Bill Bryant was, no doubt, heartened by the dissent of Judge Bazelon. He maintained that Judge Holtzoff's response to the jury was improper—"grossly prejudicial to" Mallory. Judge Bazelon found that the nearly eight-hour delay between Mallory's arrest and the first attempt to have him arraigned was not necessary. It was a "deliberate choice of the police," who "should not arrest any person on mere suspicion, hoping that, once they have him at headquarters, they can obtain from his own lips something to justify the arrest." The law, he said, "lets policemen arrest, but delegates to magistrates the judgment whether to detain. The law's requirement of arraignment without unnecessary delay is grounded upon the theory that, where policemen are judges, individual liberty and dignity cannot long survive."

There was never a doubt in Bill Bryant's mind but that he would appeal to the highest court in the land. His main argument would be the seven-and-a-half-hour delay between Mallory's arrest and arraignment.

"I wasn't even a member of the Supreme Court bar," he said years later. "I remember there was a guy named Cullinane who was over there, a deputy clerk. He used to smoke a long cigar and drink a lot of whiskey. The nicest guy you would ever want to see. There was a lady over there, I can see her now, just as nice. They shepherded me through, and got me admitted right quick."

According to the *Evening Star*, "the Supreme Court had refused to review any District cases involving claims of 'unreasonable delay' since November 1951." In late October 1956, the high court reversed course, agreeing to review Mallory's case.

Five months later, on the morning of Monday, April 1, 1957, William Benson Bryant was in the "Marble Palace," seated in that breathtaking courtroom with its forty-four-foot ceiling, mahogany furniture, ivory vein Spanish marble friezes, and Old Convent Quarry Siena marble columns. Along with spectators and other attorneys, he was awaiting the entrance of Chief Justice Earl Warren and the eight associate justices.

Having never appeared before the US Supreme Court, for a few days before he did, Bryant sat in its courtroom observing oral augments.

"Oyez! Oyez! Oyez!" declared the marshal, calling all to silence and to rise as the justices entered the courtroom. "All persons having business before the Honorable, the Supreme Court of the United States, are admonished to draw near and give their attention, for the Court is now sitting. God save the United States and this Honorable Court."

No question about it, Bill Bryant was somewhat nervous as he waited his turn to address the high court.

Chapter 10

DELAY WAS *CHOSEN*

"Mr. Chief Justice, Associate Justices, may it please the Court," Bill Bryant began, his voice somewhat flat and halting. "The case for the Court, *Andrew Mallory versus United States*, we believe presents three important questions."

Question one pertained to Mallory's alleged confessions. Had "the lower courts in the District of Columbia Circuit properly adhered to the pronouncements of this Court in *McNabb versus United States* and reiterated in *Upshaw versus United States*?"

Upshaw (1948) challenged the conviction of Andrew Upshaw for grand larceny. The police had arrested Upshaw on suspicion of robbing a furniture store in DC, and after some thirty hours in detention he confessed. Only then did the police take him before a committing magistrate. In a 5–4 decision, the high court reversed Upshaw's conviction, reaffirming *McNabb*.

Question two: Did the consent Mallory allegedly gave the police to search for certain clothing measure up "to that standard of voluntariness which the federal jurisdiction has adopted for itself?"

Question three: Was Judge Holtzoff's "no such assurance" comment proper?

Bryant proceeded to provide the Court with a summary of the early facts surrounding the case: the date and place of the rape, Mallory's arrest the following day at about 2:30 p.m., his interrogation at police headquarters, his alleged consent to take the lie detector test, and his long wait to take that test. Bryant made it a point to emphasize that the room where the test was administered was oppressively small, and that the way Mallory was hooked up to the machine was scary. He noted that it was not until sometime after 10 p.m.—after Mallory had allegedly confessed—that the police telephoned the home of US Commissioner Cyril S. Lawrence, who was unavailable. Bryant highlighted the fact that this was the very first attempt to reach the commissioner. By now his voice was more relaxed and picking up speed—more so when he took the Court through Judge Holtzoff's "no such assurance" comment. He read the jury's question and the judge's answer in full.

Justice William Joseph Brennan Jr., once described as "a slight man with a ready Irish grin," asked, "Now, what would you suggest should have been Judge Holtzoff's answer to that question?"

"I think his answer in the circumstances here should have been that is a matter which is not properly before you jurors for your consideration and I will not answer that question."

Feisty Justice Felix Frankfurter soon weighed in. "He shouldn't tell him what will influence them because that may influence them in bringing in one sentence rather than another?"

"Positively, Your Honor."

"That's your problem?"

"That's my position."

Sharp as a tack. As Dr. Michael R. Winston, distinguished historian and longtime Howard professor and administrator—and close friend of Bryant's—pointed out, "Here, in that juxtaposition you have a perfect example of Bryant's clarity of mind. He was letting Justice Frankfurter know that 'problem' was the wrong word to use. Bryant did not have a 'problem' but a *position* based on a clear reading of the law. Felix Frankfurter would have recognized in a second what kind of person was before the Court."

With his voice firm, strong, Bryant argued that in his response Judge Holtzoff "was in effect *emphasizing*" that Mallory "would be out in *no time*," and "injecting himself into that jury room."

Bryant was caught flat-footed when the ever-cordial and courteous Justice Marshall Harlan II mentioned what happened when Judge Holtzoff called counsel to the bench regarding the note from the jury. Justice Harlan read what Judge Holtzoff said: "I think as to the question they asked on number two, I shall have to say that I cannot give them any such assurance." He read McLaughlin's response of "That's right," then, said Justice Harlan, "Nothing further appears."

"That's right," replied Bryant. It quickly dawned on him that Justice Harlan was pointing out that he had said nothing, made no objection.

"Well, if Your Honor please, I might say this. That I was in an unfamiliar situation at that point and I said nothing as the record reflects. But I assure Your Honor that had I had any idea that the judge was going to say what he *did* say, I would have just . . . objected spontaneously."

When the somewhat shy Justice Charles Evans Whittaker pointed out that had he said something at the time, "it might have put your record in a little better position," Bryant replied, "Yes, Your Honor, I agree."

Reviewing this exchange, attorney William B. Schultz, who came to know Bryant extremely well years later, remarked, "This was an unusually direct response from an advocate and pure Bill Bryant—totally honest and straightforward. There was nothing more to say and it allowed him to move on, preserving precious time for the argument that ultimately prevailed."

On the issue of the long delay between Mallory's arrest and the first attempt to have him arraigned, Bryant pointed out that when cops booked Mallory at police headquarters on Indiana Avenue, NW, they were a short walk away from the federal courthouse, home to about fifteen district court judges, nine court of appeals judges, and the US commissioner. He added that the Municipal Court was just a block away and stated that all the judges there "are empowered to act as committing magistrates."

Bryant forcefully asserted that the delay did not arise from any extenuating "circumstances over which the police had no control. It was a delay which was *chosen* by the police for the purpose of interrogation." With his voice a bit softer but still resolute, he added that if "the *McNabb* and *Upshaw* cases mean what I'm certain the Court would say that they mean and if Rule 5(a) is to be observed at all, the delay in this particular case was such as to invalidate the confession."

"You said that the delay was *chosen*," remarked Justice Frankfurter. "It was designed—"

"Delay was *chosen*."

"A designed delay."

"That's right, Your Honor."

To drive the point home, Bryant repeated that the police could have taken Mallory to the US commissioner right after they arrested him. Based on his experience, the man would have been on duty until at least 4:30 p.m. Moreover, his office, located in the federal courthouse, "was about the closest office to the police headquarters."

Following more discussion about the availability of judges on the afternoon of Mallory's arrest, Justice Harold Hitz Burton asked, "Until after the lie detector test, did they have enough to arraign him for?"

"Well, if Your Honor please, they had enough to arraign him when they arrested him. Now, if Your Honor means if—did they have enough for the commissioner to hold him, I think it's a different question. I think the purpose of arraignment is to determine whether or not there's enough to *hold* him." He added that, as with Andrew Upshaw, the police did not have sufficient grounds to detain Andrew Mallory.

Said Justice Frankfurter: "That's what you mean by saying the failure to arraign was designed in order to enable [them] to get the evidence."

"That's right. The sole purpose of the delay."

Forty-seven minutes had elapsed when soft-spoken, avuncular Chief Justice Warren said, "We'll recess now."

When oral argument resumed, Bryant briefly addressed the issue of Mallory's clothing, arguing that the consent to search was not voluntary because his client was mentally ill. There was "no question about him being psychopathic," he said. Bryant also contended that the alleged consent to search was "the fruit of illegal detention." Reserving his remaining time for rebuttal, Bryant took his seat.

The lawyer representing the government was Edward L. Barrett Jr., special assistant to the US attorney general (and future founding dean of the UC Davis School of Law).

After pointing out to the high court that Mallory never claimed that he had been coerced into confessing and had, in fact, testified that he had been "treated kindly," Barrett conceded that the police could have taken Mallory for arraignment right after he was arrested, but he argued that Rule 5(a) "must be given a broader interpretation." It was not just about how much time elapsed before the police had a suspect arraigned. Barrett argued that the "delay in this case was necessary on a reasonable interpretation of the Rule and that hence the McNabb Rule does not apply to exclude this confession."

Barrett asked the justices to consider the circumstances surrounding the assault: it occurred in an apartment building's basement that could be reached only by a staircase or from the janitor's apartment; the victim said she heard no one walk down those stairs; and Mallory admitted to being in the laundry room area before the assault. "The inference at this point," said Barrett, was that in all probability "the person who committed the crime came from the janitor's apartment."

Barrett told the Court that Andrew Mallory and two of his nephews fit the general description the victim gave of her attacker. Thus, the police had "a reasonable suspicion" that one of them was the rapist and so had brought all three to police headquarters. He stressed that the young men freely agreed to take the polygraph and explained that the only reason they weren't immediately given the test was because the officer who administered it was not in the building.

"When did the lie detector machinery and its operator turn up?" asked Justice Frankfurter.

"He came about six o'clock."

When Justice Frankfurter asked if Mallory was immediately given the test, Barrett explained that the nephews were given the test first.

Justice Frankfurter also asked, "Anything in the record to suggest that the defendant was advised of his right to counsel or was—anything on that point?"

Barrett mentioned that according to the police, Mallory was told that his written confession had to be voluntary and could be used against him. Following another line of inquiry, Barrett added that "there's nothing in the record that suggests that had he wanted counsel, he could not have had it."

When Justice Frankfurter inquired about "the certainty or the confidence in which one can say, guilt was established by the proof apart from the confession," Barrett replied, "I suppose you'd have to say that it was a case of circumstantial evidence here, apart from the confession and especially if you say apart from the clothes which had seminal stains and so on which were introduced."

Chief Justice Warren followed up with a much more direct question. "Suppose you took out of the case the confession that he gave and the evidence that was obtained by the search of the house that you say was part and parcel of the same conversation while he was detained, what would be left in the case?"

First on Barrett's list was the fact that Mallory admitted having contact with the victim shortly before the assault. His list also included Mallory's testimony that he was the only person in the basement apartment at the time of the attack and Stella O'Keane's testimony that she heard no one come down the wooden steps. He repeated that Mallory "met the general description of the person who committed the rape."

Barrett soon returned to the reason that the police did not take Mallory before a magistrate right after his arrest—the reason that the McNabb Rule did not apply. "The reason the police did what they did here was to try to eliminate. Their—about the only investigative technique left to the police in this case at this time was to question the suspects." The police had no physical evidence and no eyewitnesses, Barrett told the Court. As a result of the questioning, the police "let loose the two nephews" and charged Mallory with the crime. Barrett stressed that Mallory "ultimately did confess."

Barrett stated that the government was sympathetic "with the underlying purpose of the McNabb Rule. We recognize the evils of secret interrogation, the evils of the—of the third degree." However, interpreting the McNabb Rule as being just about time went too far, making illegal "perfectly reasonable police practices, which have nothing to do with beating up the man in the back room." He added that Mallory was never "secreted away" in some back room and that the only time he was in any sort of back room was when he took the polygraph.

That last bit clearly annoyed Justice Frankfurter. "Mr. Barrett, as you well know, *McNabb* isn't merely concerned, wasn't concern[ed] merely with a fellow being beaten up in the back room."

Barrett countered that *McNabb* was not intended to bring about any "drastic change in law enforcement practices."

Justice Frankfurter shot down that notion right quick. "The McNabb Rule was intended very considerably to change conventional methods of law enforcement. That's the point of the rule."

After more back-and-forth on the intent of the McNabb Rule, Barrett insisted that Mallory's case was "a good example of the situation in which if you don't permit police interrogation of suspects, you don't convict people." The police had to question Andrew Mallory and his nephews in "the interest of society."

On Rule 5(a), Chief Justice Warren asked, "So, what do you [do] with the language of the statute that says when he's arrested he shall be taken without unnecessary delay to—to a magistrate? What do you do with that language?"

"Well, we say that—that the delay here was necessary. That it depends on how you construe, of course, the word 'necessary.'"

When Chief Justice Warren asked whether the police would have been justified in not arraigning Mallory had the US commissioner been right there in police headquarters—even in the same room with Mallory—Barrett essentially replied yes.

At one point a somewhat agitated Justice Frankfurter also had more to say about Rule 5(a): "The central concept of our prosecutorial system and the central concept that arraignment intervene in order to have the magistrate tell the fellow, 'You can keep your mouth shut. You don't have to say a thing. Do you want a lawyer? This is a capital offense. I'll give you a lawyer.'"

Further along, Chief Justice Warren asked Barrett about a hypothetical crime in a neighborhood. Would the police be justified in rounding up all the young men in that neighborhood to determine who was guilty?

"Normally I would assume that would be unreasonable. That—"

"Well, what is the difference?"

Barrett only briefly addressed the search for Mallory's clothing. Bottom line: "the search stands or falls really on the confession." As for Judge Holtzoff's "no such assurance" comment, Barrett argued that if the judge had not answered the question and Mallory was sentenced to death, his counsel could claim that *not* answering the question was prejudicial, "arguing then that, well, maybe they thought he would only get two years or five years."

When Bill Bryant returned to the lectern, he circled back to the McNabb Rule, concluding with this: "If the authorities choose to delay for the purpose of the interrogation, then that delay certainly, is at that time illegal."

"And Mr. Bryant," said Chief Justice Earl Warren, "before you take your seat."

"Yes, sir."

"The Court notices from the record in the case that you came into the case by appointment of the District Court."

"That's right."

"And that you have carried this case through for an impecunious defendant through the Supreme Court of the United States and we would have you know that we consider this a distinct service to the cause of justice regardless of what the outcome of this case might be."

"Thank you, Your Honor. It's my honor."

While Mallory was on death row, Bill Bryant had an opportunity to recoup a *tiny* fraction of his expenses. Mrs. Mallory sent him about sixty dollars, a mixture of bills and coins, which a white guy from South Carolina delivered in a drawstring Bull Durham tobacco sack. Through the DC Jail property clerk, Bryant sent the money to Mallory so that he could buy smokes and whatnot.

Three months after oral argument, on June 24, 1957, Justice Felix Frankfurter delivered the opinion in the high court's unanimous decision. He concluded with this:

> We cannot sanction this extended delay, resulting in confession, without subordinating the general rule of prompt arraignment to the discretion of arresting officers in finding exceptional circumstances for its disregard. In every case where the police resort to interrogation of an arrested person and secure a confession, they may well claim, and quite sincerely, that they were merely trying to check on the information given by him. Against such a claim and the evil potentialities of the practice for which it is urged stands Rule 5 (a) as a barrier. Nor is there an escape from the constraint laid upon the police by that Rule in that two other suspects were involved for the same crime. Presumably, whomever the police arrest they must arrest on "probable cause." It is not the function of the police to arrest, as it were, at large, and to use an interrogating process at police headquarters in order to determine

whom they should charge before a committing magistrate on "probable cause."

Reversed and remanded.

With Mallory's conviction overturned and his confession inadmissible in a new trial, US Attorney Oliver Gasch moved to have the case dismissed, and Mallory released from the DC Jail. And Bill Bryant's reputation as an extraordinary criminal defense attorney was cemented.

"I do not remember any unusual activity around the house or big celebration at that time," said Chip, "but I can only imagine that the phone downtown at his office was blowing up with congratulatory calls from other attorneys who knew him, particularly from those in the Black legal community in DC and nationally. Although there was no special family event or party that I recall, I'm sure our extended family on both his and my mom's sides, as well as our neighbors and family friends were all very proud of him, and I'd bet anything they all expressed as much to him directly at some point."

Bill Bryant did not glory in all the attention that came his way in the wake of *Mallory v. United States*. What mattered to him was that the life of a mentally ill person had been saved, that justice had been done. Ever modest, he maintained that the publicity "was really undeserving. I really hadn't cut any ground." *Mallory*, he said, "just reiterated *McNabb* and *Upshaw*."

The inadmissibility in a federal prosecution of a confession obtained from people who were not taken to a committing magistrate promptly after their arrest—the McNabb-Mallory Rule—was followed and strengthened by the Miranda Rule, established by the US Supreme Court's decision in the 1966 case *Miranda v. Arizona*.

Nearly forty years after Bryant appeared before the high court, the Supreme Court Historical Society assembled a committee of esteemed legal scholars and Supreme Court practitioners to compile a list of the "most significant" oral arguments the high court heard between 1955 and 1993—"not only important cases, but also examples of effective appellate advocacy." Bill Bryant's oral argument in *Mallory v. United States* was one of 411, out of perhaps 4,000, that made the list.[14]

Bryant's vigilance for the rights of the accused did not end with Mallory. In fact, several years later he once again faced, and prevailed against, similar government overreach. His client was James Killough, a Black postal worker originally charged with first-degree murder.

In October 1960, Killough was arrested for the murder of his wife, Goldie. Following more than twenty-four hours in police custody, the man "finally broke down and told all of it," said Bryant. The "all of it" was that, in a fit of rage over suspected infidelity, Killough had strangled his wife and buried her body in a dump near the Anacostia River. After he spilled his guts, he led cops to the body. Back at police headquarters he signed a confession and was then brought before the US commissioner for arraignment.

After that, Killough was taken to the DC Jail, where he confessed a second time to a civilian classification clerk conducting a routine intake interview. Later that day, he confessed again to a homicide detective who visited him in jail to return some clothing and to find out what he wanted done with his wife's body.

"I just knew it was all wrong," said Bryant speaking of the way the police handled Killough. As with Mallory, Bryant was all-in. DC Court of Appeals judge Theodore R. "Ted" Newman Jr., a graduate of Brown and Harvard Law who joined Bryant's firm in the summer of 1962, put it another way: "If he got involved in a case, then he wasn't in it 95 percent. It was 195 percent."

---

14. Unfortunately, Mallory's run-ins with the law continued after his release from the DC Jail. He was arrested in Philadelphia in 1960 for beating and raping a young woman. Acquitted of the rape charge, he spent eleven and a half years in prison for assault, battery, and burglary. Nine months after his release, in July 1972, police shot him dead in Philadelphia's Fairmount Park. There, armed with a .22 caliber revolver, he had allegedly made a woman undress. This was after he robbed the man she was with of about ten dollars and stole his car. Mallory was thirty-seven when he died. Paul W. Valentine, "Mallory, of Famed Decision, Slain by Philadelphia Police," *Washington Post*, July 12, 1972, A1, A9; Harriet Griffiths, "'Mallory Rule' Figure Is Slain in Philadelphia," *Evening Star*, July 12, 1972, C3; and "The Law: Andrew Mallory, RIP," *Time*, July 24, 1972, https://content.time.com/time/subscriber/article/0,33009,906164,00.html.

In Killough's first trial, his pre-arraignment confession was ruled inadmissible as it violated the Mallory Rule, but the confession to the homicide detective made it in, and in late April 1961, Killough was convicted of manslaughter and sentenced to four to twelve years in prison. On appeal Bryant succeeded in getting the conviction overturned on the grounds that the confession to the homicide detective was the fruit of the pre-arraignment confession.

The prosecution dug in, using Killough's confession to the classification clerk in his second trial. Killough was found guilty of manslaughter and sentenced to five to fifteen years. On appeal that conviction was thrown out. The court held that the confession to the clerk was inadmissible because Killough's session with that clerk came with an implied confidentiality.

James Killough's third trial began on October 8, 1964, but it did not last long. The prosecution had no confession, no eyewitnesses, and no proof that the body recovered from the dump was Goldie's. The level of decomposition had made a positive identification impossible. With a heavy heart, Judge George L. Hart Jr. directed the jury to acquit James Killough, noting that the trial had been "stripped of all competent evidence."

Judge Newman remembered that after James Killough was released from jail, he faithfully turned up at the office every two weeks, paying Bryant's fee in installments. Judge Newman could not recall how much Bryant charged Killough, but he guessed that it wasn't all that much—not commensurate with services rendered over the course of four years. If he had a flaw, laughed Judge Newman, it was that "he didn't know how to make a [good] living." He used to tease Bryant that he couldn't even charge Nelson Rockefeller a decent fee. While Bryant was no role model on charging fees, Newman, twenty-three years his junior, found him to be a great mentor on other fronts.

Bryant was a stickler when it came to confidentiality. He advised Newman to never say anything on the telephone that he did not want to see printed in the *Washington Post*. At the time, Bryant was convinced that the office phones were tapped. (And he was not being paranoid. According to Judge Newman, the police tapped the phones because of all the criminal cases Bryant handled.)

Bryant also schooled Newman on people to avoid. One was a man whose street name was Sweetenin', a "courthouse lounger" Judge Newman called him. After Bryant saw Newman chatting with Sweetenin' in the courthouse one day, he cautioned him against having any more conversations with the man. After he saw Newman on another day just standing near the guy, he told his junior partner that if he saw Sweetenin' coming down the street he was to cross the street. Bryant had good reason to believe that Sweetenin' was a police informant.

Judge Newman would never forget Bryant's "one mile rule" for remaining ethical: "If you always walk one mile from the edge, even when you stumble, you're still on safe ground."

The greatest thing Ted Newman learned from Bill Bryant had nothing to do with law, but with the power of humility. "The central feature of Bill Bryant in my opinion was that he was the most truly humble human being I ever met. He made me realize that true humility comes from genuine, deep self-confidence. This feature was the source of his ability to relate so effectively with all with whom he dealt." Because he did not crave validation from others, he could "invest in others."

Chapter 11

A MORAL ISSUE

Shortly after Killough's acquittal, Bryant told the *Washington Post*'s Susanna McBee that he hated to see the police "botch up their investigations." When they did, "then it's my job to point it out to the court." McBee observed that Bryant could be quite dramatic when trying a case. However, outside of a courtroom, he was "soft-spoken and reflective and almost reverent when talking about the integrity of the judicial process. When he does raise his voice, it is to express outrage at what he sees as injustice." There was plenty of injustice in the country in the years between Mallory/Killough and the beginning (in 1965) of Bryant's final job—forty years on the federal bench. Enough to lead Bryant to face his fear of the Deep South straight on and conquer it. Judge Newman recalled that he went south more than once to defend civil rights activists.

One was Jasper Brown, a prosperous farmer in Dan River Township, North Carolina, about fifty miles northwest of Durham. Brown, an active member of the NAACP, was one of the plaintiffs in a lawsuit that resulted in the desegregation of three previously all-white schools in his county of Caswell. This desegregation began on January 22, 1963. The first sixteen students included Brown's four children.

According to Bryant's account, after Brown dropped them off at their new schools in Yanceyville, he was harassed something awful.

"There were about three or four [white] hoodlums who followed him in a car," remembered Bryant. One was the son of the superintendent of schools. Those troublemakers trailed Brown down the road. They trailed him into a store. They trailed him inside the store. They trailed him when he got back on the road—"and after a while," said Bryant, "they tailgated him and bumped him." Brown, armed with a pistol, stopped his car, got out, and fired. He grazed the head of the school superintendent's son and the arm of another young man who was running away.

Though neither was seriously injured, Brown was, nevertheless, charged with assault with a deadly weapon with intent to kill.

"Yeah, I'll try it," said Bryant when he got the call about representing Jasper Brown. The caller was Jack Greenberg, one of the era's great crusaders for racial justice and someone Bryant very much admired. Greenberg had succeeded Thurgood Marshall as director of the NAACP LDF in 1961.

Once down in North Carolina, Bryant quickly began sizing up the situation. Considering that the two victims were unarmed, that one was running away when shot, and that the judge had a reputation "for being meaner than hell," Bryant was convinced that a jury trial was not the way to go. He managed to get the prosecutor to accept a plea of no contest to simple assault. "I figured I was protecting this man from a long time in jail, and I [knew] that that jury would find him guilty of assault with intent to kill."

After he negotiated the plea deal, Bryant spent "the better part of that evening until half of the next day, trying to convince Jasper Brown" to accept it. He succeeded and recalled that Brown was sentenced to sixty days in jail. (Other sources say ninety days.)

Though Brown accepted the plea deal, he was "madder than hell," remembered Bryant. "That's the only client that I had who was dissatisfied, and I can understand him, I mean he was wronged, he was wronged." And Jasper Brown continued to be wronged. According to a friend, "they froze him out. Whites wouldn't sell him anything—fuel oil, supplies for his farm, anything." The Brown family pulled up stakes and moved to Washington, DC.

Bryant believed that he charged the NAACP LDF $1,200 for representing Brown. "I would have felt better had I tried it for free if I could afford it. But I couldn't do it. I had to live down there."

By the time Jasper Brown was sentenced, like other Americans, Bill Bryant had lived through a whirlwind of painful and powerful days. Days of outrageous injustice.

Caswell County, North Carolina, was hardly the only place to fail to comply immediately with *Brown*. Bryant witnessed the massive resistance movement against school desegregation. The "Declaration of Constitutional Principles," better known as the "Southern Manifesto," was issued in the winter of 1956. Signed by nineteen senators and eighty-two members of the House—about one-fifth of Congress—it decried the *Brown* decision "as a clear abuse of judicial power," as a ruling that was "creating chaos and confusion." It commended "the motives of those States which have declared the intention to resist forced integration by any lawful means."

Much of the resistance took the form of illegal actions. Black people were threatened with violence—and subjected to violence—for trying to enroll their children in "white" schools. Some localities shut down public schools and funneled their funds into all-white private schools. The most notorious case was Prince Edward County in Virginia. It shut down its public school system for *five* years (1959–1964), leaving some 1,700 Black children educationally stranded and causing long-term damage.

By the time Prince Edward County shuttered its public school system, Bill Bryant had mourned the senseless murder of fourteen-year-old Emmett Till, whose mutilated body was thrown into the Tallahatchie River near Money, Mississippi, in 1955 with the seventy-five-pound fan of a cotton gin tied with barbed wire around his neck.

Chip remembered that his dad "was a total news junkie all his life, particularly legal, political, and civil rights news," so, of course, he kept up with all of this along with the news surrounding those days of Black people walking, biking, carpooling in Montgomery, Alabama, some twenty miles south of Wetumpka. How he must have marveled at Black people risking verbal attacks, physical attacks, and the loss of jobs—and contending with the fear engendered in the community on the night that the home of the bus boycott's leader, Dr. King, was bombed. Still, thousands stayed the course, remained so brave for 381 days, until the boycott was called off on December 20, 1956, after the city received a court order to end the injustice of segregation on its buses. The order came about a month after the US Supreme Court upheld the lower court's ruling in the class-action lawsuit *Browder v. Gayle* that state enforcement of the segregated but privately owned bus system in Montgomery violated the equal protection clause of the Fourteenth Amendment.

Five months after Bill Bryant's appearance before the high court, there was the early September day in 1957 when nine Black teens bravely integrated Arkansas's Central High in Little Rock and faced countless days of verbal, psychological, and physical abuse. What's more, there were all those days when Black people and white allies risked being bloodied and jailed when they protested against the injustice of whites-only lunch counters with sit-ins, whites-only pools and beaches with wade-ins, and whites-only public libraries with read-ins, when they staged kneel-ins at all-white churches, when they embarked on Freedom Rides to test rulings that banned Jim Crow on interstate buses and in bus terminals.

Later painful and powerful days included early May days in 1963 in Birmingham, Alabama, when, after scores of Black adult protestors, including Dr. King, had been jailed, more than a thousand Black children marched for social justice, braving water cannon blasts, billy club thwacks, police dog attacks. "It makes me sick," said President John F. Kennedy after seeing a photograph of a cop brutalizing a Black youth.

On June 11, President Kennedy was sickened by another disgrace in the state where Bill Bryant was born: Governor George Wallace standing in the doorway of the Foster Auditorium at the University of Alabama in Tuscaloosa to prevent Vivian Malone and James Hood from registering for classes, a right they had won by a court order that arose from an NAACP LDF lawsuit. The president federalized the Alabama National Guard and sent troops to the university to ensure that the court order was obeyed, that justice was done. Then, that evening, Kennedy addressed the American people, calling for more justice.

"We are confronted primarily with a moral issue. It is as old as the scriptures and is as clear as the American Constitution," said the president. "The heart of the question is whether all Americans are to be afforded equal rights and equal opportunities, whether we are going to treat our fellow Americans as we want to be treated." The president remarked that one hundred years after the Emancipation Proclamation, Black people were "not fully free. They are not yet freed from the bonds of injustice. They are not yet freed from social and economic oppression. And this Nation, for all its hopes and all its boasts, will not be fully free until all its citizens are free." Kennedy announced that he was going to call on Congress to enact a potent piece of civil rights legislation.

Two months later came the epic March on Washington for Jobs and Freedom. By plane and train, by car and cab, by bus and on foot people from all over the country journeyed to the capital to muster more support among the American people for that civil rights bill and to pressure Congress to pass it.

On this glorious August day, Astaire Bryant was in that crowd of roughly 250,000 with fifteen-year-old Penny and thirteen-year-old Chip. Bill was in his office with Bill Gardner and Ted Newman. All three were on-call attorneys for the NAACP in the event that demonstrators were arrested and all three were ready to perform their duty—while hoping to do so, said Judge Newman, "without being killed."

As it turned out, their services were not needed. No demonstrators were arrested. And the three didn't totally miss out on the march. They were present when Dr. King delivered his "I Have a Dream" speech.

After the March on Washington, through speeches, letters, and marches, people continued to press Congress for that civil rights bill—after Birmingham's Sixteenth Street Baptist Church was bombed on September 15, 1963, leaving four girls dead and more than twenty people injured; after President Kennedy was assassinated in Dallas on November 22; and after the new year came. The civil rights bill was "the order of the day at the great March on Washington last summer," wrote Dr. King in "A Look to 1964," an article that appeared in the *Amsterdam News* on January 4, 1964.

Five months later, on June 19, the bill finally cleared Congress. Two weeks after that, on July 2, in a televised ceremony with hundreds of guests in the East Room of the White House, Kennedy's successor, Lyndon Baines Johnson, was poised to sign that bill into law. Before he did, he addressed the American people.

The president shone the spotlight on the nation's hypocrisy. "We believe that all men are created equal. Yet many are denied equal treatment. We believe that all men have certain unalienable rights. Yet many Americans do not enjoy those rights. We believe that all men are entitled to the blessings of liberty. Yet millions are being deprived of those blessings—not because of their own failures, but because of the color of their skin." This, said Johnson, "cannot continue. Our Constitution, the foundation of our Republic, forbids it. The principles of our freedom forbid it. Morality forbids it. And the law I will sign tonight forbids it."

The landmark Civil Rights Act of 1964, which outlawed discrimination in education, employment, and in places of public accommodation—from parks to restaurants—was not only an act of justice for Black people. It prohibited such discrimination based on a person's "race, color, religion, sex, or national origin."

Many months after that powerful day on which Johnson signed the Civil Rights Act of 1964, strange things were happening at the Bryant home.

BEST EFFORT

The Bryant family no longer lived in that brick Cape Cod in Maryland, but in a three-story brick center-hall Colonial house in the Brookland section of the District.

There, at 3725 Seventeenth Street, NE, Penny and Chip heard clicks and other noises when they picked up the telephone receiver. At one point two men were parked outside their home "for what seemed like many days or maybe even weeks, off and on," said Chip. "I found all this very exciting, not really knowing what it all meant. I remember telling my buddies about it."

Equally intriguing was an invitation Bill and Astaire received to a cocktail-and-dinner party at the Cleveland Park home of two prominent DC Democrats: Gilbert Avery Harrison, owner and editor-in-chief of the *New Republic*, and Nancy Blaine Harrison, a great-granddaughter of inventor and entrepreneur Cyrus McCormick. Nancy's good works included cofounding the District of Columbia Citizens for a Better Public Education. The philanthropy of this woman, who had inherited $11 million from her grandmother Anita McCormick Blaine, was legendary.

Neither Bill nor Astaire personally knew the Harrisons and were completely taken aback by the invitation. At the party they were surprised to see that the other guests included two Black neighbors: Aubrey E. Robinson Jr. and his wife, Sarah. Aubrey was an associate judge on the juvenile court.

When Bill and Astaire returned home from the party, Chip grilled them. "I wanted a complete debriefing as to what went on and how/why they thought they were invited to attend. I think that's when my parents explained that Daddy was being considered for a very important government position, and that was why there were men spying on our house and tapping our phone—to make sure we were loyal, law-abiding citizens."

Not long after that evening in the Harrison home, on July 12, 1965, President Johnson announced his nomination of Bill Bryant to fill a vacancy on the US District Court for the District of Columbia. He also nominated Oliver Gasch to fill another vacancy on the same court.[15]

"It became obvious to my folks," said Chip, "that in addition to the standard FBI investigation and vetting of federal nominees, the Harrisons had been asked by the Democratic Party powers that be at that time, to socially vet both my parents and the Robinsons."

On the afternoon of July 15, Bryant was working away in his office when he was told that Mr. Valenti was on the phone for him.

The only Mr. Valenti Bryant was aware of was Jack Valenti, a special assistant to President Johnson (and future head of the Motion Picture Association of America). Bryant thought someone was pulling his leg, but when he picked up the phone, the person on the other end of the line introduced himself as Jack Valenti and told him that President Johnson wanted him to attend a dinner aboard the presidential yacht, the USS *Sequoia*, that very evening. After Bill hung up the phone, he still wondered if he was on the receiving end of a prank, but he called Astaire to let her know that he had been summoned to the *Sequoia*.

When he boarded the yacht, Bryant learned that he was not the president's only guest. Johnson was hosting a dinner for ambassadors and chargés d'affaires from some twenty African nations.

"And what's your country?" a white guy in his early thirties asked Bryant as he sat on a railing.

"Alabama," Bryant replied with a straight face.

"What?"

"Alabama," Bryant said again. "I have been in the District of Columbia since I was eleven months old. I have spent the rest of my life trying to forget the first eleven months." Bryant had a good chuckle with the fellow. He was another of Johnson's special assistants: the future award-winning journalist Bill Moyers.

---

15. Oliver Gasch, the US Attorney who had Mallory's case dismissed after the Supreme Court overturned the conviction, had recently entered private practice.

As the *Sequoia* sailed up and down the Potomac, Bryant did not have a lot of interaction with the president, but he remembered that Johnson "looked bad," strained and drained as he was by the nation's escalating involvement in the war in Vietnam and the escalating opposition to it among the American people.

Bryant never knew who put his name forward for the judgeship. Nancy Harrison? He also wondered if it was attorney Charlie Horsky, who in 1962 had become the first presidential advisor on national capital affairs. Bryant had worked with Horsky on several projects. One was getting the ACLU's DC branch off the ground.

Bryant had also worked on a committee with Horsky and police department lawyer Roger Robb, who became a judge on the US Court of Appeals for the DC Circuit. Bryant, Horsky, and Robb carried out a probe into the Metropolitan Police Department's practice of conducting random roundups—"arrests for investigation." This committee discovered the futility of these roundups in terms of solving crimes. Most of the folks were cut loose shortly after their arrest. At the end of their sixteen-month investigation, Bryant, Horsky, and Robb issued a 130-page report recommending that the police department put an end to this unconstitutional and worthless practice: "The cost to the community is more than the practice is worth. Legally, the practice cannot be justified. The practice should stop, and stop immediately." It did.

In his 1974 book *The Benchwarmers: The Private World of the Powerful Federal Judges*, Joseph C. Goulden maintained that the people behind Bryant's nomination included Ralph Bunche. By 1965 Bunche was not only a prominent civil rights leader but also a renowned diplomat who played a key role in the 1945 creation of the United Nations (UN). In 1950 Bunche became the first person of color to receive a Nobel Peace Prize. The award was for his work as a UN mediator brokering a ceasefire in the Arab-Israeli war that erupted in the wake of the creation of the State of Israel in 1948. In 1963 President Kennedy awarded him the Medal of Freedom. When President Johnson nominated Bryant for a judgeship, Bunche, who had been a force in the decolonization movement, was serving as UN undersecretary-general for special political affairs.

Bryant never hankered to be a judge. A few years earlier he had passed on the opportunity to be put forward to fill a vacancy on the Municipal Court's Domestic Relations branch. This devoted family man simply did not want to deal with often messy and heartbreaking divorce and child custody cases. The few times he was asked to handle a divorce, the first thing he did was try to talk the couple out of splitting up, succeeding on more than one occasion.

Chip recalled one success story. He and his dad were enjoying lunch at Lansburgh's department store one day when a man and woman came over to their table. One of them said to Bill, "We don't know where we'd be today without you." Chip said his father "was so genuinely happy to see them still together."

Bryant had also passed on an opportunity to serve on the juvenile court, but a federal judgeship was another thing altogether. With a lifetime appointment he would experience the ultimate in independence. But . . .

Back when someone from the White House telephoned telling him to expect a call from President Johnson, Bryant wrestled with whether to accept the nomination. Judge Newman recalled that he was deeply concerned that if he became a judge—and thus a referee in a courtroom—he would sorely miss being a contestant in a courtroom. Apart from his family, "his greatest joy was trying" a case, said Judge Newman. He was convinced that had Bryant not had Penny and Chip to put through college and had Astaire worked outside the home, he would have responded to the president with a polite, "Thanks, but no thanks."

People who did not know Bryant well were under the impression that if he became a judge, he would be taking a pay cut. As Bryant himself recalled, "When the word got out that I was being considered for [a seat on the District Court], I used to hear people say, 'Can Bill Bryant afford to take that job?' Hell, I couldn't afford not to." If Bryant made over $15,000 a year, he was, he said, "in clover." If confirmed by the Senate, he would earn about twice that much. (Bryant could have had many years in clover had he represented drug dealers, but that is where he drew the line.)

The largest single fee he ever earned was for his work as the executor of the estate of Charles Manuel "Sweet Daddy" Grace, the Cape

Verdean founder and bishop of the United House of Prayer for All People, a primarily Black denomination headquartered in DC. The bishop died in January 1960.

The District Court's Judge George L. Hart Jr. tapped Bryant to handle the bishop's estate at a time when Black lawyers, he said, "were usually appointed to piddling things like the estate of a veteran who dies in St. Elizabeths Hospital." Bishop Grace's estate was hardly piddling—and hardly simple. As Goulden explained, it "was tangled with far-flung potential claimants (including some in Africa) and obscure and hidden assets. . . . Bryant worked on the case for two years, found that Daddy Grace had assets of $30 million, and satisfied all claimants." Bryant also oversaw the election of the church's next bishop.

According to Goulden, when Bryant's work was done, he was prepared to submit an invoice for $30,000, and he asked a friend, "Do you think this is too much?" By law Bryant could have charged up to $300,000, or 1 percent of the assets. Said that friend to Goulden: "You can bet your ass that some other lawyers in this town would have run up the meter on this one: trips to Africa, trips to the West Coast, that sort of thing. Bryant played it tight and honest. He's that kind of guy."

Dr. Michael R. Winston contended that there "is more than one explanation for Bryant thinking that $30,000 might be 'too much' to charge for handling a thirty-million dollar estate. His integrity was always beyond question, and he would not have 'run up the tab' by taking unnecessary trips or by any other device. But he had been extremely limited in his practice by the segregation of the Bar." Dr. Winston added that Black lawyers with offices on F Street, NW (so-called Negro lawyers' row) "were very capable people, but they simply did not handle estates of the size of Bishop Grace's. They had no experience of big or small white law firms." For those F Street lawyers, "$300,000 was unimaginable as a fee, even though that would have been permissible by law."[16]

Bryant's nomination for a seat on the District Court met with hostility in some quarters, according to Goulden. "Because of his background in criminal defense work, especially that of the Mallory case (a decision which the police establishment considers the Pearl

16. Where "Negro lawyers' row" once stood now stands the Capital One Arena.

Harbor of law enforcement, or worse), Bryant's nomination drew much underground opposition, especially from the Washington field office of the FBI. According to reliable accounts from within the Justice Department, the FBI report contained so much unconfirmable adverse rumor that Bryant's appointment was fleetingly in doubt. But when department officials finished sorting through the information, and evaluating it, 'there wasn't a piece of dirt the size of a toothpick.'"

On the morning of Friday, July 23, 1965, Bill Bryant was in room 2228 of what is today known as the Dirksen Senate Office Building, before the Subcommittee of the Committee on the Judiciary.

The committee chair was a champion of civil rights, Democrat Philip Hart of Michigan, known as the "The Conscience of the Senate" and after whom the Senate's third office building was named in 1976. The other members of the committee were Democrat Quentin Burdick of North Dakota, Democrat Birch Bayh of Indiana, moderate Republican Hugh Scott of Pennsylvania, and liberal Republican Jacob Javits of New York.

At the start of the hearing, Senator Hart asked, "May I ask if there is present anyone who desires to testify against this nomination?"

Silence.

"I would repeat that. Is there anyone who desires to testify against the nomination."

Silence.

"I assume, then, that this large crowd is at least neutral and very probably all for the nominee."

That large crowd then heard from four people fiercely in favor of the nomination. The first was Paul McCardle, president of BADC, the organization that denied Black people membership when Bryant began practicing law. McCardle declared Bryant "exceptionally well qualified" for the judgeship. He rated him one of DC's "most outstanding attorneys."

The committee then heard from Frederick Evans, president of the Washington Bar Association. Cofounded by Charlie Houston in 1925, it was one of the first Black bar associations in the nation. Evans was certain that Bryant would bring to the bench "unquestionable legal ability, impeccable integrity and sound judicial temperament." He noted that Bryant had served the Washington Bar Association and

BADC "in a number of important committee assignments" and that he was currently on the board of directors of the Neighborhood Legal Services Project (NLSP). With several offices in Black neighborhoods, the NLSP provided legal services for indigent people.

Joe Waddy was the next person to champion Bill Bryant. Waddy had left the firm he shared with Bryant and Gardner in 1962 after his appointment to a seat on the Municipal Court's Domestic Relations branch, the judgeship that Bryant had declined to pursue.[17]

"I know from personal experience that this man is of the highest integrity," declared Judge Waddy. "I know that he has exceptional ability, and I know that if he is confirmed, he will carry on in the highest traditions of the judiciary." He remarked briefly on Bryant's domestic life, his "lovely wife" and "two well-adjusted children," and was convinced that all this spoke "very highly of the type of family life that this man has, and of his own personal character."

Astaire and Chip were at the hearing. Penny was at her summer job, working at an NLSP office, where she did client intake and typed letters and legal briefs to be filed in court. When asked if his parents were nervous as they left home for the hearing, Chip replied, "If my folks were nervous, they probably would not have let me know or see that. They were very protective."

After introducing himself to the committee, John J. Carmody, a past president of the DC Bar Association, stated, "I have appeared before this august tribunal many times, quite a few times, may I say, in opposing nominees." That said, Carmody declared Bryant "one

17. By 1965 the Municipal Court had become the DC Court of General Sessions, which was later combined with the juvenile and tax courts for the making of the DC Superior Court. At the time of the hearing, the firm was composed of not only Bryant, Gardner, and Newman, but also future DC Superior Court and DC Court of Appeals judge, Annice M. Wagner, a Dunbar High graduate who earned her bachelor's and law degrees from Wayne State. Joining the firm later was Howard Law graduate Emmet G. Sullivan who would serve on the DC Superior Court, DC Court of Appeals, and the District Court. William C. Gardner was appointed to the DC Superior Court in 1980. The first member of the firm to become a federal judge was the nation's first Black federal judge: Charlie Houston's second cousin William H. Hastie, a Harvard Law graduate under whom Bryant studied at Howard Law. In 1937 President Franklin D. Roosevelt appointed Hastie to the US District Court for the District of the Virgin Islands, where he was its first Black governor (1946–1949). Hastie also served on the US Court of Appeals for the Third Circuit (1950–1976).

of the best nominees for this position we have had in many, many years." Carmody had first gotten to know Bryant and "to appreciate his work" when Bryant served on the Committee on the Revision of the Federal Rules, and Carmody was its chair. After his experience with Bryant, when Carmody was unable to take on cases for whatever reason, he delighted in sending them to Bryant, "because I knew that they would be handled well." Carmody added that along with his "extensive knowledge of law" Bryant "possesses judicial temperament. I have seen it reflected in his law practice. I have seen it reflected in his courtroom tactics."

After Carmody concluded his remarks, Senator Hart again asked if anyone wanted to speak in opposition to the nomination.

Silence.

When invited to address the committee, Bryant was brief.

"Sir, at the risk of undoing some of the things that have already been said, I think I am compelled to say that as you know this is quite flattering to have the President of the United States express this much confidence in you." He added, "It is a great honor. It is also a great responsibility. The only other thing I can say is that if it is the pleasure of this body to recommend my confirmation, I shall always give this matter my best effort."

Shortly before the committee adjourned, Senator Hart had this to say: "Next time we meet, I am sure I shall address you as Judge."

"Thank you very much, sir."

The hearing lasted all of twenty-five minutes.

An article celebrating the nomination appeared in the *Afro* the next day. It called Bryant "a criminal case dynamo with a homespun wit, a sparkling laugh, an enthusiastic air, a sense of humor, and the common touch" and pointed out that "nearly everybody calls Attorney Bryant 'Bill.'"

Bernice Gordon, the receptionist-secretary at Bill's firm, told the *Afro*. "I am just so thrilled about the appointment I don't know what to do. He is such a wonderful person. It couldn't have happened to a nicer one."

In its pen picture of Bryant, the *Afro* told its readers that he was fifty-three, five feet, nine inches tall, kept his weight between 153 and

155 pounds, and, oddly, that his neck size was 15½. His hair was "just beginning to show touches of grey."

Readers learned that Bryant was color blind, had never gone fishing, and didn't really have any favorite foods. Also that he loved his wife's cooking—but "I like to take her out dining every so often, though she probably doesn't think it is often enough."

On the movies: "I like it when I can get there. My wife and I go every now and then, particularly when a certain movie's publicity strikes our attention."

On television: "I have no program favorite. I try to catch the news, of course, and the Sunday sports telecast."

On music: "Well, I can relax and enjoy almost any kind. Not being a teenager, rock and roll doesn't particularly appeal to me, but I don't have an intolerant attitude toward it." (Bryant wasn't being totally open with the *Afro*. For example, when it came to music he was really into the blues and Benny Goodman-style jazz. He loved watching westerns, and his favorite evening-news anchor was Walter Cronkite. "He liked pecans a lot," said Penny.)

About two weeks after the hearing and that *Afro* piece, on August 11, the Senate confirmed Oliver Gasch and the man with the common touch. At the time there were fewer than ten Black federal judges in a nation with several hundred, and Bryant was only the second Black person appointed to the DC District Court since it was established in 1863. His confirmation came just days after another milestone moment in the Civil Rights Movement.

On August 6 President Johnson signed into law the landmark Voting Rights Act of 1965, aimed at ending the suppression of the Black vote. Among other things, the Voting Rights Act banned obstacles to voting such as literacy tests and made provision for federal examiners to supervise voter registration in places where voting rights were trampled. Moreover, jurisdictions where discrimination in voting was pervasive would be banned from altering voting procedures and practices without approval from the Justice Department or from the

US District Court for the District of Columbia, on which Bill Bryant would soon serve.[18]

He and Oliver Gasch were sworn in to serve on the "big court" on August 16. Bryant was, understandably, a bit anxious. "You know," he said to Gasch, "I've been a lawyer for many years, but putting on this robe, I don't feel so sure. This is a serious responsibility."

"Bill, I don't think it's going to be that hard for you," Gasch replied with a smile. "You know right from wrong."

---

18. This "pre-clearance" provision was Section 5 of the Voting Rights Act. It was made null and void in *Shelby County v. Holder* (2013). In a 5–4 decision, the US Supreme Court ruled unconstitutional the formula in Section 4(b) used to determine where pre-clearance was required. After the *Shelby* decision, many localities devised an array of tactics to further voter suppression in certain communities—especially Black ones—such as rigid photo-ID laws, unjust voter roll purges, shortening hours for voting in certain neighborhoods, and closing polling stations in certain neighborhoods.

DAY AFTER DAY, TRYING CASES

When Bill Bryant became a member of the US District Court for the District of Columbia in the summer of 1965, its chief judge was Matthew Francis McGuire, on the bench since 1941. Judge McGuire was known as a quick decision maker and for his "wry sense of humor," said a reporter. In addition to Oliver Gasch, Bryant's fellow associate judges included Burnita Shelton Matthews, before whom he had defended Lefty Winston; Richmond B. Keech, before whom he had defended Matthew Harrison; and Alexander Holtzoff, who presided over Mallory's trial. Also on this court was its first Black judge, and Judge Bryant's friend, Spottswood W. Robinson III, a native of Richmond, Virginia, who graduated from Howard Law three years after Bryant.[19]

Things were kind of "hectic," said Judge Bryant, reflecting on his early days on the bench. "When I first came on the court and for some years thereafter, they didn't have the individual calendar system. You might get a civil case that had been in the hands of four or five or six other judges before it gets to you if you are going to try it. Or you might have a motion in a case that you had no previous experience in, and after you deal with the motion you are not going to have any more experience in. A kind of haphazard kind of business."

19. Robinson, who in *Brown v. Board of Education*, along with Oliver Hill, argued the Virginia school desegregation case, *Davis v. County School Board of Prince Edward County*, and who served as dean of Howard Law 1960–1963, was appointed to the court in 1964 and would be elevated to the US Court of Appeals for the DC Circuit in 1966, the year that Bryant's friend and neighbor Aubrey E. Robinson Jr. would join him on the District Court. In 1967 Joseph C. Waddy would become a member of this court. This was the same year that Thurgood Marshall became the first Black US Supreme Court justice.

During these hectic days, the cases that Judge Bryant dealt with ranged from petty larceny and assault to arson, rape, and first-degree murder. Just as when he was an assistant US attorney, Judge Bryant stayed busy: "Every day from 9, 9:15 to 9:30 right straight through the day. Day after day, trying cases."

When it came to dispensing sentences, there were those who, unlike Judge Oliver Gasch, did not think that the Honorable William Benson Bryant knew right from wrong. Early on he was "tagged as the most lenient sentencing judge of the court," reported the *Sunday Star*'s William Basham. "He soon found himself swamped with guilty pleas." At the time, "judge shopping" was allowed: defense attorneys with clients willing to forgo a trial and plead guilty could choose the judge they believed would go easiest on their clients. Basham's article ran on March 31, 1968, the day before judge shopping was set to end in the District Court, as he reported.

Noting that Judge Bryant "had distinguished himself as a tireless trial attorney," Basham remarked that it "was obvious that he needed this stamina to shoulder what soon became the heaviest criminal caseload in the court." Court employees and colleagues on the bench believed, wrote Basham, that his "case burden has been wearing him down, despite his show of energy. Some say he agonized too long over each case at the time of sentencing—that crucial period when a judge holds awesome power over a defendant."

Agonizing over each case often had Judge Bryant in the courthouse until after midnight carefully reading presentence reports. (A *Washington Post* article from the previous year stated that he "pays closer attention than some judges to the defendant's background and tries to tailor the sentence accordingly.") Of course, with each case the judge was bringing to bear his experience as both a prosecutor and a defense attorney. Moreover, Judge Bryant had not been raised like chickens on wire. The man who now occupied the federal courthouse's Courtroom 16 had known adversity and was attuned to the adversities everyday folk often faced.

In cases of nonheinous crimes, Judge Bryant granted probation 50 percent of the time to defendants who took a plea deal. More than any of his colleagues, he availed himself of the Youth Corrections Act that allowed him to sentence men age eighteen to twenty-two to the

Lorton Youth Center in Fairfax County, Virginia, instead of to the DC Jail. The Lorton Youth Center, which opened in 1960, had been designed to look less like a prison and more like a college campus (with inmates wearing suits and ties). School dropouts could earn the equivalency of a high school diploma. Those without academic aptitude could learn a trade.

For his article, William Basham spoke with more than a few prosecutors and defense attorneys who pushed back against the charge that Judge Bryant was overly lenient and a coddler of criminals. "Most favor either 'fair' or 'humane.'" In any event, at sentencing the judge could be quite stern.

Take the case of eighteen-year-old Donnell Jackson, who pleaded guilty to snatching a woman's purse, striking her in the process. According to his lawyer, Jackson didn't have a juvenile record and was estranged from his family at the time of the crime. Since then he had been on the straight and narrow. He was holding down a steady job and had reconciled with his parents. Judge Bryant told Jackson that his victim had "the right to walk the streets in safety. You not only took her pocketbook, but you hit her in the mouth." After this rebuke, instead of giving Jackson jail time, he sentenced him to three years' probation. "If you cross the line, you're going to the penitentiary. Keep your hands off people . . . off property."

To twenty-year-old Ralph Maniscarco, who pled guilty to robbing someone at knifepoint, the judge said, "Whatever impulses you had that night, you'd better get rid of them. It's stupid." Like Donnell Jackson, Maniscarco had no priors and was gainfully employed at the time of sentencing. Judge Bryant placed him on probation for three years.

He gave repeat car thief Joseph Martin, also twenty, a suspended sentence of twenty months to five years in prison and placed him on probation for five years. Judge Bryant told Martin that he might have "wheel syndrome" but that he had better understand that if he was nabbed again for stealing a vehicle within the next five years, his butt would end up behind bars. "You are walking out of here today with the keys to the penitentiary in your pocket. When you switch on one of those cars, you are opening the door of the nearest penitentiary."

The year that Basham's article appeared was the same year that Judge Bryant had mercy on Donnell Jackson, Ralph Maniscarco, and Joseph Martin, and the year that progressive Americans celebrated the Fair Housing Act of 1968, which banned discrimination in housing—from sales and rentals to financing—based on race, religion, national origin, and sex. It was also the year that Boeing rolled out the 747 jumbo jet; that Frank Borman, Jim Lovell, and Bill Anders orbited the Moon aboard *Apollo 8*; and that the controversial rock musical *Hair* opened on Broadway. However, more than anything else, 1968 was a year of great tumult and more tragedies than anyone cared to count.

On January 23, 1968, North Korean forces seized a US Navy intelligence vessel, the USS *Pueblo*. Dunnie Tuck, one of the dozens of Americans held captive for eleven months, recalled, "We got terrible beatings. Head beatings, rifle butts and broomsticks—I had two chairs broken over my head."

A week after the capture of the *Pueblo*, in the early hours of January 31, the North Vietnamese and Vietcong forces launched phase one of the Tet Offensive, a series of attacks on more than a hundred South Vietnamese cities, towns, and villages—including the capital city of Saigon. Though North Vietnam ultimately failed to control the territory it invaded, the Tet Offensive blew a hole through the US government's claim that South Vietnam was winning the war.

Between the start of the Tet Offensive and its end by early March 1968, US and South Vietnamese forces suffered some 12,000 casualties, roughly 2,600 of them deaths. Added to that were the deaths of some 7,000 South Vietnamese civilians and the wounding of more than 18,000. Tens of thousands of North Vietnamese and Vietcong soldiers were killed. More Americans were growing sick of the carnage, sick of so many members of the US armed forces returning home in body bags, sick of the millions and millions of dollars spent on war. More Americans agreed with Dr. King's powerful pronouncement in his remarkable 1967 speech at New York City's Riverside Church, "Beyond Vietnam—A Time to Break Silence": "A nation that continues year after year to spend more money on military defense than on programs of social uplift is approaching spiritual death."

On March 31, 1968, President Johnson shocked the nation, and the world, when he announced that he would not seek reelection. Just a few days later, thirty-nine-year-old Dr. King was assassinated as he stood on the balcony of the Lorraine Motel in Memphis, Tennessee. In the wake of the murder in Memphis, Black rage was on display in the streets of Judge Bryant's DC and scores of other cities. The looting, the burning, the hurling of stones and Molotov cocktails were not only in reaction to the killing of Dr. King. As had been the case the year before during the "long, hot summer of 1967," the root of the violence was rage over opportunities denied, over persistent inequities in housing, education, employment—in just about every aspect of life. And over police brutality.

Two months after Dr. King's assassination, progressive Americans were grieving again. Forty-two-year-old Bobby Kennedy, a champion of civil rights and a contender for the Democratic presidential nomination, was assassinated as he celebrated his victory in the California primary at L.A.'s Ambassador Hotel.

It was also in 1968 that, at the historically Black South Carolina State College (now University) in Orangeburg, state troopers fired into a crowd of peaceful civil rights demonstrators, killing three and wounding more than twenty (many shot in the back).

The year also saw thousands of L.A.'s Hispanic high school students stage a walkout in protest of subpar education.

It saw NYU students picket a recruiting event by Dow Chemical, the US military's supplier of napalm.

It saw a ninety-minute shootout in Oakland, California, between Black Panthers and the police.

It saw Columbia University students take over several campus buildings in protest, among other things, of the university's affiliation with the Institute for Defense Analyses, a weapons R&D company.

There was unrest at Judge Bryant's alma mater too. In March 1968, Howard University students chanted "Beep, beep! Bang, bang! Unga-wa! Black power!" outside the Mordecai Wyatt Johnson Administration Building before taking it over, demanding, among other things, a comprehensive Black studies program.

All around the world—Brazil, Czechoslovakia, France, Mexico, South Africa, Spain—the year 1968 saw rebellions in which thousands of political protesters were bloodied and killed. And in August of that year, during the Democratic National Convention in Chicago, people around the world saw bloody battles between antiwar demonstrators and the police. *The Year That Rocked the World* was the perfect subtitle for Mark Kurlansky's history book about 1968.

The theme of *Esquire* magazine's October 1968 issue was "Salvaging the 20th Century." Acknowledging that "man's inhumanity to man" is all too common, one article declared, "If the human race is salvageable and in fact worth saving it is not because of any lovable traits that we exhibit en masse, but because there are some, a few, individuals who give evidence that selfless behavior is not a genetic impossibility." This article, titled "Twenty-Seven People Worth Saving," offered readers examples of selfless souls "in the hope that if the Great Originator of all this is thinking of wiping it out and starting over he may, for a while at least, stay his hand."

Judge William B. Bryant was the first person on this list of twenty-seven people worth saving. Among the others on the list: civil rights activist Ella Baker and labor leader César Chavez. "Twenty-Seven People Worth Saving" celebrated Judge Bryant as "the man behind the Mallory rule" and saluted him for "his lifelong concern with providing legal defense for the poor, usually at a personal financial sacrifice." Though no longer doing so at a personal financial sacrifice, the judge was in a sense still defending the poor by dispensing mercy, not to hardened, vicious criminals, but to those charged with crimes such as purse snatching and car theft.

Astaire Bryant was engaged in work on behalf of the needy as well. She was a member of the Friends of the Juvenile Court, an all-volunteer organization established by Dorothy Goldberg, wife of Arthur Goldberg, US Supreme Court associate justice from 1962 to 1965. Initially created in response to a need to spruce up the juvenile court's waiting room, the organization went on to launch a number of initiatives to aid at-risk youth and their families. Astaire's involvement with the Friends of the Juvenile Court included working in its Georgetown thrift shop. Astaire had met Dorothy Goldberg through Nancy Harrison. Astaire and Nancy had become quite friendly after that dinner party in the Harrisons' Cleveland Park home.

Meanwhile, Astaire's husband was dealing with more than street crime cases.

In the spring of 1969, Judge Bryant had before him an ACLU case against the Department of the Interior (DOI) on behalf of several organizations. They included the Women Strike for Peace, Clergy and Laymen Concerned about Vietnam, and the Quaker Action Group. The lawsuit challenged the hundred-person limit on demonstrations in front of the White House and the five-hundred-person limit on demonstrations in Lafayette Park across the street. These limitations had been put in place in August 1967 when protests against the Vietnam War were on the rise.

The National Park Service maintained that having more than a hundred people demonstrating before the White House would "distract motorists on Pennsylvania Avenue, force pedestrians into the street and possibly block the White House driveways." As for Lafayette Park, the argument was that having more than five hundred people there at one time would lead to "injured shrubs and other plants."

One can imagine the judge rolling his eyes at those claims. On April 26, 1969, he ruled that limiting the number of demonstrators in Lafayette Park and before the White House infringed on people's First Amendment rights: "rights to freedom of speech and to assemble peaceably and petition the Government for a redress of grievances." Judge Bryant pointed out that before the regulations, during one demonstration "between 10,000 and 30,000 persons passed in orderly procession along the White House sidewalk" while upward of 30,000 had demonstrated in Lafayette Park. "Despite the large numbers of persons present during past demonstrations at almost no time have disruptions to the orderly flow of pedestrians or traffic along the White House sidewalk or through or around Lafayette Park occurred or been reported."

The government had also maintained that the regulations were "in the interest of the security and safety of the executive residence, its occupants and contents." In response to that the judge pointed out that "thousands of tourists pass through the White House itself every day." Moreover, in the rare instances of arrests during demonstrations there was "no correlation to the number of demonstrators."

Judge Bryant's injunction against DOI's numerical limitations was challenged, and the challenges were challenged. Eventually the DOI was allowed to limit demonstrations and special events before the

White House to 750 people at one time and those in Lafayette Park to three thousand at one time, with applicants for permits having the possibility of receiving a waiver of numerical limitations.

Another of Judge Bryant's high-profile cases was *Hodgson v. United Mine Workers of America* (UMWA). It stemmed from the union's disputed December 1969 elections in which W. A. "Tough Tony" Boyle, president of the roughly 200,000-member union since early 1963, beat out Joseph "Jock" Yablonski.

A little over a week after the election, Jock Yablonski contacted the Department of Labor (DOL) and implored that agency to look into election fraud. Shortly thereafter, Yablonski, his wife, Margaret, and their daughter, Charlotte, were shot dead in their Clarksville, Pennsylvania, home. In March 1970 the DOL sued to have the elections overturned.

In this bench trial, Judge Bryant found evidence of gross violations of several aspects of the Labor-Management Reporting and Disclosure Act of 1959. In his opinion, delivered on May 1, 1972, he stated that to find otherwise, he "would be forced to swim upstream against the tide of evidence too strong to resist." That evidence included the fact that the union's official publication, *The United Mine Workers Journal*, had been "used as a campaign instrument for the incumbents. The issues from March 1 through June 1 are replete with speeches, statements and pictures of Boyle, Titler and Owens." Titler was UMWA vice president George T. Titler. Owens was the union's secretary-treasurer John Owens.

"The April 15 issue," continued Judge Bryant, "even carried a convention song for Tony Boyle to be sung to the tune of 'Hello Dolly.'" The judge also noted that before Jock Yablonski announced his candidacy, "he had been mentioned and pictured in the *Journal* on several occasions" and that "Yablonski's announcement of his candidacy, though featured in the commercial press, was accorded not one word of mention in the *Journal*."

Financial malfeasance included pay raises for certain union employees, the judge found, "for the purpose of securing their support for the incumbent officers." Also, a little more than nine thousand dollars of union funds had been spent on five thousand ballpoint pens that advertised Boyle, Titler, and Owens. About a week before the election, District 23 had spent funds to hold a political rally in Madisonville, Kentucky. It had been billed as a black-lung event, but after a brief discussion of the disease and safety measures, the main event was Boyle "making an extensive attack on Yablonski."

Judge Bryant declared the 1969 elections "null and void." He ordered new elections under the supervision of the DOL, whose chief was James D. Hodgson. Among other things, the judge's order gave the DOL oversight over all union financial transactions and the power to post representatives at each of the union's more than twenty district headquarters and at UMWA headquarters in DC. The judge's order was the "strongest order for a union election within memory," said the *Washington Post.*

While just doing his job, Judge Bryant, being one of just a handful of Black federal judges at the time, demonstrated remarkable courage and bravery by issuing such a strong order against the UMWA, whose top leadership had ordered a successful mafia-style hit on the Yablonskis. Such was the judge's iron will in his commitment to justice.

As for "Tough Tony" Boyle, in 1973 he was arrested and charged with ordering the hit on the Yablonskis. Sentenced to three consecutive life terms, he died in prison in 1985. Eight co-conspirators, including the three hit men, also went to prison.

By the time Judge Bryant ruled in the UMWA case in 1972, he had suffered a profound personal loss. On July 11, 1970, his mother, Alberta Wood Washington, died. She was in her late seventies.

At the time of her death, Alberta was living in an apartment in Brookland a few blocks away from her son. Long before she passed, Astaire regularly prepared dinners for her, meals sometimes delivered by Bill, sometimes by Chip and Penny.

When asked how her dad took his mother's death, Penny replied, "My father, of course, was very sad, and quiet."

Bill had lost his stepfather, George Washington, and his grandparents, Lizzie and Charlie Wood, many years earlier. Astaire's father and stepmother had also died years earlier.

Nearly three years before his mother passed, Bill was at home, in his kitchen with Astaire and Chip, when he received a call from New York City. His biological father had died. Bill knew that Benson Bryan, a World War I veteran nicknamed "Buddy," had remarried and had stepchildren. He also knew that the father he never laid eyes on also had a daughter. Benson was seventy-eight when he passed.

"He got off the phone and told us the news," said Chip. "My mother asked him, 'Well, Bill, what are you going to do?' He hesitated, and then answered her, 'I'm not going to do anything.'"

Chip continued: "Obviously, he never forgave my grandfather, who we were never allowed to meet, for abandoning him, and I later totally understood. I always felt that having been abandoned as a child by his father was one thing that motivated him to be such a great father with his own family."

Chapter 14

IS IT RIGHT? IS IT RIGHT?

When Alberta passed, the Bryants were still living at 3725 Seventeenth Street, NE, in that brick three-story center hall Colonial-style house with its three main bedrooms and a living room with a fireplace. On the third floor was a guest bedroom, along with a room Astaire had made into an office for Bill. As he rarely used it, that room became the place where young Chip often did his homework. Naturally, a house like this had a dining room, but the family used it only on special occasions. They ate most meals in the kitchen.

They did a lot of their living in the basement family room, a knotty-pine-paneled room with a gas fireplace to keep it cozy on the cold days, and with a large tropical fish tank to delight the eye no matter the season. It's where the family watched television and set up the annual Christmas tree. It was also where Bill enjoyed playing his collection of vinyl records on his stereo, grooving to Big Band–era tunes, digging the soulful sounds of Nat King Cole or Ella Fitzgerald. His all-time favorite singer was gospel great Mahalia "Move-on-Up-a-Little-Higher" Jackson.

Bill and Astaire hosted many a card party in their basement. In its kitchen, where Astaire dished up finger food for their guests, she also made homemade applesauce from store-bought apples and grape jam from the grapevines that grew in a corner of the backyard. That basement was also home to Bill's prized Brunswick solid-slate-top pool table, which he purchased one Christmas and on which he taught both Penny and Chip to shoot pool.

Along with fond memories of his father teaching him to shoot pool, Chip would never forget how that large fish tank came to be a fixture in the basement. When he was seven or eight, Bill took him along on a visit to his friend and fellow attorney Frankie Bourne and his wife, Ivey. Chip went wide-eyed over the couple's several marvelous aquariums. Months later, on Christmas morning, Chip was very happy and excited when he discovered a fish tank up and running "complete with an operating filter, and air bubbles blowing up from beneath the colored gravel, and all sorts of tropical plants and fish." Bill had pulled it off with the help of Frankie Bourne. "I'll never forget my dad conspiring with Mr. Bourne to surprise me that Christmas."

Both Penny and Chip would never forget the Friday night treat of dinner out. One favorite restaurant was the Hot Shoppe on Rhode Island Avenue, a short drive from their home. The legendary Hogate's Seafood Restaurant on DC's Southwest waterfront was something of a destination for family celebrations. Back in 1960 Bill treated Astaire, Penny, Chip, his aunts, and his first cousin Johnny Edwards (Aunt Josephine's son) to a grand dinner at Hogate's on the occasion of Johnny's graduation from Howard Med. It was a most memorable event for Chip: "I was ten at that time and it was my first time eating lobster."

Later, Bill sometimes splurged on dinner at the Occidental, the upscale surf-and-turf restaurant on Pennsylvania Avenue, NW. Bill and Astaire both loved good seafood, so much so that they regularly went to the fish market on Maine Avenue, SW, on the Waterfront to buy fish just off a boat. Remembered Chip: "Ninety percent of the time my dad would be the one to cook it. Always broiled or baked, hardly ever fried."

Bill was still not big on vacations, but the family did enjoy getaways. They included get-togethers with two couples Bill and Astaire had known since before Chip and Penny were born: Chauncey and Edna Artis (he an attorney, and she at one point a secretary) and Inez and George Herman Dabney (she a federal employee and one of Astaire's best friends, and he a brick mason by trade turned general contractor).

During warm-weather months Chauncey and Edna Artis often hosted card parties at their vacation home on Columbia Beach, Maryland, one of several resorts Black professionals established during the days of Jim Crow in their quest to partake of simple pleasures many white Americans of means enjoyed. En route to Columbia Beach, Bill had a habit of stopping at a roadside store where he indulged in some one-armed-bandit action (legal in Maryland then). "My dad definitely enjoyed an occasional game of chance, whether it be penny-penny poker, the slots or the ponies," said Chip. He added that his father had stopped betting on horse races at Astaire's insistence.

While visiting Chauncey and Edna Artis at Columbia Beach, the family also spent time on Deale, the next beach over, where Inez and George Dabney had a small cabin cruiser. The Dabneys loved to fish, said Chip, "and I loved boats, so my mother would brave sea sickness to take me on their boat to go fishing. My dad never got on the boat. I think he was prone to seasickness worse than my mom." Makes you wonder if Bill had some excruciating moments on that July night in 1965 when he was aboard the USS *Sequoia* at President Johnson's request.

When the Bryants moved to Brookland in the mid-1950s, it was a peaceful, largely white neighborhood of well-kept homes of various sizes and styles. Remembered Chip: "We were among several younger Black families—doctors, attorneys and other professionals, government workers, and small business owners—who were integrating the neighborhood at that time." In addition to Aubrey and Sarah Robinson, who lived around the corner, their Black neighbors included the family of Georgetown Law graduate H. Carl Moultrie I, a member of George E. C. Hayes's firm.[20]

Brookland was home to more than a few Black people of note well before the 1950s. They included two renowned Howard University professors: historian Rayford W. Logan and poet and literary critic Sterling A. Brown, DC's first poet laureate (1984). Bill's mentor Ralph Bunche, who left Howard in 1941, lived in Brookland 1941–1947 in a home designed for him in the International Style by the prominent Black architect Hilyard R. Robinson, a Howard professor of architecture who also designed Logan's home. Bunche's home at 1510 Jackson Street, NE, was about a two-minute drive from the Bryant home.

By the 1970s Brookland was predominantly Black and still a wonderful family neighborhood, and Bill and Astaire still loved their home, but during the summer of 1973, said Chip, "my parents decided that

---

20. In 1972 Moultrie became an associate judge of the DC Superior Court and served as its chief judge from 1978 until his death in 1986, shortly after which its courthouse on Indiana Avenue, NW, bore his name.

their home on Seventeenth Street, with its three full flights of stairs, was not a viable option for their future." Bill and Astaire were in their early sixties.

The Bryants moved to the Chevy Chase section of Northwest DC, to 2920 Northampton Street. Home was now a midcentury colonial rambler with a huge bay window on the front. It was a spacious home: five bedrooms and a den.

When the weather was nice, Bill and Astaire took most of their meals on the elevated screened porch off the kitchen in the rear of the house. That porch overlooked a large yard filled with flowers and flowering trees. The front of the house was graced with dogwoods and crepe myrtles along with two concrete pots on either side of the front door. These pots overflowed with flowers spring, summer, and fall.

This home's daylight basement with its large windows looking out into the backyard was where many bridge and poker games were played and where, remembered Chip, "many of my father's signature Bourbon Whiskey Sours were consumed." Bill, by the way, didn't drink. When, in his younger days, he was at a party where folks did not know that he was a teetotaler, he could be found with a drink in hand, but when no one was looking he poured his drink into a plant. "I killed a lot of plants," he later joked with a law clerk.

It was also in the basement of the Northampton Street home that Bill's prized Brunswick pool table had a room of its own. Bill had added golf to his pastimes but had not lost his passion for pool. Even though he had his own pool table at home, he had never stopped shooting pool on Seventh Street. Not even when he became a judge. Initially, that is.

He did eventually curb his enthusiasm for some eight-ball action at the Stage Door pool hall. This was after, said Chip, "some of the regulars there persuaded him to give it up because they didn't want his reputation compromised in the event that a fight were to break out" or some other ugly incident were to occur. No one wanted to see a headline like "JUDGE BRYANT CAUGHT AMID POOL HALL BRAWL."

For the rest of his life, Bill would miss those games with the Seventh Street Regulars.

The year after the Bryants moved to Northampton Street, the judge was presiding over *Dellums v. Powell.* It was another case involving antiwar protesters. Its plaintiffs had been among the roughly thirteen thousand demonstrators arrested in the capital in early May 1971.

In *Dellums v. Powell* the ACLU represented some 1,200 people arrested on May 5, 1971, as they listened to antiwar speeches on the steps of the Capitol. The lead plaintiff was one of the speakers: Ron Dellums, the long, tall, unabashedly radical California congressman. Dellums, a founder of the Congressional Black Caucus, had not been arrested but, as one newspaper reported, "complained that he had been deprived of his free speech when the authorities took away his audience." (The lead defendant was James M. Powell, chief of the Capitol Police at the time of the arrests.)

The plaintiffs were seeking damages for violations of various constitutional rights, chiefly their First Amendment rights to freedom of speech and freedom of assembly. They also charged that the arrests had been part of a conspiracy hatched by top White House officials with President Nixon's approval. The ACLU wanted White House tapes from April 16 through May 10, 1971. In mid-November 1974, Judge Bryant ordered the White House to surrender said tapes. Nixon was, of course, no longer in the White House, having resigned in August over the Watergate scandal. By the time the trial started in mid-December, President Ford's White House counsel and attorneys for former President Nixon had managed to find ways around complying with the judge's order for those tapes.

Even without the tapes, the ACLU still won a major victory. At the end of the six-week trial, in January 1975, a jury of three men and three women awarded the plaintiffs $12 million in damages (about $60 million in today's dollars). Each plaintiff was to receive $7,500 for violation of First Amendment rights. The amounts varied for violations of other constitutional rights. For example, those who had been subjected to false imprisonment (a Fourth Amendment violation) were entitled to $300 to $1,200, depending on how long they were held in jail.

The *New York Times* reported that the "award by a jury in the United States District Court for the District of Columbia was thought to be one of the largest ever in a civil liberties suit." The court of appeals deemed it too much. Eventually the total award was reduced to north of $2 million.

For every high-profile case there were countless cases that never made national news—a multitude of "little" cases in which Judge Bryant was just as bound and determined to see that justice was done. As attorney John W. Nields Jr. said, "his love of justice was like, it was in his body. I mean you could—his body would react to good things that were happening in the courtroom and bad things that were happening in the courtroom."

Back in 1969, there was the case of Mark Kravik, whom Selective Service had ordered to report for induction on March 12, when he was in the middle of his second year as a graduate student at American University. Judge Bryant ruled that Kravik be allowed to finish the academic year.

In 1970 Chesapeake and Potomac Telephone Company employee Richard Levi faced losing his job if he did not get a haircut in compliance with a company rule that male employees could not have hair that fell over their ears or below their shirt collars. Judge Bryant did not believe that anyone should be fired "solely because of hair."

It was also in 1970 that the judge had before him the case of a sixteen-year-old boy who had been shafted by the juvenile court. In September the boy pleaded guilty to possession of a dangerous weapon (a hunting knife). He was released into the custody of his parents while he awaited sentencing. Before that happened, police arrested the teen for robbery based on an anonymous tip that the perpetrator had "bumps on his face" and a "scar over one eye." The boy fit the description, but there was no positive identification by the victim of the robbery. Still, the boy was sent off to the DC Receiving Home without having had a hearing. When a public defender presented the boy's case before the judge, the lad had been stuck in this overcrowded, crime-ridden juvenile detention center on Mt. Olivet Road, NE, for about two weeks.

According to the *Washington Post*, Judge Bryant spent nearly an entire day on this case. "There is so much room for injustice in this type of case," he said during his hearing. "It seems to me that before committing a person, you would at least have to have an identification by the [victim]. I don't see how, from reading the [police report], a judge could commit this fellow without running a substantial risk of unfairness." He reckoned that "there may be 50 kids around with 'bumps on the face' and 'a scar over the eye.'" Finding no probable cause for the boy to be held, the judge ordered him to be released into the custody of his parents.

Another case that surely made the judge's blood boil was one an attorney with the Neighborhood Legal Services Project brought on behalf of Mrs. Jarice Parrish, her seven children, her disabled sister, and her sister's three children.

In late fall 1970, this family had been evicted from their home on Sixth Street, NW, because the landlord wanted to sell the property. They lived in a shelter while Mrs. Parrish searched for a new home. Through a referral by the shelter, she found a house to rent on Seventeenth Street, NW. The place needed a lot of work, but when Parrish handed over her security deposit of $150, the rental agent assured her that all would be in order when the family moved in on December 4. When that day came and all was *not* in order, the family stayed at the shelter but were soon forced to leave. Living on a monthly welfare check of $385, the family had no choice but to move into the house on Seventeenth Street, NW.

When the case became before Judge Bryant in January 1971, the house had no heat, no hot water, no working stove. The upstairs tub, sink, and toilet were still clogged. Other problems included missing window panes letting in wintry wind. Some of the children had been sent to Junior Village, an awful orphanage near a dump in Southwest DC that would be shut down in 1973.

In the Parrish case, on January 14, 1971, Judge Bryant ordered the homeowners and the rental agent to have heat in the house by 10 the next morning and to have a hot water heater and stove installed and all other repairs completed later that day, by 5 p.m.

"I saw an unforgettable expression of compassion on Judge Bryant's face as he looked at the plaintiff," remembered Harry W. Goldberg with regard to a different case. The plaintiff in this one was Goldberg's client Andrew Husovsky.

In the summer of 1968, Husovsky was rendered a paraplegic after part of a ninety-foot, ten-ton rotting tulip poplar came crashing down on his Volkswagen as he drove through Rock Creek Park. Husovsky was just months away from earning his PhD in analytical chemistry from Georgetown. That expression of compassion swept across Judge Bryant's face when a jury found the District liable and awarded Husovsky $250,000.

There was another defendant, the National Park Service (and so the federal government), tried before Judge Bryant. He found that it was also liable for the negligent maintenance of that tree. Taking into account Husovsky's world of woes—from his not being able to have children as he had once dreamed to his lost earning capacity, ongoing medical bills, and the prognosis of a shortened life span—Judge Bryant ordered the federal government to compensate Husovsky in the amount of $975,000 (equivalent to about $4.5 million in today's dollars). The US Court of Appeals upheld the award.

While Judge Bryant was serving on the bench, he was also being of service in another arena. As it turned out, he who, years earlier, had dismissed the idea of attending Miner because he had no interest in becoming a teacher, was called to classroom teaching after all. Shortly after he became a judge—and when he did not need the money—he became an adjunct professor at Howard Law and proved to be a master teacher.

On Saturday mornings he taught trial advocacy. In teaching rules of evidence and other matters pertaining to a jury trial, to class after class, Judge Bryant stressed that attorneys were duty-bound to be prepared—*very well-prepared*—when they entered a courtroom on behalf of a client. He called an unprepared attorney "a walking travesty of the Sixth Amendment," an advocate not truly fulfilling his or her duty to provide a defendant with effective "Assistance of Counsel" as the Constitution guarantees.

Judge Bryant also advised students that there might be times when they would need to challenge a statute or a precedent. "After you look at the facts," he'd tell them, "and after you look at the law, you have to ask yourselves, 'Is it right? Is it right?'"

A VERY DISTINCTIVE DIGNITY

On March 21, 1977, twelve years after he ascended to the bench, as seniority dictated, William Benson Bryant became chief judge of the US District Court for the District of Columbia—its first Black chief judge. According to the *Washington Post*, he was "one of four blacks across the US to head a trial-level federal court."

The day before Judge Bryant became chief judge, the *Washington Star* ran a piece about his stance on how society should treat its people addicted to heroin. "After watching heroin addicts and low-level pushers parade before him for nearly a dozen years, US District Court Judge William B. Bryant has concluded that 'the time has come to reassess whether we should continue to try dealing with heroin in the criminal context,'" reported the *Star*'s David Pike. Heroin use had been on the rise around the nation since the early 1960s, becoming an epidemic in the 1970s.

So many alleyways strewn with needles.

Track marks scarring so many arms.

Countless men and women—even teens—in parks, under overpasses, in hallways, in deep knee-bend nods, in bobbing-up-and-down nods, and in leaning-over nods on stoops with heads snapping back up before they hit the ground.

On street corners, in bars, and the likes of chicken-and-waffle joints, so many puffy hands peddling jewelry, transistor radios, cameras, cassette players, cutlery, hub caps—all manner of boosted goods.

Judge Bryant told Pike that if heroin were decriminalized and addicts were provided the drug in conjunction with a treatment program, burglaries and other street crimes would be reduced by 40 percent or more. "If addicts were maintained on drugs and then treated, they wouldn't have to be constantly running like wild dogs to get the money they need to support their habits." He pointed out that roughly 95 percent of the inmates at the Women's Detention Center and roughly 75 percent of those at Lorton were there for drug offenses or drug-related crimes.

"There is no doubt the current system is not working," Judge Bryant insisted. "Trying to control heroin use under the criminal process is like trying to shoe a running horse."

It was mostly the addicts and low-level pushers who ended up behind bars. The drug kingpins—the ones making "tremendous profits"—not so much. "By providing drugs to addicts and treating them, there no longer would be a market for organized crime. It's like a banana peddler; the way to put him out of business is to make it unprofitable to sell bananas." Judge Bryant was adamant that criminalization of heroin was a "tremendous waste of time, money, and human lives. What society is doing is choking itself with its own hands."

He referenced Prohibition—and how that backfired, with members of organized crime doing big business in bootleg booze and not at all pleased when Prohibition (Eighteenth Amendment ratified in 1919) was repealed in 1933 (Twenty-First Amendment). Said the judge: "I'm sure that organized crime is quite happy to see the current laws on the books. They gain the profits with little or no risk."

Pike stated, "Other judges reportedly have spoken out on the question in recent years, but the fact that Bryant, as the first black chief judge of the US District Court here, has done so was seen as significant by several persons familiar with the issue." Significant, yes, but Judge Bryant's stance was not universally applauded. Pike added: "A number of black community leaders have strongly opposed heroin maintenance programs, suggesting that they were intended to 'enslave' inner-city blacks in a life of drug dependency. They have advocated a crackdown on pushers and a greater emphasis on abstinence programs, like that run here by RAP, Inc."[21]

According to Pike, Judge Bryant's stance horrified some of his District Court colleagues. "One judge said it would be 'criminal' to provide heroin to anyone who wanted it. He also contended that

---

21. RAP, Inc.—Regional Addiction Prevention, Inc.—was founded in 1970 by Ron Clark, once a bass player for Charles Mingus's band and a recovering addict himself. RAP, Inc. offered people struggling with substance abuse a drug-free, Afrocentric path to wellness.

treatment programs have been a failure and that tougher law enforcement was the only answer to the problem."

In "Everybody Likes Judge William Bryant," a separate article that ran in the same issue of the *Star*, Pike told readers that a veteran defense attorney called the judge "a lawyer's lawyer." Many judges and lawyers Pike interviewed "echoed" the same sentiment. "And other praise was usually added. In fact, no one uttered a negative comment about the soft-spoken Bryant as a person." However, some did criticize him for something he was criticized for almost from day one: his slowness in deciding cases and his tendency to hand out light sentences.

Another lawyer told Pike that Judge Bryant "is the most human being I've ever known." This lawyer added, "That implies that his judgment about people and legal situations is unflaggingly right; he's the kind of person you turn to if you need advice."

Still another lawyer said, "He's an extremely humble man, which is not always the case in people in such powerful positions. For example, this appointment [as chief judge] brings him something he always dreaded, the likelihood of big testimonials and other praise. It's the last thing in the world he wants."

When Judge Bryant spoke with the *Star* reporter, he was rather matter-of-fact about becoming the District Court's first Black chief judge. "This has some significance cosmetically from the public's point of view, but from my view, the administration of the judiciary is not color oriented. If I've been doing the job long enough to be chief judge, it shouldn't have any significance." He understood that it was "historic for the city, but it has greater significance for the public than it does for me."

As for the administrative part of his new position, Judge Bryant did not think it would be as taxing as it had been for chief judges before him. "I think we have a good court now, the shop is run well, much better than when I came here. The clerk's office is well equipped, and the administration of the judiciary depends on support personnel. But we have no weakness there." His salute to the court's support staff is telling.

Judge Bryant planned to cut back on the number of civil cases he handled, but not on criminal cases. He had also decided to give up one task traditionally handled by the chief judge: information pleas, that is, pleas to criminal charges where there were no grand jury indictments.

"I'm frank to say that I thought about that one, and people [the other judges] agreed with me," Judge Bryant told Pike. "All criminal cases are assigned on a random basis, and the plea to an information [criminal charge] is no less a criminal case. All should be assigned on a rotating basis. It has the appearance of fairness, and it is fair that way."

When asked if being chief judge would bring changes to his lifestyle, Judge Bryant replied, "I don't contemplate any basic changes in my day-to-day existence. I'll just do the best I can to keep the shop running. . . . I'll be satisfied to keep it in the same shape I found it, and no doubt, I'll have a lot of support from the other judges." After a pause, he added, "It ought to be a pleasant piece of business." The judge uttered these words, wrote Pike, with "his eyes twinkling and a slight smile crossing his angular face." In agreeing to the interview, Bryant had categorically refused to allow a photo shoot in his chambers. He did, however, provide a headshot to accompany the article. Reluctantly.

Several months after Bryant became chief judge, at its annual Law Day celebration the Washington Bar Association awarded him its highest honor: the Charles Hamilton Houston Medallion of Merit.

While carrying out his duties as chief judge—from handling motions and special proceedings to overseeing the grand jury, appointing his colleagues to various committees, keeping check on caseloads, and chairing meetings of his fellow District Court judges when policy decisions had to be made—Judge Bryant was in no way tyrannical. He was his usual easy-going self. Judge Joyce Hens Green, a trailblazer for women in the law, who joined the court in 1979, remembered that in conversation with Judge Bryant, "You always knew that you were in a safe space. You may not always agree but you were in a safe place." He "was gold," said Judge Green.[22]

22. Judge Green's major cases include the BCCI bank fraud case (1993) and Guantanamo Detainee cases (2004–2005).

Cases over which Judge Bryant presided during his first year as chief judge include *King v. Andrus*, about a particular right of defendants in the US territory of American Samoa. As attorney Daniel A. Rezneck explained, at issue "was whether there was a constitutional right to jury trial in criminal cases in the courts of American Samoa." He added: "To my surprise, I found that the Supreme Court had never definitively decided the famous question: Does the Constitution follow the flag?"

Rezneck was representing Jake King, a US-born newspaper publisher living in American Samoa. Denied a jury trial, King had been convicted of tax evasion by a panel of Samoan judges. Rezneck brought the case in the District Court by filing the lawsuit against Cecil Andrus, secretary of the Department of the Interior, which oversees US territories.

"The Department of Justice pulled out all the stops," remembered Rezneck. "An array of Samoan chiefs came to court in full regalia to testify. All of them swore that it was unthinkable to have a jury system in Samoa—it just would not work."

Rezneck recalled that through Judge Bryant's own questioning, he "realized that what was truly at stake was the dominance of the old ruling class of chiefs, who were increasingly being challenged by the younger members of Samoan society. For this young generation, trial by jury symbolized the right to participate in popular government." Added Rezneck: "Judge Bryant quickly perceived the similarities between the changes taking place in American Samoa and the early civil rights movement in the United States."

The government's star witness was anthropologist Margaret Mead, whose first book, *Coming of Age in Samoa* (1928), was an instant bestseller. Mead, who had not been to American Samoa since the 1920s, was out of touch, according to Rezneck. She still "carried in her head an image of the Samoans as helpless children incapable of self-government and lucky to be ruled by the chiefs."

Rezneck recalled that with her long-winded speeches in response to questions, Mead "gave Judge Bryant fits as a witness." The judge did his best to handle Mead with his "customary tact and politeness," but at one point he lost his cool.

"Dr. Mead, will you just answer the questions!"

In the end Judge Bryant ruled that American Samoa had to adhere to a defendant's right to a jury trial as guaranteed by the Sixth Amendment. How could it not, given how much the American Samoan government paralleled the US government?

"American Samoa has its Constitution with a Bill of Rights," said the judge in his thirteen-page opinion. "The latter contains all of the procedural protections of our own Constitution for criminal defendants except the grand and petit jury requirements. These include protection against unlawful search and seizures, the exclusionary rule against the admission of illegally seized evidence, the protection against double jeopardy, the privilege against self-incrimination, the right of cross-examination and confrontation, the presumption of innocence, the right to bail, and the right to the assistance of counsel, and the time-honored writ of habeas corpus."

He noted that American Samoa's court system "follows the American system of trial. It is an adversary system with a prosecuting attorney on one side and defense counsel on the other; witnesses testify under oath and are cross-examined. The Federal Rules of Criminal Procedure apply fully except for the jury trial provision. And finally the Samoan substantive law is a virtual transplant of the American. Title 15 of the Code of American Samoa defines the basic crimes and virtually all of them are derived from our Title 18." (Title 18 is the US federal government's main criminal code.)

Judge Bryant also pointed out that the "educational advances in American Samoa during the last ten or fifteen years have been extraordinary. School attendance is compulsory through age 18 or graduation from high school, and there is an increasing emphasis on higher education. A community college, opened in 1971, is well attended, and since 1972 has graduated between 100 and 130 persons annually. In addition, a substantial number of American Samoans have been educated in schools in the United States. Some have returned with law degrees and master's degrees."

Finding prospective jurors would not be like searching for needles in haystacks. "The evidence indicates that there are about 7,000 registered voters with the vast majority of them situated on the main island of Tutuila where the courthouse is located. Available transportation eliminates any problem of access to the courthouse. A roll of registered voters is maintained by the election department of the government and this should provide an adequate pool of prospective jurors who are most likely to be literate and educated."

The people of American Samoa were not the helpless children Margaret Mead made them out to be. They were more than ready for jury trials.

Gilbert Morgan, charged with murdering his wife, mother-in-law, and seven-month-old daughter. . . . California congressman Richard Hanna, charged with conspiring to commit bribery. . . . Folksinger-activist Joan Baez's Freedom of Information Act lawsuit against the National Security Agency. . . . Jim "Yazoo" Smith's lawsuit against the NFL and the Washington Redskins (now the Washington Commanders) contending that the draft violated the Sherman Anti-Trust Act—this is just a sampling of the variety of cases over which Judge Bryant presided during his early days as chief judge.

Another was the two-month trial of Linwood "Big Boy" Gray, reportedly the boss of a $30 million heroin smuggling ring. Along with drug charges, Gray was charged with tax evasion. The government was convinced that Gray, described by one reporter as a "burly, 250-pounder," was responsible for two shootings and five murders, but it did not have enough to charge him with these crimes.

On July 18, 1979, a jury acquitted Gray of the drug charges but convicted him of income tax evasion—of not paying taxes on $300,000 of income. A month later, Judge Bryant sentenced Gray to a twenty-month-to-five-year bid. He had rejected US Attorney Carl Rauh's recommendation that Gray get the maximum for tax evasion: ten years. Rauh insisted that this was a "major tax case." He had also argued that Gray was a "dangerous man" and a "threat to the community," insisting that he was responsible for those five murders and those two shootings. AUSA Barry Leibowitz was one of the people who survived a shooting. In the fall of 1978, while investigating the drug ring, Leibowitz had been shot in the back right outside the federal courthouse.

Tragic, yes. But Judge Bryant could not sentence Gray to the maximum for tax evasion as a way of punishing him for crimes for which he had not been convicted. It wasn't right.

To be sure, Linwood Gray was a dangerous dude. During the trial Judge Bryant had a special detail of US marshals. "He didn't like it," said Diane Steed, his secretary starting in April 1979. "So he would evade them, go out the back door, get on the Metro, go wherever he wanted to go. When they said, 'We're trying to protect you,' he'd say, 'I don't need any protection. Nobody's going to bother me.'"

In 1980 Judge Bryant presided over the trial of two former high-ranking FBI officials: W. Mark Felt and Edward S. Miller. Felt had been J. Edgar Hoover's second-in-command. Miller had been chief of the FBI's domestic intelligence division.

In the early 1970s Felt and Miller had given FBI agents the green light for a series of break-ins of people's homes—"black-bag jobs" in FBI speak. The break-ins occurred in New York and New Jersey, in the homes of relatives and friends of Weather Underground members. The FBI was on the hunt for the leaders of this radical left-wing group that had declared war on the US government and executed a series of bombings, including that of the Capitol in 1971 and the Pentagon in 1972. (No one was killed or injured in the bombings, but the damage was considerable. In the case of the Capitol, $300,000-worth.)

Before he had the case, Judge Bryant had never heard of a black-bag job. His description of it years later makes one shudder: "A black-bag job is where somebody can come in your house and search it from stem to stern, photograph anything they want in the house, leave the house, you go in it and you never know that anybody's been in the house. I mean, it is undisturbed, everything is where it was, so you don't have any idea that anybody has burglarized your house. No authority, no warrant, no nothing."

During Felt and Miller's eight-week trial, witnesses included former president Nixon. Remembered Judge Bryant: "Nixon testified for the defendants, and Nixon testified to the effect that if something is illegal, and the president says you can do it, you should do it. That took out the illegality." He added, "I almost had to clap my hand over my mouth."

Another unforgettable moment involved a victim of a black-bag job, the father of a Weather Underground member. As this man made his way from the witness stand, he turned to Felt and Miller and said, "All you had to do is ask, I would have let you in."

Judge Bryant was convinced that this elderly man's outburst was "spontaneous." He did not think that anyone had put him up to it. "If he had known that it was an improper thing to do, I'm satisfied that he never would have done it. He was an unassuming man, a nice old man. But he said it, and there was nothing I could do then. What admonition do you give the jury? I'm looking out the window, I don't know what to say but, 'Call your next witness.' The best prophylactic to that situation is, 'Call your next witness.' There was nothing I could say. I remember that, sometimes, you got band-aids for almost anything that happens in a courtroom, but sometimes there's really nothing you can do." Had he instructed the jury to disregard the outburst, it probably would only have made matters worse—drawing more attention to it.

On November 6, 1980, a jury found Felt and Miller guilty of violating the civil rights of the people who were on the receiving end of those black-bag jobs. As punishment they could have received up to ten years in prison and a fine of ten thousand dollars.

On December 15 Judge Bryant handed down a sentence that surprised, even shocked many: no prison time. Felt was fined $5,000, Miller $3,500.

The judge had wanted to impose jail time, but, he said, he thought that "the convictions in that case were important." He wanted to give them no strong basis for an appeal. As he put it, all through the trial he did not want "any air to hit" the case. "I gave them everything they wanted, everything they asked for I gave them. Damn near every request they made, I gave it to them. I may be exaggerating, but I mean I leaned over backwards to accommodate them, so when they went to the Court of Appeals, they had damn little."

However, W. Mark Felt and Edward S. Miller had President Ronald Reagan. In the spring of 1981, he granted them full, unconditional pardons. He stated that they had served the FBI "and our nation with great distinction" and contended that what they did "grew out of their good-faith belief that their actions were necessary to preserve the security interests of our country. The record demonstrates that they acted not with criminal intent, but in the belief that they had grants of authority reaching to the highest levels of government."

President Reagan noted that his predecessor, Jimmy Carter, had granted "thousands of draft evaders and others who violated the Selective Service laws" unconditional pardons. "America was generous to those who refused to serve their country in the Vietnam war. We can be no less generous to two men who acted on high principle to bring an end to the terrorism that was threatening our nation."[23]

By the time Reagan pardoned Felt and Miller, for a year Judge Bryant's official portrait had been gracing the walls of his courthouse's Ceremonial Courtroom on the sixth floor. It was unveiled on the afternoon of Friday, April 18, 1980, before a crowd of some two hundred to three hundred people—attorneys, government officials, former law clerks, friends, and family. The judges in attendance included Bryant's fellow Black trailblazers Spottswood W. Robinson III, Theodore R. Newman Jr., and H. Carl Moultrie I.

Astaire was beyond proud, "all smiles and beaming," remembered Chip. Initially he was not certain that he would be able to attend the ceremony, given his West Coast work obligations. Having earned his bachelor's from Wesleyan University and his JD from George Washington University Law School, Chip was a program development officer with Neighborhood Reinvestment Corporation in San Francisco. Once he knew that he *would* be able to attend the wondrous event honoring his dad, the family kept it a secret from Judge Bryant. It wasn't until a few minutes before the ceremony commenced—

Surprise!

Penny was there as well, and beyond proud too. And she was not living some three thousand miles away from her parents, but still residing in the District. Having earned a bachelor's degree in education from American University and master's degree in special education from Southern Connecticut State University, Penny was a teacher and diagnostician in Maryland's Montgomery County Public School system.

Also present were Judge Bryant's niece/adopted daughter Beatrice and her husband, Ed Jones; Aunt Elizabeth, who had never left DC;

---

23. In 2005 W. Mark Felt acknowledged that he was Deep Throat: the critical informant who enabled *Washington Post* reporters Bob Woodward and Carl Bernstein to break open the Watergate scandal.

and Aunt Josephine, who had returned to the DC area from Detroit after her husband passed.

Presiding over the ceremony was Judge Bryant's fellow District Court judge John Lewis Smith Jr., on the bench since 1966. Like Bryant, he was renowned for his fairness.

The first person Judge Smith called upon to address the gathering was David L. Bazelon, still a judge on the US Court of Appeals for the DC Circuit. Judge Bazelon was known far and wide as a champion of the rights of defendants and a proponent of more emphasis on rehabilitation versus punishment in the criminal justice system. Judge Bryant had appeared before Bazelon a number of times when he was a trial lawyer, well before Mallory's conviction was upheld on appeal with Bazelon dissenting. After Bryant joined the District Court, the two men came to know one another better and, not surprisingly, became good friends.

Judge Bazelon sometimes took Judge Bryant to his favorite lunch spot, "Mr. K's," a dining room in the V Street, NE warehouse of wholesale liquor distributor (and philanthropist) Milton S. Kronheim. In this off-the-beaten-track, take-off-your-jacket, no-tablecloths space, the prominent and the powerful—including US Supreme Court justices—enjoyed scrumptious meals with no worries about their conversations being leaked to the press. Given Judge Bryant's love of seafood, he no doubt especially relished the famed crabmeat gumbo served up at Mr. K's.

At the portrait unveiling, Judge Bazelon remarked, "Even before I knew him personally, I wanted to know Bill Bryant. In the courtroom, I was struck not only by his sharp intellect, sincerity, and candor, but I noticed a very distinctive dignity—a quality the combines humility, wisdom, and purpose. His every move invited confidence. Once I told him I thought he ought to be a judge. He laughed, modestly. Now, we enjoy reminiscing about it together." Bazelon called Bryant a "district judge *par excellence*," one who "elevates the institutions, the organizations, and the people that he touches."

Next to speak was another legend: Pine Bluff, Arkansas, native Wiley A. Branton, a World War II army veteran who became one of the University of Arkansas School of Law's first Black graduates. Other highlights from his life in civil rights include serving as chief counsel for the "Little Rock Nine." From 1962 to 1965 Branton headed the Atlanta-based Voter Education Project, an initiative that resulted in nearly 700,000 Black registered voters in the South. Branton was in his second year as dean of Howard Law when he spoke at the unveiling of Judge Bryant's portrait.

Dean Branton praised Judge Bryant's dedication as an adjunct professor. "I don't know how he does it, with his other duties, particularly with his duties at the court, but during the fall semester, he's generally there from 9:00 in the morning until 12:00 or 1:00 o'clock every Saturday." When moot court trials were held in the Spring, Judge Bryant was often there from 9 a.m. until 5 or 6 p.m. "And sometimes I try to urge him to take a break and have a little lunch or relax or something."

Judge Bryant's former law partner Bill Gardner, who regarded him "as a brother," stated that this brother, "both as a lawyer and a judge, has always been mindful that laws have practical human consequences, that laws affect real people, and that laws have to be enforced by real people." Gardner also hailed Judge Bryant as "a fabulous talker." The judge did not so much overwhelm people with words, did not monopolize conversations, "but he does dominate, and he dominates by pleasing and by delighting. His humor, his style, and his range make him the center of the group, both as a listener and as a talker." Attorney Henry F. Greene reminded the crowd of the 1968 *Esquire* magazine piece that had Judge Bryant at the top of the list of twenty-seven people worth saving. Greene, who clerked for Judge Bryant in the 1960s and later appeared before him as an AUSA, said that knowing the man "invariably leaves one richer and more confident in the fundamental values that transcend the law and the courtroom, and matter most: Decency and respect for the rights of our fellow human beings."

Greene soon invited Astaire and Penny to step forward and unveil the portrait.

The room erupted in rapturous applause at the unveiling of the large, elegant oil painting of a hero to hundreds in attendance and to thousands beyond the Ceremonial Courtroom, beyond the courthouse, beyond Washington, DC.

In the portrait Judge Bryant's hair, along with his mustache, has more than some touches of grey. His black robe has a graceful flow.

He looks to his left as if gazing upon a far horizon. His face, with its telltale signs of the Creek in him, radiates warmth and wisdom. He holds a pair of eyeglasses in one of his long, strong hands that once ran a freight elevator, operated a switchboard, and laid bricks.

After a few words of praise for the portrait and for the person, Judge Smith asked, "Bill, would you say a few words?"

Judge Bryant, thus far sporting broad smiles throughout much of the ceremony, was at that moment overwhelmed with emotion.

To Judge Smith: "Ever since I found out that this ceremony was to take place, I have been apprehensive about the fact that if anybody came to attend, I would probably choke up and not be able to say anything. Well, that's exactly what has happened to me."

To those who honored him with their presence at this solemn and joyous occasion: "When I look around and see all of you, my immediate family, my extended family of law clerks, my wonderful colleagues and my many, many, many wonderful friends, I can say only, Thank you. Thank you very much. I am really choked up. Thank you very much."

It was a memorable moment for everyone, especially for Judge Bryant's family. Some forty years later, Chip had this to say: "I think he must've been feeling proud of his achievement, but also humbly grateful for everything that day represented at that point in his life. My dad was by nature a very strong and genuinely secure personality but with a lot of humility—a quiet strength and comfort and security in his own skin that allowed him to be emotional if that was what he was genuinely feeling. And he was feeling it that day."

Willie Benson circa 1919. Courtesy of Astaire A. Bryant and William B. Bryant Jr.

Willie Benson with his mother, Alberta Wood Washington, and his stepfather, George S. Washington, circa 1919. Courtesy of Astaire A. Bryant and William B. Bryant Jr.

Teenaged Bill, circa 1925. Courtesy of Astaire A. Bryant and William B. Bryant Jr.

US Army officer Bill Bryant, circa 1943–1947. Courtesy of Astaire A. Bryant and William B. Bryant Jr.

The Bryant family on August 16, 1965, right after Bill was sworn in to serve on the US District Court for the District of Columbia. Courtesy of Astaire A. Bryant and William B. Bryant Jr.

Judge Bryant with former law partners Joseph C. Waddy (far left) and William C. Gardner, on August 16, 1965, the day of his swearing in. Courtesy of Astaire A. Bryant and William B. Bryant Jr.

Bryant in the front room of his office at 615 F Street, NW, with law partners Theodore R. Newman Jr. (far left) and William C. Gardner. This photo was taken around the time that Bryant became a judge. Courtesy of Astaire A. Bryant and William B. Bryant Jr.

This circa 1965 photograph was taken at what was for decades DC's premier Black-owned photography studio, Scurlock, launched by Addison Scurlock in 1904. Courtesy of Astaire A. Bryant and William B. Bryant Jr.

Judge Bryant in his chambers, circa late 1960s–early 1970s. Courtesy of Astaire A. Bryant and William B. Bryant Jr.

Astaire Bryant in the living room of the Seventeenth Street home, seated before draperies she made, circa 1970s. Courtesy of Astaire A. Bryant and William B. Bryant Jr.

Judge Bryant's official portrait by Richard Henderson. It was unveiled on April 18, 1980, in the Ceremonial Courtroom of the E. Barrett Prettyman United States Courthouse. Courtesy of the E. Barrett Prettyman United States Courthouse.

Four DC chief judges in 1981. With the US District Court for the District of Columbia's Chief Judge William B. Bryant are (left to right): Spottswood W. Robinson III, chief judge of the US Court of Appeals for the District of Columbia Circuit; Judge Bryant's former law partner Theodore R. Newman Jr., chief judge of the DC Court of Appeals; and H. Carl Moultrie I, chief judge of the DC Superior Court. Courtesy of Astaire A. Bryant and William B. Bryant Jr.

Bill and Astaire at his surprise seventieth birthday party in his chambers, September 1981. Astaire, the judge's secretary, Diane Steed, and the judge's law clerks planned the party. Courtesy of Astaire A. Bryant and William B. Bryant Jr.

Judge Bryant and his colleagues during his tenure as chief judge of the US District Court for the District of Columbia (1977–1981). Seated, left to right: John Lewis Smith Jr., George L. Hart Jr., Richmond B. Keech, William B. Bryant, Burnita Shelton Matthews, Howard F. Corcoran, and Oliver Gasch. Standing, left to right: Norma Holloway Johnson, John Garrett Penn, Louis F. Oberdorfer, Barrington D. Parker Sr., John H. Pratt, Gerhard A. Gesell, Aubrey E. Robinson Jr., June L. Green, Charles R. Richey, Thomas A. Flannery, Harold H. Greene, and Joyce Hens Green. The photograph was taken in the Ceremonial Courtroom of the E. Barrett Prettyman Courthouse. Courtesy of the E. Barrett Prettyman United States Courthouse.

Spring 1983. In the forefront, left to right: Judge Bryant, Judge Luke C. Moore (the DC Superior Court), Justice Thurgood Marshall, Howard Law's Dean Wiley A. Branton. The young man standing behind Branton is Arthur T. Matthews, president of Howard Law's Student Bar Association. The photo was taken at Howard Law, where Justice Marshall gave a talk, cosponsored by the Student Bar Association. Courtesy of Astaire A. Bryant and William B. Bryant Jr.

Astaire Bryant in the home of a friend or relative, circa 1988. Courtesy of Astaire A. Bryant and William B. Bryant Jr.

Judge Bryant addressing a crowd at a dinner in the US Supreme Court Building, 1990. The dinner was organized by his law clerks to celebrate his twenty-fifth year on the bench. The room was filled with most of his law clerks, many of whom flew in from great distances to be there, including his first law clerk, Richard "Dick" Cahill from Texas. Seated to Judge Bryant's right is his wife, Astaire Bryant. To Justice Thurgood Marshall's right is his wife, historian and civil rights activist Cecilia "Cissy" Suyat Marshall. Seated far left is Chip (with the beard). Courtesy of Astaire A. Bryant and William B. Bryant Jr.

In this photograph of the 1990 dinner celebrating his twenty-fifth year on the bench, Judge Bryant is with the Marshalls and three former law clerks. The woman is Bernadette Oddiah, the man behind her Morad Eghbal. Far right: William B. Schultz, who clerked for the judge in the mid-1970s and conducted a series of interviews with the judge in the 1990s for the Historical Society of the District of Columbia. Courtesy of Astaire A. Bryant and William B. Bryant Jr.

Astaire and Bill with daughter Penny, son Chip, and grandchildren, Vaughn and Lauren, at Channel Inn's Pier Seven restaurant on DC's Southwest Waterfront, circa 1990–1991. Courtesy of Astaire A. Bryant and William B. Bryant Jr.

Bill and Astaire's niece/adopted daughter, Beatrice, and her husband, Ed, at their golden wedding anniversary celebration, which Bill and Astaire attended, 1994. Courtesy of Astaire A. Bryant and William B. Bryant Jr.

Astaire Bryant in the Northampton Street home, circa 1992–1994. Courtesy of Astaire A. Bryant and William B. Bryant Jr.

Judge Bryant in his chambers with his spirit shining through, circa 1992–1994. Courtesy of Astaire A. Bryant and William B. Bryant Jr.

Judge Bryant at a DC Circuit Judicial Conference, date unknown. Closest to him are two very dear friends: John H. Ferren, associate judge on the DC Court of Appeals 1977–1997 and a senior judge on that court 1999–2023, and in front of him, his wife, Linda Ferren, executive director of the Historical Society for the District of Columbia Circuit 1990–2021. Behind Mrs. Ferren is Katherine Mazzaferri, CEO of the DC Bar 1982–2017. Next to her: legendary civil rights attorney Bill Taylor. Courtesy of Astaire A. Bryant and William B. Bryant Jr.

At a DePriest Fifteen Ladies Night Dinner Dance, late 1990s. Seated next to Judge Bryant is John Garrett Penn, a fellow member of the US District Court for the District of Columbia. Standing left: historian Dr. Michael R. Winston. Standing right: Chip. Courtesy of Astaire A. Bryant and William B. Bryant Jr.

Judge Bryant receiving a Washington Bar Association award, circa 2000. Far left: Donald A. Thigpen, the president of the association. Far right: Annice M. Wagner, former Houston firm attorney who served on the DC Superior Court, from 1977 to 1990, after which she was appointed to the District of Columbia Court of Appeals, serving as its chief judge from 1994 to 2005, and as senior judge from 2005 to 2013. Courtesy of Astaire A. Bryant and William B. Bryant Jr.

Happy ninetieth birthday, Bill Bryant! The birthday boy with his trusty "horse" has just arrived at the party Vernon Jordan hosted in his home in 2001, and which was attended by many of the judge's closest male friends. The judge stands between his son, Chip, and Julian R. Dugas. Far right: Ed Jones, the husband of Bill and Astaire's niece/adopted daughter, Beatrice. Courtesy of Astaire A. Bryant and William B. Bryant Jr.

Chip and Judge Bryant with two others at the ninetieth birthday party: one of the judge's earliest law clerks, Henry F. Greene, a senior judge of the DC Superior Court (far left), and Richard Kirkland "Kirk" Bowden, who had distinguished careers with the Metropolitan Police Department and with the US Marshal Service. Courtesy of Astaire A. Bryant and William B. Bryant Jr.

Judge Bryant at his ninetieth birthday party with Dr. Victor "Vick" Assevero, a prominent and beloved DC pediatrician. Courtesy of Astaire A. Bryant and William B. Bryant Jr.

Another photograph from the stag ninetieth birthday party in 2001. Judge Bryant is seated at the head table in the Jordan dining room. Far left: host Vernon Jordan. To the judge's left: Judge Louis F. Oberdorfer, and Dr. Burke "Mickey" Syphax, Judge Bryant's friend since their days at Dunbar High in the 1920s. Other attendees included William B. Schultz. Courtesy of Astaire A. Bryant and William B. Bryant Jr.

The William B. Bryant United States Courthouse Annex on Constitution Avenue, NW. Left of the Annex is the E. Barrett Prettyman United States Courthouse. Courtesy of the US General Services Administration.

Chapter 16

FEEL THEMSELVES GROW

Federal judges cannot serve as chief judges after turning seventy, and so on September 18, 1981, Judge Bryant's tenure as chief judge of the District Court ended. He was succeeded by John Lewis Smith Jr.

Shortly before Judge Bryant stepped down as chief judge, he granted *Washington Post* staff writer Laura A. Kiernan an interview in his chambers. She reported that the judge "is not looking back to see where he has left his mark. He doesn't think in those terms, he says." Kiernan also told her readers that the judge "says he will leave it to history simply to record the things he has done in the long years since he was, by his own description, 'the busiest poor lawyer in the city.'"

During the interview Judge Bryant told Kiernan, "Sometimes I tell my children that I guess we are equipped to move forward and you don't have much time to be thinking about what happened last week." The judge was also fond of saying this: "There is no end to the good a person can do if he is willing not to receive the credit."

Two months after his tenure as chief judge ended, Judge Bryant informed the White House that he would be taking senior status on January 31, 1982. Federal judges sixty-five and older who have served on the bench for at least fifteen years can opt for senior status, which is basically semiretirement. Judge Bryant took senior status at Astaire's urging. He had been working for more than fifty years. Time to slow down.

When Judge Bryant took senior status, he had been on the bench for nearly seventeen years and was one of the most respected jurists in the nation. Years later the equally highly respected Judge Louis Oberdorfer, who joined the District Court in 1977, declared, "Judge Bryant wasn't just good at the facts. He mastered the law." This cofounder of the Lawyers' Committee for Civil Rights Under Law (1963) and a native of Alabama, maintained that there were "only two people in the world who really understood the Constitution" and its impact on American lives. Judge Bryant was one. The other was someone for whom Judge Oberdorfer had clerked: US Supreme Court Associate Justice Hugo Black, a member of the high court when Bill Bryant made his oral argument in *Mallory v. United States*.

As it turned out, when it came to Judge Bryant's days in semiretirement, Astaire didn't exactly get her wish. Her husband worked almost as hard as ever, presiding over case after case after case—still on fire about justice being done, still asking, "Is it right? Is it right?"

In May 1982 he definitely did not think that a jury's conviction of the Floridian Richard Kelly was right. Kelly, a former federal prosecutor and circuit judge, was a member of Congress when convicted of bribery and conspiracy. For bribery he faced a maximum of fifteen years in prison and a $20,000 fine. For conspiracy, a maximum of five years in prison and a $10,000 fine.

This Republican was one of several politicians snared in Abscam, short for Abdul Scam: an FBI operation intended to ferret out corrupt public officials. FBI agents pretending to be Arab sheiks or their underlings offered politicians bribes in exchange for favors. In Richard Kelly's case, he was charged with taking $25,000, as a down payment on the work he was to do to help a sheik with an immigration problem. There were promises of future Arab investments in his district in central Florida.

There was no doubt that Kelly had taken the money. There was a videotape of him stuffing packets of cash into his pockets. This was after he had been pressured twice.

During his seven-week trial Kelly testified that when he finally accepted the cash he did so for a very good reason. As Judge Bryant explained, "Congressman Kelly presented the bizarre, nearly farcical defense that he was conducting his own investigation of the reason why he had been surrounded by shady characters."

What the FBI agents did to Kelly vexed Judge Bryant far more than Kelly's bizarre defense. Abscam disgusted him. "It has an odor to it that's going to be cleared before anybody gets convicted," he said at one point during the trial when he had opposing counsel at the bench. "It has an odor to it that is absolutely repulsive."

After the jury found Kelly guilty, Judge Bryant had the courage of his convictions in this high-profile case to dismiss the indictment and enter a judgment of acquittal. In his memorandum he stated, "The function of law enforcement is to prevent crime and catch criminals. Conversely, law enforcement exceeds its bounds when it manufactures crime and creates criminals. The manufacture of crime and creation of criminals have been specifically prohibited by numerous cases." When the FBI targeted Kelly it had no evidence that he had or was on the verge of engaging in any criminal activity. The judge's main point: when Kelly turned down the bribe the first time, the FBI should have left him alone.

One imagines sparks flying off Judge Bryant's pen: "Government agents, hard about the business of corrupting public officials who are free of suspicion, essentially subvert our government; and on its face this presents an unwholesome spectacle. This is particularly true with respect to the manner in which Kelly was handled." What was done to him, "creates a whole new type of crime that would not exist but for the government's actions," declared the judge, echoing his take on what the police did to his client Lefty Winston years earlier.

Judge Bryant was overruled.

In a 3–0 decision, the US Court of Appeals for the DC Circuit instructed him to reinstate the indictment and the jury's verdict. In the opinion he issued in May 1983, Judge George MacKinnon asserted, "Considering the genuine need to detect corrupt public officials, as well as the difficulties inherent in doing so, we conclude that the FBI's conduct in furtherance of its Abscam operation, insofar as it involved Kelly, simply did not reach intolerable levels."

In a separate opinion, Judge Ruth Bader Ginsburg, ten years away from an appointment to the US Supreme Court, concluded, "The importuning of Congressman Kelly and the offers made to him, extraordinary and in excess of real-world opportunities as they appear to have been, did not involve the infliction of pain or physical or psychological coercion. We are therefore constrained to reverse, although we share the District Court's grave concern that the Abscam drama, both in its general tenor, and in 'the [particular] manner in which Kelly was handled,' unfolded as 'an unwholesome spectacle.'" (The third judge, Spottswood W. Robinson III, who had become the DC Circuit's first Black chief judge two years earlier, issued no opinion.)

With a heavy heart, Judge Bryant sentenced Richard Kelly to a six-to-eighteen-month prison sentence and three years' probation. And he didn't hold his tongue at Kelly's January 1984 sentencing. "What the government has done has been to bring about the downfall of a man" who probably would have "lived out his life without committing a crime."

Richard Kelly served time first at a prison camp at Eglin Air Force Base in the Florida Panhandle, then at a halfway house in St. Petersburg. He was released in 1986 after serving thirteen months. When he died in 2005 at the age of eighty-one, the *Tampa Bay Times* reported that he had "lived for almost 20 years in a sort of self-imposed exile."

While Judge Bryant could be quite fierce, biting even, in his memoranda and opinions, in his courtroom he was typically still even-tempered and gracious, not prone to snap at people the way he snapped at Margaret Mead. He treated all in his courtroom—defense attorneys, witnesses, prosecutors, stenographers, marshals—with respect.

He was also ever a teacher to attorneys who came before him, not in an overbearing way, but with a soft touch. According to Roger Adelman, an AUSA from 1968 to 1988, who appeared before Judge Bryant numerous times, this was especially true with defense attorneys. He remembered Judge Bryant telling defense attorneys, "Don't ask a 'why' question of a hostile witness." He then explained: "If you ask the 'why' question, you're going to have to sit down and take the answer because the guy's going to tell you why." The judge was schooling that attorney on Cross-Examination 101: Never ask a question on cross unless you know the answer. Moreover, asking a why question can easily result in a witness going on and on and on, leaving the attorney with no basis to cut the witness off on the ground that he or she is not answering the question.

As well, Adelman recalled the judge telling defense attorneys, "The old folks would say, 'If you've got a lot of questions to ask, don't ask any.'" An attorney with a raft of questions probably does not have many—or any—key questions. The judge also advised against long, drawn-out cross examinations, urging attorneys to "just get in and get out," which had been his MO as a defense attorney.

Adelman recalled that Judge Bryant always paid close attention during a trial. "He tracked every case. He was there watching the lawyers, and he was trying the case in his head. And many times he called us to the bench, and he'd lean forward and look to the defense attorney and say, 'I don't want to tell you how to try your case but . . .'"

The judge was also known to pull a defense attorney's coattails with a question such as, "Do you really want to call any more character witnesses?," advising against overkill and wasting everyone's time.

One day Adelman asked Judge Bryant, "Well, why don't you give me some advice?"

"You don't need it," replied the judge.

Adelman, who became a defense attorney in the late 1990s, declared that this was "probably the highest compliment I have ever gotten from anybody on the bench or anywhere else for that matter. High praise."

Wheels always turning, the judge sometimes called Adelman to the bench to inquire why he asked a particular question or why he put a certain witness on the stand.

"And I'd tell him. To rebut this or to set this up. And he, the tactician, would say, 'Okay.' Wouldn't say anything, but he was satisfied. He wasn't testing me. He was just sort of learning his way through my mind here."

Adelman remembered Bryant telling him about lawyers who really had him shaking his head. One involved two men charged with robbery, Defendant A and Defendant B. Defendant A had an alibi: that he was at work. His attorney put witnesses on the stand who confirmed that. Defendant B claimed that at the time of the robbery, he was on a boat fishing in the Chesapeake Bay. His attorney produced the captain of said boat, who confirmed Defendant B's story.

As a courtesy Judge Bryant asked Defendant A's attorney if he had any questions for the boat captain.

This rather prominent attorney replied, "Oh, yes, your Honor." He then asked the boat captain, "Was my client on the boat?"

"Yes," replied the boat captain.

After the witness left the stand and with the attorneys at the bench, Judge Bryant asked Lawyer A which alibi he intended to use. Remembered Adelman: "And not only did he let A know that he had made a blunder, but he gave the prosecutor his closing argument. And the prosecutor later got up and said to the jury, 'Ladies and Gentlemen, you can't have it both ways. You [can] be at work or you [can] be fishing. And if you've got to choose, he's guilty.'"

Beth Perovich Gesner, who clerked for Judge Bryant in the early 1980s, recalled his encounter with another attorney who was not ready for prime time in a lawsuit against the District.

After the suit was filed—crickets.

The District had not responded to the complaint.

The plaintiff's attorney had taken no further action.

Remembered Gesner: "Judge Bryant decided to set the case in for a status hearing at which he intended to explore with plaintiff's counsel what his intentions were given the inactivity in the case."

Gesner was observing from the jury box when the hearing began and Judge Bryant asked the plaintiff's attorney about the status of the case. The attorney "quickly responded that he was ready to try the case. Judge Bryant, surprised at this response given that the defendant had not even answered the complaint, paused and looked quizzically at the file in front of him." He called Gesner to the bench.

"Is that man a lawyer?" he asked.

Gesner, a summa cum laude graduate of Indiana University of Pennsylvania with a JD (cum laude) from Georgetown Law, went on to become a US magistrate judge in Maryland.

While at work, Judge Bryant made time for random acts of kindness. Carol Garfiel Freeman remembered a day in the 1970s when she, a Criminal Justice Act defense lawyer at the time, had a hearing before him. Her son Alan, about age five, was with her, because he was too sick to go to school and she was, presumably, unable to find a babysitter.

"I was at the bench showing Alan where the reporter sat, etc., when the judge came out unannounced. I was, of course, embarrassed and we quickly returned to our seats."

Judge Bryant was not at all irritated. In fact, after the hearing he called Freeman and her son to the bench "and he showed Alan the features of the judge's part of the bench. He then brought us back to chambers for a few minutes." Alan Freeman, who grew up to be an attorney, never forgot that day, never forgot Judge Bryant "allowing me to play around the bench, in his chair and in his chambers." That experience "forever 'humanized' the judiciary in my mind."

November 1, 1987, was a sad, maddening day for Judge Bryant. That was when the Federal Sentencing Guidelines went into effect. The guidelines abolished parole for people convicted of federal crimes regardless of whether they had priors or were first-time offenders, established longer minimum sentences, and mandated that judges adhere to a strict formula in sentencing based on, for example, the degree of damage the crime caused and the defendant's criminal record or lack thereof.

Judge Bryant was dead set against the guidelines. As Ned Miltenberg, who clerked for the judge in the 1980s, explained, the judge felt that the guidelines "robbed judges of their ability to act like judges, of their right and obligation to see—and sentence—criminal defendants as individual human beings and not just the numbers in the US Code. To him, the Guidelines were an affront to the separation of powers and the height of arrogance."

In protest of the guidelines, Judge Bryant, now seventy-six, refused to take any criminal cases. If a colleague had a serious backlog, he might preside over the trial, but if the defendant was found guilty, he handed the case back over to the original judge for sentencing. (The guidelines became advisory in 2005, when the US Supreme Court ruled that mandatory sentencing guidelines were unconstitutional.)

It was also in 1987 that Roger Adelman and Professor Sherman Cohn of Georgetown Law visited the judge's chambers to seek his support in establishing an American Inn of Court. They wanted not only his support in establishing this fellowship of judges, attorneys, law professors, and law students but also his permission to name the inn after him.

American Inns of Court are modeled on English Inns of Court that started in the Middle Ages. The first American Inn of Court was chartered in 1980 (in Utah). The fact that a mere seven years later there was a movement to name an Inn of Court after Judge Bryant is a testament to how revered he was.

Judge Bryant's support for a new Inn of Court was immediate, but it took some persuading before he agreed to allow it to bear his name. In November 1987 the William B. Bryant American Inn of Court embarked on its mission "to promote civility, professionalism, ethics, education and mentoring in the legal profession."

The Honorable William Benson Bryant absolutely embodied all of this.

Deputy US Marshal Kirk Bowden, awed by AUSA Bill Bryant in the 1950s, recalled, "There was not a person in the [courthouse] he did not know by name. He spoke to each and every person he passed regardless of their status of employment."[24]

Bowden was the first deputy marshal assigned to Judge Bryant's courtroom, but the two first came to know each other in 1959 when Bryant was in private practice and Bowden was a police officer. After Bowden testified in a case in which a Bryant client was on trial, when Bryant later saw him in the hall, he went out of his way to go up to Bowden and shake his hand. "Young man, I want to congratulate you for the way you conducted yourself on [the stand]."

During the several years that Bowden served in Judge Bryant's courtroom the two men became good friends, with Bowden, twenty-four years younger than the judge, calling him "Uncle Bill"—and forever grateful for all that he learned from him. "I got to sit in on some of the discussions between law clerks and the Judge as they dissected the cases that were before him. And oftentimes they would ask my input because of my experience as a law enforcement officer, which gave me an opportunity to grow as a law enforcement officer, gave me an opportunity to listen and learn the intricacies of the law."

---

24. Early on in his career as a deputy US marshal, Bowden's duties included providing security for James Meredith, a fellow Air Force veteran who integrated the University of Mississippi in 1962. White marshals watched over Meredith when he was on campus. Bowden and other Black marshals watched over him when he was off campus. Bowden was also part of the security detail for the March on Washington.

Bowden marveled at how the judge would "simplify the most complex and complicated case so that even I could understand."

After Bowden was transferred to the Court of General Sessions, the two remained very good friends. What's more, Bowden served as a professional witness in Judge Bryant's courses at Howard. Years later, when the judge's mind was still razor-sharp but his body was giving him a little trouble, Bowden sometimes drove his Uncle Bill to and from the courthouse.

Back in 1977 the *Washington Star*'s David Pike observed that Judge Bryant "retains a mixture of informality and decorum in his bench style." He was often even more informal behind the scenes. He cultivated a peaceful atmosphere in his chambers. The "dynamic had to be calm just like his home was," said his secretary, Diane Steed.

For years, no degrees, no certificates, no awards hung upon the walls of his office. He didn't even have the commission for his judgeship framed until Chip saw to it in the 1990s.

Where had it been the whole time?

Diane Steed found it, along with several of Judge Bryant's awards, in a box in a closet in his office. Even after Chip had the commission framed, it hung not in the judge's office but in Steed's. Chip also later took it upon himself to dust off some of his dad's awards and hang them in his office: a 1965 DC Public Service Award . . . a 1969–1970 Justice Byron R. White Award . . . a 1975 Washingtonian of the Year Award . . . a 1976 Howard University Distinguished Alumni Award . . . that 1977 Charles Hamilton Houston Medallion of Merit . . . a 1977 Howard Law Martin Luther King Jr. Award . . . a 1978 Federal Judicial Center Award . . . a 1980 Stuart Stiller Memorial Award . . . a 1981 Bar Association of DC Award. He appreciated his awards. He was deeply moved by each and every one, but displaying them was simply "not a priority for him," explained Chip.

Judge Bryant, who tended to make his own phone calls, cared not for *any* kind of fuss or fanfare in his chambers. Diane Steed recalled that he did not want anyone to help him into or out of his robe. He insisted on carrying books into and out of his courtroom himself. "He didn't want anyone to feel that they were subservient to him," she explained.

His office, not surprisingly, was modest. He had been given a budget for furnishings and was free to use his own money to purchase anything that would put him over budget, such as an antique desk, Persian rug, or pricey work of art. Judge Bryant came in under budget, outfitting his formal office with a standard executive desk and chair, a blue leather sofa, and two blue leather chairs. "Judge Bryant's focus was always on the law and fairness," not on furnishings, said Steed.

When contemplating the law and fairness or when writing his opinions, he hardly ever did so in his office. He preferred to work in the small, narrow library/conference room. That room was also where he read cases, which he read, said Steed, "the way other people would read the Bible."

The judge's sense of fairness and common decency definitely extended to his staff. There was a time when Steed, for family reasons, needed to work a half-day on Fridays. No problem.

"He treated me with such respect," she recalled—as he did everyone who worked for him. Respect and love. "We were all family."

Judge Bryant seldom ate lunch with fellow judges in the small room reserved for them inside the dining room down the hall from his chambers. He preferred to spend lunchtime with his law clerks in the portion of the dining room where guests were allowed.

Lynne Bernabei, who clerked for the judge in the late 1970s, remembered lunches with him in which he shared "decisions he was about to make, and the law that he was turning over in his mind. He would intersperse his ruminations on the case he was considering, with vignettes from his life, which always perfectly illustrated the points he was making in his opinions."

When it came to those opinions, he was "very precise. He labored over every sentence," said Steed. A *Howard Law Journal* article described the judge's opinions as "models of clarity, with complex reasoning rendered in plain language, well-documented and painstakingly detailed."

As for Lynne Bernabei, who cherished lunchtimes with the judge and who had earned a bachelor of arts (magna cum laude) from Harvard and a JD (cum laude) from Harvard Law, she went on to practice civil rights litigation and employment law.

William B. Schultz, who clerked for the judge in the mid-1970s and in the 1990s conducted a series of extraordinary interviews with him for the Historical Society of the District of Columbia Circuit's Oral History Project, had "vivid memories of sitting in his chambers engaged in conversation, which ranged from politics to life, to an interesting insight about animals learned from a program the Judge had seen on TV." These conversations, Schultz continued, "were a gift in many ways, but one way was that no matter who you were, no matter what you were doing, you left Judge Bryant's chambers feeling good about yourself and good about the world in general."

Schultz remembered that one thing Judge Bryant did not feel good about was the Washington Redskins, because the team's owner, George Marshall, "was a total racist. So he had no interest in the Washington Redskins." This was not the grumbling of an angry Black man but simply a matter of principle. Schultz added, "I always thought Judge Bryant was a little bit like Nelson Mandela in that way, in that you never saw any bitterness or hostility or tremendous negativity even though he grew up in a completely segregated society."

Schultz also remembered that as a boss the judge "was not a hard-driving taskmaster at all." He did not micromanage. "He would give you assignments, tell you what to do and he expected you to know how to get the job done."

Schultz, who had earned a bachelor's in economics from Yale and a JD from the University of Virginia School of Law, eventually specialized in health care and Food and Drug Administration (FDA) law. After clerking for Judge Bryant, he worked at Public Citizen Litigation Group for fourteen years, which, said Schultz, "Judge Bryant encouraged; it was always clear that he loved that I chose public interest law." During the Clinton administration, Schultz was deputy commissioner of the FDA, and during the Obama administration, he served as the Department of Health and Human Services's general counsel.

Judge Bryant was a most patient, forgiving boss. Ned Miltenberg recalled that early in his clerkship, he drafted an order "in a relatively minor civil case." Miltenberg was quite proud of his work. He believed he had drafted it "with care." However, a few days after Judge Bryant signed that order Miltenberg read a court of appeals decision "that made it plain my draft—and his order—were in error. Mortified, I told him what I'd found and apologized as profusely as I could." Miltenberg braced himself for a stern upbraiding—and even a request for his resignation.

No worries. That was the essence of Judge Bryant's response.

After Miltenberg drafted a new order, the judge lifted up a pencil and asked him what was on the end of it. "When I stammered 'an eraser,' he said that the old folks had told him that erasers are affixed to the end of every pencil because 'everyone makes mistakes.'"

Miltenberg, who had earned a bachelor's of arts from Cornell and a JD from the University of Michigan Law, became a constitutional lawyer.

John Spiegel, who like Miltenberg clerked for Judge Bryant in the 1980s, recalled how gracious his boss was when he made a colossal blunder not long after he started on the job. The incident occurred at the beginning of a hearing on "a big case, and the courtroom was filled with lawyers, spectators, and some journalists. Right after taking the bench, the Judge gestured to me to come over to him." When Spiegel reached the bench, Judge Bryant whispered, "John, I forgot the jacket. Can you go to my office and get it? It's sitting right on the desk."

Spiegel hurried to the judge's chambers, where he quickly spotted his boss's suit jacket folded over his chair. "I picked up the jacket, walked right into the courtroom and right up to the bench, holding up the suit jacket like a trophy."

"What are you doing with my suit coat?" asked a very puzzled Judge Bryant.

"'Judge,' I answered, 'You asked me to get the jacket. Here it is.'"

Judge Bryant stared at Spiegel "momentarily in disbelief. Then a look of amusement crossed his face."

Judge Bryant said softly, "The jacket. The jacket. The 'jacket' means the court file. I left it on my desk." Judge Bryant then "laughed softly, eyes sparkling, and in a louder voice said, 'Counsel, we'll take a short recess.'"

Spiegel also bore witness to the fact that the judge was not above letting his clerks see just how human he was. He recalled him crying in his presence twice. The first time was when, at the end of a day, they were chatting about American history. Judge Bryant mentioned attending Marian Anderson's concert on the steps of the Lincoln

Memorial on April 9, 1939, that remarkable concert arranged by First Lady Eleanor Roosevelt after the Daughters of the American Revolution refused to let Anderson sing at its Constitution Hall because of the color of her skin.

On that historic day at the Lincoln Memorial, the extraordinary contralto sang seven songs. Judge Bryant's recollection of one in particular had him tear up. It was Anderson's rendition of "My Country 'Tis of Thee," the first song she sang.

Spiegel recalled that as Judge Bryant recited the lyrics, "tears began to roll down his cheeks. He paused, made an effort to compose himself, and then, with a slight shrug, gave up the effort and cried softly. 'I don't know how she found the strength to sing that song,' he finally said."

Having earned a bachelor of arts from Stanford and a JD from Yale Law, Spiegel became a staff attorney at the US Environmental Protection Agency, then practiced family law before opening a mediation practice.

Judge Bryant's law clerks remembered him as the consummate teacher, so often in subtle ways.

Robert P. Watkins III, who clerked for the judge in the 1960s, recalled, "Very early in my clerkship, after a hearing on a motion to suppress evidence in a criminal case, Judge Bryant came into my office, took off his robe, sat down, put his feet up on my desk and said: 'What do you think of X?,' one of the propositions that a lawyer in the hearing was propounding. I answered. He then said: 'What do you think of Y?,' another fact in the case that I had not thought about. I answered again. He then said, 'What do you think of Z?' I answered again."

The conversation "went back and forth for about an hour with no resolution. Judge Bryant got up and left my office. At that point I realized that I had some legal research to do."

In retrospect Watkins realized that the judge knew the answers to each question. "He was guiding me and teaching me how to approach legal problems." Watkins added that these conversations had "a profound effect on my legal career." His year with Judge Bryant, was "a pivotal moment in my career because I learned things from him by being exposed to him. I learned things that I wouldn't have learned anyplace else."

Watkins, with his bachelor of arts from Harvard, a JD from Columbia University Law, and a diploma in criminology from Cambridge University, became one of DC's top trial lawyers.

William Richard "Rick" Hyde Jr., who clerked for the judge in the late 1970s, would never forget the day that he was taken aback by a particular piece of advice. "I reeled as I listened to him analogize me to a 'lost ball in high weeds' if I continued taking notes on testimony instead of listening to the testimony and remembering it. As I listened to his good natured chastisement, I recalled courthouse folklore about the Judge as a trial lawyer trying entire cases with a blank yellow pad and a paper clip with perfect recall of the testimony."

Initially Hyde was daunted by the prospect of following the judge's advice. "However, as I matured the wisdom of his lessons slowly sank in—always trust yourself and listen."

Equally memorable were the times when during a recess Hyde was with Judge Bryant in his chambers "to discuss, to my relief, not any error on my part, but some nuance in his swing which would produce great results in his next round of golf. He would not hesitate to demonstrate his new swing, fully clad in judicial gown, for my critique."

Hyde, who had earned a bachelor's degree in architecture and urban planning at Princeton—where he was the first Black varsity golfer in the Ivy League—and an LLB (cum laude) from Howard Law—where he took Judge Bryant's trial advocacy course—became a sports, entertainment, and finance attorney and a professor of sports law at Howard.

"It goes without saying that he taught each of us how to be better lawyers and to fully analyze any legal issue," stated Magistrate Judge Gesner. "Perhaps, more importantly though, he taught us, through example, how to be better people. He taught us about common sense and compassion—two qualities that would serve us well in whatever we chose to do." What's more, the judge taught his law clerks, Gesner added, "that family ('your folks,' as Judge Bryant would say) always, always comes first."

Like Hyde, Gesner had golf stories. "I'll always hold dear the daily golf sessions we shared." After he learned that she golfed, the judge brought in an extra club. "Virtually every day around 4:30 or 5:00

p.m., Judge Bryant would yell for me across the two offices between his office and my office. When I would arrive in his office, he would have the two golf clubs and his latest swinging gadget out to show me the latest trick 'some guy' had shown him. Thank heavens for the high ceilings in his chambers."

Whether listening to his ruminations on a case, having a wide-ranging conversation with him, being forgiven for a mistake, watching him weep, being asked, "What do you think of X?," being on the receiving end of some "good-natured chastisement," or engaging with him on his golf swing, Judge Bryant's law clerks could feel themselves grow. And he took great delight in displaying their photographs on the walls of his library/conference room.

Law clerks of other judges also had the benefit of his wisdom and generosity of spirit. Back in 1968 Paul L. Friedman, who clerked for Judge Aubrey E. Robinson Jr., then for Judge Roger Robb, sought Judge Bryant's advice when he was trying to decide next steps at the end of his clerkship.

"'Go to the US Attorney's Office,' he said. 'It's a great office.' And more importantly, he said, 'A prosecutor with a good heart can do more justice every single day than the defense lawyer, by deciding which cases merit prosecution and which cases do not, by negotiating fair pleas both to protect society and, at the same time, recognizing that almost every human being is salvageable.'"

Friedman did serve as an AUSA for several years in the early 1970s, then as assistant United States solicitor general before entering private practice. In 1994, he joined Judge Bryant on the District Court and continued to cherish him. He found that "there was nothing better for perking you up or making you feel more optimistic about life or giving you hope for the future than spending half an hour late in the afternoon after a busy day in court talking with Bill Bryant."

Judge Friedman had this to say as well: "And because Judge Bryant believed in the rule of law and the limitations and constraints on a judge, he'd remind us that, as judges, we're not just free to do whatever we want to do. We must follow the law, and we must follow precedent. But as Judge Bryant used to say, even so, every once in a while you can strike a blow for justice."

It was also in 1994 that James Robertson, a corporate lawyer and a former head of the Jackson, Mississippi, office of the not-for-profit Lawyers' Committee for Civil Rights Under Law, joined the bench. His chambers were next door to Judge Bryant's. "He welcomed me immediately—all the judges did—with the standard invitation to consult about anything I wanted to. I did a few of those consultations with other judges. They were very nice, very accommodating, but I have to say not all that helpful. I would ask some question, and they would say, 'Hell, Robertson, you're an Article III judge; do whatever you want to do.'" (Article III judges are judges with lifetime appointments—barring bad behavior—as outlined in Article III of the Constitution.)

"Do whatever you want to do" was not the sort of response Judge Robertson received from Judge Bryant when he sought his advice on a couple of occasions. These were times when Judge Robertson was, he said, "wrestling with a decision of real public importance, a decision I knew would be controversial." Judge Bryant "never failed to stop what he was doing, read carefully, consider deeply, and tell me exactly what he thought."

Judge Robertson also recalled Judge Bryant telling him this: "Jim, a district judge can't go out looking for cases. You've got to deal with the ones that come to you. But a district judge is kind of like a cannon on top of the mountain, guarding the harbor. Every once in a while something comes within range and the bearing is right, and boom. You hit it."

Just as Judge Bryant did with his children, so with Diane Steed, his law clerks, and his colleagues on the bench, he relished sprinkling wisdom into their lives in the form of aphorisms, often prefaced with the words "as the old folks say."

"In the land of the blind the one-eyed man is king."
"It's hard to take ink out of milk."
"Whenever you try to put too much English on the ball, you miscue."
"Where a worm comes out of an apple depends on where he goes in."

Remembered Judge Friedman: "When he thought I was working too hard, he would say, 'If you burn the candle at both ends, it will burn twice as bright but last half as long.'"

Outside the courthouse, Judge Bryant never went about on a high horse. When interacting with strangers, he did not introduce himself as "Judge Bryant" but as "Bill Bryant" or simply "Bill." He never used his position to get, say, a better table at a restaurant.

Ned Miltenberg remembered that the judge would "stand in line for hours at the offices of the DC Water Department waiting patiently to see a clerk in order to contest an incorrect bill; although others might have announced that their important public position warranted special treatment, asking for such treatment, or even accepting it when offered, was foreign to his faith." When the judge arrived at his doctor's office, if a staffer offered to let him jump the line, his reply was "I'll wait my turn. I'll wait my turn."

And he still got his hair cut at a barbershop on Seventh Street, just as he did when he was a pool-playing teen.

Chapter 17

I'LL BE THERE

When Bill hit the links, he did so mostly with the DC Pro-Duffers, which he joined in the late 1960s.

This Black men's golf club first teed off in 1954, when Black people could play only at two of the DC metro area's many courses. One was the East Potomac Golf Links, a public course in Southwest DC that was desegregated in 1941 after Black people staged a golf-in. The other was the Langston Golf Course in Northeast DC, built for Black golfers in the 1930s and named after John Mercer Langston, Howard Law's founding dean (1868) and Virginia's first Black member of Congress (1890–1891). Langston was where the DC Pro-Duffers mostly played until other courses in the DC metro area desegregated in the 1960s.[25]

Mordecai Johnson, still president of Howard, was one of the nine men who got this group of proud professional duffers off the ground. Another was general surgeon William Richard "Bill" Hyde Sr., a Dunbar and Howard graduate who trained under blood plasma preservation pioneer Dr. Charles Drew, at Howard Med, commanded a MASH unit during the Korean War, and in 1958 became the first Black surgeon at Washington Hospital Center. Hyde's son Rick was the law clerk Bill cautioned against becoming "a lost ball in high weeds."

As much as Bill loved golf, he "practiced more than he played," said Rick Hyde. He also remembered that, along with chipping and putting in his office between hearings, when Bill could get away from the court for an hour or two he headed over to the Soldiers' Home Field to practice his short iron game. But Bill needed more than an hour or two to play a game of golf. "Playing a round of 18 holes took

25. The Black community began campaigning for a new golf course in the 1920s when it became clear that the construction of the Arlington Memorial Bridge over the Potomac would doom the only course for Black golfers, the rather shabby nine-hole one near the Lincoln Memorial.

five or more hours," explained Rick Hyde. Added to that was the DC Pro-Duffers' post-round camaraderie, which included drinks. Hyde recalled that every now and then Bill was able to play on a Wednesday afternoon. Mostly he played on Sundays.

Whether on a Wednesday or on a Sunday, whether he played at Langston, DC's Rock Creek Park Golf Course or at courses in Maryland such as Falls Road, Bill had a terrific time with his band of brothers, a spirited group that engaged in friendly wagers and much trash-talking. According to Hyde, these men "accepted their poor play graciously" and celebrated their "successful shots with gusto" and with "the conviction that since able to hit the shot successfully once they should be able to do it all the time."

Kirk Bowden recalled that Bill "often compared the game of golf with life: it is preparation, tenacity, concentration, talent, seizing the opportunities, and being prepared for the unknown." Bowden also remembered that Bill "often talked about the time he met and played a round of golf with Lee Elder," the first Black person to play in the Masters Tournament (1975).

Along with Bill Hyde, Bill Bryant was also a member of the Brookland Literary and Hunting Club, another group of Black professional men. This one organized in 1942. The club's name was a bit of mischief. It was simply a poker club that met in members' homes. "It was literary because of discussions we'd have—of the civil rights and so on," explained Dunbar High and Howard graduate Thomas Taylor, who had a remarkable career as a social worker and was known as the "godfather of daycare" in the DC area.

Hunting?

Bill Bryant—hardly a great golfer but definitely a great poker player—like Bill Hyde, Thomas Taylor, and the other club members were, said Taylor, "always hunting" for a good hand in their games of five-card stud. Those others included Dr. Paul Cornely, the first Black person in America to earn a PhD in public health (from the University of Michigan in 1934). In 1970 this warrior against racism in healthcare became the first Black president of the American Public Health Association (founded in 1872).

There was so much history around those poker tables, as was the case when the DC Pro-Duffers hit the links—stories of striving, overcoming, of Black men doing their damnedest in the face of daunting odds.

The same is true of the DePriest Fifteen, to which Bill also belonged. Founded in 1933, this Black men's social club was named after the twentieth century's first Black member of Congress, Oscar Stanton De Priest of Chicago, whose son, Oscar Jr., was a member of Howard's class of 1932 along with Bill. At the start the DePriest Fifteen was something of a fraternity of legal professionals. Early members included Charlie Houston's father, George E. C. Hayes, and Judge Armond Scott, whose nephew, Alfred, steered Bill to Wesley Williams for that internship when he was studying for the bar.

The DePriest Fifteen hosts an annual black-tie affair, Ladies Night, and an annual picnic (a stag event). Its heart and soul is a monthly Saturday night dinner with no set agenda. Conversation has always been based on whatever was on the minds of these men of mark, typically ranging from matters in DC and the state of the nation to global affairs.

The men with whom Bill engaged in these wide-ranging conversations included DC's first Black mayor, Walter Washington (1975–1979), and Dr. Burke "Mickey" Syphax, Bill's friend since his Dunbar High days. There was also Bill's longtime friend Julian R. Dugas, DC's first city administrator when Washington was mayor. With Bill, Dugas, himself a graduate of Howard Law, co-taught trial advocacy. (At one point, the team included Luke C. Moore, a former chief US marshal for the District of Columbia appointed to the DC Superior Court in 1972.)

DePriest Fifteen member Dr. Michael R. Winston remarked that George E. C. Hayes "was the most intent, most focused listener I had ever encountered, until I met Judge Bryant, who was his equal in that. When you spoke with Judge Bryant, with his penetrating look upon you, you worked hard to be succinct, factual, and analytic. He tended to say things like 'Is that a fact?' or 'Really?' Sometimes it took no more than a squint for him to express some skepticism about what was being said."

Dr. Winston regarded "equanimity" as another of the judge's "distinguishing characteristics." He stated, "Although he had a close acquaintance with what some would call the 'realities' of modern life, they could not push him into the arms of cynicism or the equally unsatisfactory embrace of easy optimism. He faced life with a steady gaze. He could also freeze the moment, and you, with no more than a steely-eyed look, from the Bench or from across a pool table."

For Dr. Winston, listening to this most focused listener, was an amazing experience. "One had the sense of being in the presence of that rare phenomenon, a wise and unpretentious man, whose sharp insights were tempered by knowledge of the world as it is." Dr. Winston went on to say, "Many of his qualities could be appreciated without any significant knowledge of his past. One could apprehend at once his quiet dignity, his inner firmness, the absence of the easy bonhomie that often is a substitute for real interest in other people. It was only when one knew some of the facts of his earlier life that many of his most impressive virtues emerged in bold relief."

Pulitzer Prize–winning *Washington Post* columnist Colbert I. "Colby" King recalled that it "was a pleasure just to be in Bryant's company and to hear him trade war stories with the more senior members about the early days in Washington, when the city was, by law and custom, divided by a strict color line."

Details on those war stories? What was specifically said at a DePriest Fifteen dinner stayed at a DePriest Fifteen dinner. From its inception the club's number-one code of conduct was confidentiality.

One of Bill's closest friends outside of the Pro-Duffers, the poker club, and the DePriest Fifteen was Vernon Jordan, the venerable civil rights leader turned corporate lawyer and DC power broker.

Like Bill, Vernon Jordan had grown up in a city where segregation was intense (Atlanta). Also, he had not been born with a silver spoon. He waited tables as a teen for extra cash. While a student at DePauw University, where, in a class of four hundred, he was the lone Black student, he had worked as a chauffeur and waiter in the summers. Another thing the two men shared was Howard. Jordan earned his JD from Howard Law in 1960, three years after Bill's triumph in *Mallory*.

"Vernon and my dad talked about the law, civil rights, politics, family and golf," remembered Chip. They talked in Bill's chambers; they talked on the phone. Christmas after Christmas, Jordan sent Astaire a beautiful poinsettia and personally delivered to Bill a pound cake baked by his wife, Ann Dibble Jordan, a social worker by training and prominent in her own right. She served as a director of Johnson & Johnson for a number of years, for example, and as a member of the Brookings Institution's board of trustees.

Whenever the dapper, dignified Jordan was a guest speaker at Howard's Rankin Chapel, Bill was sure to be there. And when the Reverend Dr. Gardner C. Taylor, civil rights leader and longtime senior pastor of Brooklyn, New York's historic Concord Baptist Church, was scheduled to preach at Rankin Chapel or anywhere else in the DC area, "Vernon would call my dad to urge him to attend," said Chip.

"Where? What time? I'll be there," Bill typically responded.

Wherever "there" was, Bill "thoroughly enjoyed the sermons," said Chip. One would have a hard time finding anyone who did not savor a sermon by Reverend Taylor. As one reporter said, he was "a rumbling, rhythmic orator who marshaled Scripture, mystical allusions and the art of plain talk into sermons of emotional power."

Vernon Jordan never forgot how Bryant was there for him when he was subpoenaed to appear before a grand jury in 1998. This was in connection with independent counsel Kenneth Starr's investigation of President Bill Clinton that led to his impeachment.

Jordan, a close friend and advisor to Clinton for years, was put through the wringer by many in the press. News outlets reported that Starr had him in his sights for obstruction of justice. Jordan had urged Monica Lewinsky to lie about her affair with the president when she was a White House intern—or so the story went. According to a Pew Research Center piece, the "allegations against Jordan also spawned profiles that often depicted him as an amoral character." Moreover, shortly before Jordan testified, *Meet the Press* "aired a rumor" that Starr had granted Jordan limited use immunity, "which suggested that he needed shielding from a criminal charge." At the time Jordan was a partner at a prestigious DC law firm.

Jordan recalled, "Every night, before my testimony, the Judge called from home and simply asked: 'You alright, boy, you alright?'" Penny remembered that Jordan "would call my dad in the evenings to debrief and get encouragement."

In the end, after hours of testimony during five appearances before the grand jury in March, May, and June, Vernon Jordan was all right, never charged with any wrongdoing.

When it came to Bill's life outside the courthouse, nothing was more precious than time with family. "He really enjoyed spending time with all of us, especially at family holiday dinners," said Chip. Astaire and her niece/adopted daughter Beatrice Jones alternated hosting Christmas and Thanksgiving dinners. Christmas after Christmas, Thanksgiving after Thanksgiving, around a table laden with roast turkey, stuffing, ham, mashed potatoes, sweet potatoes, kale or collard greens, corn on the cob, cranberry sauce, hot rolls, and gravy—and with the prospect of apple or pumpkin pie—the Bryant-Jones family laughed and loved, with Bill and Ed often steering conversations to politics or sports, especially golf.[26]

These Bryant-Jones holiday dinners included Beatrice and Ed's three children, Edina, Debbie, and Eddie. Starting in 1979 Bill and Astaire had a grandson at those holiday tables, then, starting in 1984, a granddaughter: Penny's children, Vaughn and Lauren, who called their grandparents "Papa" and "Mama."

When those holiday dinners were at Beatrice and Ed's, the family was literally close-knit. Beatrice and Ed's dining room was smaller than Astaire and Bill's. But the family made it work! "We all squeezed in to sit at one large extended table!" remembered Chip, for whom home was once again DC, starting in 1988.

At one point Bill and Astaire spent a great deal of time with their grandchildren. This was in the mid-late 1980s when Penny was going

26. Ed had a long career as a supervisor for Howard University's Grounds Keeping Division, co-owned a floor maintenance company with his brother, and at one point taught at Melwood, a not-for-profit that provides job training and other support services to people with disabilities. Beatrice had a long career at the Library of Congress, including as a secretary in its law library and as an administrator. Deborah Jones Taborn, email to author, July 8, 2022.

through a separation, then a divorce. She, Vaughn, and Lauren lived in the Northampton Street home.

"It was good growing up there," said Vaughn. His fond memories include Papa sometimes driving him to school and the family taking evening meals together. He also never forgot being aware that every morning and every night, Papa got down on his knees in silent prayer.

After Penny and her children moved back into their home in Brookland, Bill and Astaire continued to see a great deal of Vaughn and Lauren. Penny and the kids often had dinner at their house. During some of his after-school visits Vaughn had a good time playing gin rummy, blackjack, or tunk with Mama, whom he would forever remember as elegant and full of grace.

Like her brother, Lauren had fond memories of Papa driving her to elementary school. Penny was still an educator in Montgomery County, and because her workday started before Lauren's schooldays began, she dropped her daughter off at her parents' before she went to work. Frozen waffles always awaited Lauren, waffles she prepared herself and enjoyed with a big glass of milk. "Knowing that the waffles would always be there [meant a lot]." So did Papa's words of comfort during those drives to school.

Young Lauren was quite shy and often apprehensive about going to school, especially at the start of a school year. Having had a mean teacher one year and being one of the few Black children at her school didn't help. Papa always assured her that everything would be just fine. He also always encouraged her to have confidence in herself. She would be forever grateful to him for other things as well. The value of hard work, resilience, and perseverance were among the things he taught her, not through lectures but by his actions, his example—"just by what he did day to day." Papa's life was also a lesson in the importance of walking in humility. "Regardless of how much he accomplished, he never boasted about anything."

"Right from wrong" is at the top of Vaughn's list of things he credits Papa with instilling in him. "Try to live pretty much righteous. And I think that's what he pretty much tried to do." Vaughn remembered that his grandfather was acutely, painfully aware of all "the suffering in the world" and that his message here was, "You may not be able to change everything but do what you can."

Vaughn often went on drives with Papa, when his grandfather wanted to check out a location connected to a case before him or because he simply wanted to show his grandson different parts of the city. During these drives Papa would point out certain things such as a group of people who were clearly inebriated. He didn't condemn them; instead he asked Vaughn questions such as "What do you think about that?" or "How do you think they fell into that?" If traveling through a troubled part of the city, he might ask, "Why do you think it's poorer over here than in other parts of the city?"

After Vaughn learned to shoot pool, he and Papa hung out around that Brunswick slate-top pool table, and over the years the two spent countless hours in Papa's den watching sports, from football to golf. The sound was often turned off, because Papa had no patience with commentators who served up more hype than facts. He felt, said Vaughn, "that they didn't know what they were talking about." In his mind these commentators were saying things that were not *right*, plain and simple.

Vaughn couldn't recall ever hearing Papa complain about anything. "He knew how much suffering there was in this world. He knew how blessed he was." Another thing that always stuck with Vaughn is that Papa was "always thinking before he spoke." He never said anything "reckless."

During any given summer, and especially on Mother's Day, the Fourth of July, and Memorial Day, the family gathered at Beatrice and Ed's home for bang-up barbecues. Beatrice and Ed's home was an average-size house in the Woodridge section of the city, but it was set on a *very* large lot, which meant a very large front yard and very large backyard, with patios, flower beds, and a vegetable garden.

In this idyllic setting, with the aroma of hot dogs, hamburgers, and chicken on the grill wafting in the air and with bowls and trays of potato salad, corn on the cob, and salad delighting the eye, Bill and Ed sometimes indulged in endless rounds of horseshoes—"until they could no longer walk," recalled Vaughn. Beatrice and Ed's middle child, Debbie Jones Taborn, remembered times when her Uncle Bill just chilled. He "chatted, laughed, listened, and took his quick naps."

The family also enjoyed dips in a large pool—except for Astaire and Bill. Neither could swim.

As for the couple's time alone, things remained low-key. They had no need for extravagant vacations. Their simple pleasures together included going out to dinner and taking in the occasional play at the Arena Stage, the National Theatre, or the Kennedy Center. "My parents were porch people," said Chip. "They really enjoyed hanging out on their porch."

Astaire remained the ardent gardener, something Bill continued to adore. Life was good and full of bliss. That bliss was shattered, however, one warm day in 1991 when Astaire, age eighty, suffered a stroke.

"She was conscious, and scared," said Chip recalling his mother's condition when he arrived at Washington Hospital Center immediately after getting the call from his father. "Back then, they didn't have the interventional drugs they have today to minimize the damage of a stroke, so you had to just wait and let the stroke run its course—very frustrating and frightening." Astaire had some difficulty with her speech, a bit of a pinched cheek, and some balance issues when it came to walking. She had also lost the use of her left arm, which rendered her "depressed and easily brought to tears."

Astaire spent five or six weeks at the National Rehabilitation Hospital (NRH), with Bill having dinner with her every day, every day, every day. "The NRH did a great job with my mom," said Chip. Bill stopped spending long hours at the courthouse, and while at work, said Diane Steed, "he didn't wear his pain on his sleeve." People who were not close to him never knew how much he was hurting.

Astaire did her utmost in pushing back to strength. When the NRH discharged her, the pinch in her cheek was gone, she was speaking clearly and walking pretty well without the use of a cane. Though her left arm was not as strong as it once was, she had regained full use of it. And there would be home visits by a physical therapist to aid Astaire's recovery.

Bill hired a housekeeper and companion for Astaire: Sonia Avalos, a native of El Salvador. Monday to Friday Sonia was at the Bryant home early in the morning to help Astaire get ready for the day and to prepare breakfast for the couple. In and around dusting, vacuuming, or doing a load of laundry, Sonia often watched television with

Astaire and, if the weather was nice, accompanied her on a walk. By the time Sonia left at around 3 or 4 p.m., she had prepared dinner, which Bill later heated up, having done his best to get home by 5 or 6 p.m. Although Astaire was quite comfortable being home alone for an hour or so, Penny, Lauren, and Vaughn were often at the house between the time Sonia left and Bill arrived.

All along Diane Steed was also a source of support and not just in arranging Bill's schedule so that he could head home early in the evenings. "Judge Bryant came in one day and had this big bag of bills and looked at me and he said, 'I don't know what to do with this.'" He was clearly overwhelmed at the moment, and Steed was more than happy to help out. For some time, she used part of her lunch hour to prepare checks for his signature, then readied payment slips and checks for Chip to pick up for mailing. Chip worked at the Department of Labor, across the street from the courthouse.

After Astaire had the stroke, Bill not only stopped spending long hours at the courthouse but also gave up teaching trial advocacy at Howard. Typically after that Saturday morning class, he headed over to the courthouse to read up on current cases. He stopped doing that too. However, Bill did not give up all his passions. He continued to make it to those monthly poker games and to DePriest Fifteen dinners. Once or twice a month, he donned a pair of khakis, a polo shirt, and a short-brimmed hat, and, with his top-of-the-line golf clubs, headed to the links. This set of clubs was a gift from law clerks in celebration of the judge's tenth anniversary on the bench. (Chip recalled that his father occasionally splurged when adding clubs to his set. For example, at one point, "at the urging of Vernon Jordan, my dad bought the latest and greatest driver at that time, Big Bertha. Bill was still very frugal, but when it came to certain things he was a firm believer in the adage, said Chip, "You get what you pay for.")

Seven or eight months after her stroke, Astaire was getting out of the house more and more, enjoying such things as luncheon-bridge parties with girlfriends. She even mastered a new card game, pinochle, which Beatrice taught her and Sonia.

Remembered Chip: "So my mom would practice at home playing with Sonia, so she'd be ready to play with Beatrice's small pinochle group. Beatrice's card buddies became very fond of my mother. They got a kick out of her because she had a good sense of humor and was young at heart." And Astaire absolutely adored her new card buddies.

Astaire had also relearned how to drive, but, said Chip, "she stopped driving on her own because she drove slowly and didn't want people honking at her. She told me it was just a matter of her proving to herself that she could do it. She wanted to get her confidence back, which she partially did."

Bill and Astaire were also back to enjoying dinners out. By then their number one go-to was O'Donnell's Sea Grill in Bethesda, Maryland. And these porch people still had their beautiful flower gardens to enjoy, thanks to the Black, family-owned lawn service company the Bryants had been using for years.

As Bill carried on presiding over cases and caring for his wife, at one point he was contending with quite a bit of pain in one of his hips, which forced him to give up golf and led to a hip replacement in 1995, when he was eighty-four.

About a year later, Astaire, by then walking with a cane, became, explained Chip, aphasiac, "whereby she could understand what was being said but found it increasingly difficult to speak and articulate her thoughts." Lauren remembered that Mama's eyes were so alive. "She never looked out of it."

In time Astaire went from getting about with a cane to using a walker. She also needed more personal care. It came from trusty Sonia, by then a licensed personal caregiver and much loved by Penny, Chip, Beatrice—the whole family—"because of the way she took care of my folks," said Chip.

There came a point when Bill hired a woman for the night shift but she didn't last long. "He said he wasn't going to pay anyone to sleep in his house," recalled Steed. Instead, he hired a woman to be on hand for a few hours in the evening, a Mrs. Johnson, who left after getting Astaire ready for bed. Bill was more than willing to be there for his wife, to attend to any needs she might have between the time Mrs. Johnson left and Sonia arrived in the morning.

On the morning of Wednesday, September 17, 1997, twelve days after her eighty-sixth birthday and the day before her husband's eighty-sixth, Astaire Gonzalez Bryant—Bill's darling, his soulmate, his beloved wife of sixty-three years—passed away. She died peacefully in her sleep at Washington Hospital Center. Bill was at her side.

On September 22, Astaire lay in state at the Blessed Sacrament Catholic Church on Western Avenue, NW, and was then buried at Fort Lincoln Cemetery in Brentwood, Maryland. Those who had wished to send flowers had been asked to make donations in her memory to the Hospital for Sick Children instead. Astaire had been a board member for several years.

That year the family had both Thanksgiving and Christmas at Beatrice and Ed's, where, said Chip, "We did not dwell on my mother's absence. No one wanted to risk putting my dad in a sad mood." As the family mourned, togetherness remained strong. Penny, Chip, Vaughn, and Lauren visited the Northampton Street home regularly and there were frequent family dinners at Clyde's of Chevy Chase, a short drive from Bill's home. Chip recalled that his dad "did sometimes go to the Channel Inn for dinner by himself after my mom passed, but when I heard about it, I started going with him most Thursdays." Chip still worked across the street from the courthouse.

Bill had other kin looking out for him. They included Debbie Jones Taborn. "I remember one Friday night, my husband and I were going to a restaurant in Bethesda, one that Uncle Bill had introduced us to. On our way up the beltway we called him to see if he wanted to join us. Without hesitation, he said, 'I'm at the door!' That really made me realize how lonely he was."

Many a Friday or Saturday night, often well past midnight, after hanging out at a friend's house, teenaged Lauren drove the long way home so that she could pass by Papa's house. If the house was dark, she drove on home. If there was a light on, she went inside. If she found her grandfather asleep, she headed to the kitchen and washed up any dishes that might be in the sink, then set the table for his breakfast in the morning. If she found him awake in his den reading a newspaper or watching television, "Papa, you gotta go to bed," she'd say. After talking with him a bit more, she went home. "I enjoyed doing that. Every moment of it." (Like Lauren, Vaughn, Penny, and Chip had keys to the house.)

Vernon Jordan called Bill more regularly and occasionally stopped by the house to check on him. Moreover, for several years Jordan sent Penny and Beatrice beautiful poinsettias at Christmas. He also continued to have one sent to Bill's home. Bill would call him up and say, "Astaire's poinsettia came today. Thank you."

Sonia Avalos was also part of Bill's support system. After her mom passed, Penny asked Sonia to take care of her dad, and she did, as housekeeper, as family friend.

After his beloved was laid to rest, for at least two years Bill visited her grave every morning, and sometimes in the evening. Early on he took flowers a few times a week. While the visits eventually became less frequent, they never stopped until he was laid to rest beside her.

When Bill visited Astaire's grave, perhaps he reflected on the day they first laid eyes on one another, the shows they took in at the Howard Theatre, and the start of their married life in a single room in the home of Ed and Lucy Simon. Raising Beatrice . . . the joy of Penny's arrival after fourteen years of trying to have a baby, and then nearly a year and a half later the joy of Chip's arrival . . . the bridge and poker games they hosted in their home . . . their getaways to Columbia Beach . . . their trips to the fish market on the Waterfront—surely all this and more floated across his mental sky, along with Astaire's steady, unfailing support of his pursuit of a life in the law. Through thick and thin.

At moments Bill may simply have meditated on the wondrous flower gardens Astaire created when they lived on Kenilworth Avenue in Beaver Heights, then on Seventeenth Street, NE, and, finally, at their Northampton Street home, where he now lived alone with a permanent ache, an everlasting void.

Chapter 18

NOT TO BE TOLERATED IN A CIVILIZED SOCIETY

After he lost his wife, on weekdays Judge Bryant typically arrived at the courthouse late morning and sometimes stayed at work as late as 10 p.m. He was a night owl by nature. Besides, he had no reason to head home in the early evening, as Astaire was not there. When Diane Steed knew that the judge would be working late, before she left for the day she often brought him a dinner from the cafeteria to take home. She also let marshals know that he was still in his chambers so that they could watch out for him when he left the building.

By then the judge's home away from home had been renamed in honor of Judge E. Barrett Prettyman Sr., who served on the US Court of Appeals for the DC Circuit 1945–1971. It just so happens that back in the 1950s, Prettyman spearheaded the creation of the sculpture in front of the courthouse: the Trylon of Freedom, which pays homage to the nation's founding documents. This twenty-four-foot-high three-sided granite obelisk includes bas relief images representing freedom of speech, the proscription against cruel and unusual punishment, the prohibition against illegal search and seizure, and other fundamental legal rights enshrined in the Constitution, a pocket copy of which Judge Bryant almost always had within easy reach. He also kept in his chambers a volume of worship and wisdom: a book that combined the Old Testament's Psalms and Proverbs.

In 2001, at age ninety, Judge Bryant endured a second hip replacement. He also said goodbye to the blue Toyota Cressida he had been driving for years and purchased a Subaru Outback. Some of his colleagues took that purchase as a sign of his abiding optimism. Perhaps.

According to his family, he bought the Outback because he needed a car that was easier for him to get into and out of. "When he was 89 years old," recalled Chip, "my father told me, 'Chip, if I live to be 90, I'm going to do two things—get a new hip and a new car!' He did both!" The judge loved his Subaru, explained Chip, "because he said the driver's seat was at the perfect height for him to ease himself against it and 'just sit down' without having to bend or lower his body. Although he could manage to walk, he continued to use a walker after his surgery for balance. He called it his 'horse' and he would lift that lightweight aluminum walker into the rear passenger side seat, and he was off wherever he wanted to drive."

By then plenty of people had often asked Judge Bryant when he was going to retire. Chip remembered that his dad "would always reply that when President Johnson gave him a lifetime appointment, he took him at his word." The judge saw neither age nor a body growing frail as a reason to retire. The mind was another matter. William B. Schultz recalled that Judge Bryant "often asked former clerks to tell him if he was too old to continue to be a judge. He was very concerned that he would not be aware if his mental ability diminished. It never did." As long as he remained sharp of mind, Judge Bryant wanted to keep on going, keep on serving the cause of justice.

His chief judge, Thomas F. Hogan, on the bench with him since 1982, absolutely had his back. "The day I became Chief Judge [on June 19, 2001] I called and asked to meet with Bill," recalled Judge Hogan. "He was turning 90 and I think he might have felt the new chief was going to ask him about his retirement plans but said, 'Come right up.'" Judge Bryant's retirement was the last thing on Judge Hogan's mind. "My visit was to tell him as long as I was chief he had a home at the court as long as he wished and then I asked him for advice. We sat and talked, or rather I listened, until the sun left the sky."

Nearly two years later, on March 21, 2003, Judge Bryant's longest-running case came to an end: oversight of the DC Jail. This arose from two class action lawsuits over the horrendous conditions men endured at the jail: *Campbell v. McGruder*, filed in 1971 on behalf of pretrial detainees, and *Inmates of DC Jail v. Jackson*, filed in 1974 on behalf of men convicted of crimes. At the time the jail housed men convicted of both misdemeanors and felonies. The DC Jail, built in the 1870s and later expanded, was located at Nineteenth Street and Independence Avenue, SE.

Judge Bryant, who remembered that in the late 1940s and early 1950s, "you could damn near eat off of the floor in the jail," ruled that the conditions violated the Eighth Amendment's prohibition against cruel and unusual punishment.

On November 5, 1975, in *Campbell*, the judge ordered inspections for—and prompt remedy of—violations of building codes, plumbing codes, fire codes, housing regulations, health regulations, and food regulations. At a time when inmates were responsible for laundering their underwear—and two cellblocks lacked hot water—the judge ordered the jail to supply inmates with clean clothing (including underwear), towels, and bed linen once a week at minimum. Also, inmates had to be granted at least one hour of recreation out in the fresh air every day.

Astonishingly, the DC Jail had no clear classification system establishing which inmates required maximum security and which did not. As a result, wrote the judge, "many unsentenced inmates who do not require maximum security are housed in the maximum security areas of the Jail under the most stringent living conditions." He mandated the creation of "a classification system which will make it possible to determine a) which inmates of plaintiff class require maximum security confinement; and b) which members of class can enjoy contact visits without jeopardizing the security of the facility." In contact visits, inmates are allowed some physical contact with visitors instead of only being able to see them through glass and speak to them by phone.

Judge Bryant's order also called for humane treatment of inmates suffering from mental illness. Psychiatrists were to examine inmates showing signs of disorders within twenty-four hours. A person found to be mentally ill was to be sent to a hospital with a psychiatric facility within forty-eight hours. Moreover, while that inmate was still in the jail, there was to be no use of restraints without a doctor's approval and then only for up to twenty-four hours without a doctor's reauthorization. (When the judge issued the order, one mentally ill prisoner had recently been shackled to a bed for *two weeks*.) The judge also prohibited the use of unpadded leg irons and handcuffs.

In an earlier order (March), Judge Bryant ordered an end to the overcrowding in the jail. Its capacity was a little over 600 but it had 950 inmates, with many pretrial detainees—inmates not yet convicted of any crime and who were in jail only because they could not make bail—double-celled: two men in a forty-eight-square-foot cell intended for one. Addressing the overcrowding required the jail to transfer scores of inmates to other facilities, mostly to the Lorton complex in Virginia.

"These conditions simply are not to be tolerated in a civilized society, much less in our national capital," he thundered in his May 24, 1976, memorandum and order in *Inmates v. Jackson*. "These are conditions which turn men into animals, conditions which degrade and dehumanize. In some senses the punishment they inflict is more painful and enduring than the stocks or the rack, long since discarded as barbaric or primitive. Imprisonment in conditions such as these absolutely guarantees that the inmates will never be able to return to civilized society, will never feel any stake in playing by its rules."

In this stunning cri de coeur, the judge declared that "where a man may be stuffed into a tiny cell with another, surrounded by the nocturnal moans or screams of mentally disturbed but untreated fellow inmates, plagued by rats and roaches, sweltering by summer and shivering by winter"—all this and more "can only have one message for him: society does not acknowledge your existence as a fellow human being." He ordered the correction of all remaining violations and many of the same things he ordered in *Campbell*.

A new DC Jail had opened in March in the 1900 block of D Street, SE, but because of overcrowding the old jail remained up and running for a time. Judge Bryant continued to issue rulings addressing the conditions of the jails.

Before he ruled on *Campbell* and *Inmates*, the judge had heard from some inmates about how degraded they felt. Back on the evening of October 11, 1972, he was about to head home when he was called to slip back into his black robe for an emergency hearing.

Around 1 a.m. that morning about fifty inmates had seized control of the DC Jail's cellblock 1, taking hostages: eleven guards and Corrections Director Kenneth Hardy. The inmates demanded to see New York congresswoman and presidential candidate Shirley Chisholm, who became a key negotiator. The inmates started out demanding their freedom. In the end they agreed to release the hostages if some of them were heard by a federal judge and if none were punished.[27]

The six men representing the inmates were bused to the courthouse and appeared in Courtroom 16 around 6:30 p.m. According to the *Evening Star*, each man "was permitted to talk as long as he wished."

Robert N. Jones told Judge Bryant, "I feel I'm being treated like an animal and I don't belong there."

Alvin McCoy, sentenced by Bryant to five-to-fifteen on a manslaughter conviction about two years earlier, expressed the same thing: "They don't think we're people . . . like we lost all our sense of being a human being." Like several other men, McCoy spoke up for the sixteen- and seventeen-year-olds lumped in with adult inmates. "You take a 16-year-old kid and stick him in there with someone who's been in Leavenworth, or Atlanta for 30 or 40 years . . . and it ruins the kid," he said, suggesting that these teens were inevitably sexually preyed upon.

As Judge Bryant heard the inmates out, he stressed that individual grievances could "only be brought effectively before the court, and properly before the court, by a lawyer."

"I wrote you three or four letters," said McCoy. "I never received a reply. What can I do? You say come properly. I tried."

Judge Bryant promised McCoy that he would have an opportunity to speak with a lawyer that evening. And by the time the hearing ended around midnight, he had issued an order for lawyers with the Public Defender Service to inspect the jail within two days, for the cellblock 1 inmates to be interviewed by lawyers before midnight, and for the immediate segregation of sixteen- and seventeen-year-olds from adult inmates.

During the tenures of the District's first Black mayors—Walter Washington, Marion Barry, Sharon Pratt Kelly, and Anthony A. Williams—Judge Bryant issued order after order for the DC Jail to do *right* by its inmates. The District repeatedly missed the mark.

---

27. Shirley Chisholm, the first Black woman elected to Congress, had been involved in negotiations in the wake of an uprising at the Queens House of Detention in 1970 and once again called for prison reform after the uprising at Attica in 1971.

Overcrowding was a constant problem. In the summer of 1985, the judge gave DC officials responsible for the jail forty days, then ninety days to reduce its population from roughly 2,600 to a little under 1,700, sending the city in a scramble to transfer inmates to halfway houses, Lorton, and federal prisons in Virginia and other states. He issued this order on the heels of an unannounced visit during which he observed "massive overcrowding" and its deleterious effects. The "pressures have intensified, the opportunities for respite and relief have diminished, and the expected tensions and problems of incarceration have been exacerbated. The safety valves are now sealed shut." What he saw literally made him sick!

Hundreds of inmates sleeping in jerry-rigged cells in aisles of the jail.

Filthy showers and toilets.

Mattresses "fouled with urine, fecal material, food and vomit."

All this and more had contributed to a sharp rise in violence. Judge Bryant declared that the failure to "alleviate the overcrowding and the resultant inability to protect prisoners from violence inflicted unnecessary and wanton pain" on inmates, violating their rights.

This was not his first visit to the jail—and with no fear for his safety. William B. Schultz, who accompanied the judge on a surprise visit when he clerked for him, recalled that there was no jeering or any other kind of ugliness from inmates, a number of whom the judge had sentenced. "They were quiet and respectful," said Schultz.

In July 1995, Judge Bryant put the jail's medical and mental health services in receivership. A court-appointed special officer had reported a "long-standing pattern of grossly deficient care." That special officer's medical expert had found that the "quality of medical services is deplorable, the physical condition of the medical areas are horrible, and the infirmary is a disgrace." The mental health expert had found "the mental health care that is provided is frequently substandard and at times dangerous and negligent."

It was when Judge Bryant took control of the jail's medical and mental health services that he famously declared that he had been listening to city officials' promises since "the Big Dipper was a thimble."

The *Washington Post* reported that Judge Bryant's "action came as public outrage has intensified over the death of Richard C. Johnson, 39, an AIDS-stricken inmate who was tied to a wheelchair with a urine-soaked sheet."

The judge's action also came at a time when the District was going through a tough time. The crime rate, largely fueled by the crack epidemic of the 1980s and early 1990s—that led to the city being dubbed the "murder capital"—was declining but there was an abundance of other problems. Unlike other cities, DC had not recovered from the recession of the early 1990s. Ongoing federal job cuts caused tens of thousands of businesses and residents to leave the city. Moreover, many agencies did not have their houses in order. As the *Post* reported, Judge Bryant was "the third judge to take over a significant part of city government." In August 1994, a DC Superior Court judge had taken control of the Department of Public and Assisted Housing. In May 1995, Judge Hogan had seized control of the child welfare system. Added to that, DC was, said the *Post*, "under dozens of court orders, covering such areas as human services, juvenile detention and most facilities at the Lorton Correctional Complex."

Judge Bryant told the *Post* that he certainly did not relish the situation. "I have some concern about the fact that the city is virtually operating [with] receivers. . . . That is an awful reputation for the capital of the nation to have, and I don't like to contribute to it. . . . But I just can't sit idly by and see this nose-thumbing."

The *Post* reported that City Administrator Michael C. Rogers "called the judge's action unfortunate. He said he believes that Bryant did not adequately consider the effect of the District's financial crisis on its ability to keep its promises. If city officials had a receiver's blank check, 'we could all be superstars,' Rogers said." In early 1995 former civil rights activist Mayor Marion Barry had announced that DC faced a budget shortfall of roughly $722 million. Having served as mayor for three consecutive terms (1979–1991), Barry had made one of the most unlikely political comebacks in the 1994 election, four years after he was caught on videotape smoking crack cocaine in a hotel with a woman not his wife. (Convicted of misdemeanor cocaine possession he was fined $5,000 and sentenced to six months in prison.)

Control of the DC Jail's medical and mental health services ended in 2000. Those services received national accreditation in 2003 when Judge Bryant terminated *Campbell* and *Inmates*, thus ending more than thirty years of court oversight of the DC Jail. Mayor Anthony A. Williams declared, "Ending one of the longest-running court interventions in the city's history is truly a big win for the Department of Corrections, the Office of the Corporation Counsel, and the people of the District of Columbia." A Department of Corrections press release stated that "a number of significant improvements, initiated as a part of a six-year, $30 million capital improvement plan, were major contributing factors to finally ending court intervention in the daily operations of the facility."

Many people may have thought that Judge Bryant would opt to retire now that the DC Jail case was over. But, no. In 2004, he maintained a heavy docket of trials.

It was also in 2004 that, unbeknownst to Judge Bryant, Judge Hogan paid a visit to DC congresswoman Eleanor Holmes Norton with a very special request.

Chapter 19

A GOOD FIGHT

Back in 2002 the groundbreaking was held for the annex to the E. Barrett Prettyman US Courthouse. Judge Hogan believed with every fiber of his being that there was no better name to grace the annex than that of the trailblazing William B. Bryant. His colleagues on the District Court wholeheartedly agreed. Thus, Judge Hogan's visit to Eleanor Holmes Norton.

Like Judge Bryant, Norton had devoted her life to the doing of justice. As a young woman, she was a member of SNCC who lent her brains and bravery to the 1964 Black voter registration drive in Mississippi, Freedom Summer. She went on to become the first woman to head New York City's Human Rights Commission and in 1977 the first woman to chair the Equal Employment Opportunity Commission, appointed by President Jimmy Carter.

Norton, elected to Congress in 1990, was more than willing—and eager—to introduce a bill to name the annex after Judge Bryant. He had long been a hero, an inspiration to this DC native and Dunbar graduate. She had studied *Mallory v. United States* while earning her LLB from Yale in the early 1960s.

"I came home one year from law school and phoned [him]," she recalled, "and asked if I could come and meet with him. I told him how much I admired his work in the law, and I said I wanted to work for him." Bryant "wouldn't hear of it." Instead, he "encouraged me to reach much higher and to reach for a whole lot more money." In his recollection of their meeting, Judge Bryant called Norton "one of the brightest persons" he had ever met. Had the firm not been "long on reputation" but short on money, he would have hired her on the spot.

"I know Judge Bryant personally," said Congresswoman Norton when she introduced HR 4294 on May 5, 2004. "I know his reputation in this city and on the law. I know that the request to name the annex for Judge Bryant reflects deep respect for his unusually distinguished life at the bar." The bill passed in the House on July 21 by, which time Patrick Leahy of Vermont had sponsored it in the Senate, where it met with opposition. Republican James Inhofe of Oklahoma, chair of the Senate Environment and Public Works Committee, was against the naming because the judge was still serving on the bench.

In the meantime Judge Bryant kept on living, kept on going with his life in the law, moving about the courthouse on his "horse" and needing the strong arm of a clerk to take his seat on the bench. He was flattered by the campaign to name the annex after him but expressed his usual modesty in an interview with the *Washington Post*. "There are so many people who were really giants. I stand on their shoulders," he said in a piece that appeared on September 16, 2004, two days before his ninety-third birthday, under the headline "A Lifetime of Faith in the Law."

In March 2005 Congresswoman Norton and Senator Leahy reintroduced the naming bill with this change: the annex would not bear Judge Bryant's name until after he retired. But there was another problem: the Senate Environment and Public Works Committee had a rule against naming a building after a living person. On October 27, 2005, Senator John W. Warner, the once-young law clerk captivated by AUSA Bill Bryant's mastery of the law and his skill at trial, came to the rescue. He fought to make Judge Bryant an exception to that rule based on precedent. Warner reminded fellow senators, "Prior to the current Chairman of the Committee, the rule was waived in certain instances and I certainly feel that the case of Judge Bryant warrants such discretion." By then the naming bill was attached to another bill Warner cosponsored: naming a federal building in Detroit after civil rights icon Rosa Parks who died on October 24.

That bill cleared Congress on November 2, 2005. President George W. Bush signed it into law on November 11.

Late Sunday, November 13, or early the next morning, after nearly sixty years of a life in the law, forty of them as a federal judge, the Honorable William Benson Bryant, age ninety-four, passed away. He was found in his den seated in his favorite easy chair. The TV was on.

When Congresswoman Norton learned of the news, she issued a press release, stating, in part "In Judge Bryant's closed, segregated Washington, a Black lawyer could not achieve what he did by the protests we are used to today. He was left on his own with only his excellent, disciplined mind, his understanding of the meaning of justice, his determination to succeed and his zeal for public service. In this city, where the federal District Court on which Judge Bryant served wields disproportionate power, residents were the direct beneficiaries of his service. The nation and the law itself, however, are equally in his debt as the William B. Bryant Annex will now attest."

A grieving Judge Hogan told the *Washington Post* that Judge Bryant was "the soul of the court."

Penny, Chip, Beatrice, and Diane Steed made the funeral arrangements with DC's venerable McGuire's Funeral Home, a Black-owned mortuary that opened in 1912, the same year that an eleven-month-old boy born in Wetumpka, Alabama, was brought to the nation's capital. In lieu of flowers, people were invited to make donations to Howard University School of Law.

Vernon Jordan, Julian R. Dugas, and Howard's president, H. Patrick Swygert, coordinated the service and repast at Howard Law's Dunbarton Chapel, where Ella Marie Edwards, the wife of Judge Bryant's cousin Dr. John W. Edwards Jr., sang "Ave Maria" and all the other hymns during the two-hour service held on Friday, November 18, 2005.

Penny, Chip, Lauren, and Vaughn, seated in a front-row pew, did their best to bear up, at times holding back tears, at times letting them flow, as they listened to those hymns and to speakers extolling the man they so cherished and adored.

The speakers included Judge Henry F. Greene, a member of the DC Superior Court, who clerked for Judge Bryant 1966–1968. Judge Greene spoke on behalf of other former law clerks, recalling what a joy it was to work for the judge, recounting some of his "old folks" sayings, remembering how they all learned so much from him. "Bill Schultz recalled how all of us seldom spent much time in chambers because Judge Bryant wanted us to learn in the courtroom. And learn we did, never failing to be awestruck by how the Judge routinely summed up legal issues succinctly with uncommon insight and eloquence. And whatever we learned right about what to do in a courtroom invariably was the result of the Judge explaining to us in chambers, after court, how we had just seen it done wrong."

Judge Greene paid tribute to Judge Bryant's trademark humility. "Bob Watkins recalls that because the Judge never lost the common touch, he was loved by those who knew him well, and liked by everyone else—in part, Bob observed, 'because he was serious about serious things, but never about himself.'"

"He was a special person, an unparalleled character," declared Judge Hogan. "Judge Leonard Hand wrote of the great Judge Cardozo words that fit Judge Bryant: 'that he was wise because his spirit was uncontaminated, because he knew no violence, or hatred or envy, or jealousy, or ill will.' That was our judge. Indeed, the harshest I ever heard him critique a person was his statement about a famous lawyer and judge—that 'humility and compassion never came closer than 1,000 feet of this man.'"

After alluding to the fact that Judge Bryant came up during the days of segregation and intense discrimination, Judge Hogan reflected, "Perhaps the most remarkable feature of his remarkable life was his indomitable spirit. Judge Bryant did not regard life as a passive activity but, rather, seized life, enjoying each moment, turning challenges into opportunities and conquering difficulties." In closing, Judge Hogan offered a slight variation on something he said right after Judge Bryant passed. "He was the soul of our Court and we shall miss him so." As he uttered those words, Judge Hogan's voice was "growing thin," said the *Washington Post*.

Vernon Jordan delivered the main eulogy. He did so, reported the *Post*, "from a podium overlooking Bryant's simple cherry wood coffin and hundreds of judges, lawyers and former law clerks," in a service that was "as understated and dignified as the judge himself."

Six-foot-four, seventy-year-old Vernon Jordan, steeped in the oratorical traditions of the Black church and possessed of a booming baritone voice, began with this: "To measure the life, work, accomplishments and meaning of Judge William B. Bryant is as if one would take a thimble and try to empty an ocean." He continued: "It would be as if one sought to measure the expanse of the heavens with the span of the human hand. Something vast and noble has passed from among us. It is like a mighty oak has fallen, leaving an empty and gaping and glaring space against the sky where he stood."

Jordan proclaimed that his friendship with Judge Bryant was "one of the great privileges and pleasures of" his life. He was an eternally grateful beneficiary of Judge Bryant's "advice, counsel, wisdom, wit and experience. Like so many here I was the mentee, the clerk, the intern, the student, the younger Howard Law graduate who drank from his full fountain."

Jordan reminded the gathering that Judge Bryant was the consummate family man. "While the Judge loved the law and the courts, his first love was his family." The judge's face "always lit up" whenever he was asked about Penny, Chip, Beatrice, Vaughn, Lauren, or Kaniya, Vaughn's three-year-old daughter, a constant source of delight during the judge's final years.

Jordan recounted the rather tough time he had persuading his friend to let him host a dinner celebrating his ninetieth birthday. "After much deliberation he said OK on one condition—no women. I asked why. He said because Astaire cannot be there."

Vernon Jordan had visited Judge Bryant's chambers two weeks before the funeral. "And toward the end of our visit, I inquired about his health. He told me about the aneurysm and that the doctors said there was nothing that could be done." Judge Bryant looked his friend straight in the eyes and said, "Vernon, I feel the mist of the River Jordan. . . . I'm ready to cross over." Drawing on the apostle Paul's words in 2 Timothy 4:7, Judge Bryant, whom Jordan aptly described as a man with a "great but quiet faith," added: "I've fought a good fight. I have finished my course. I have kept the faith. I'm ready."

After the great Frederick Douglass died in his Washington, DC, home in the winter of 1895, the Providence, Rhode Island, *Sun* declared, "We do not expect to see another Douglass, but the lesson of his life is to us a legacy worth preserving."

In June 2006, during the District of Columbia Circuit Judicial Conference in Pennsylvania that included a tribute to Judge Bryant, Judge Louis F. Oberdorfer expressed the same sentiment about someone he had known for nearly thirty years, someone he regarded as a mentor, as a friend: "It is unlikely that there will ever be the likes of William B. Bryant again."

Although he did not say it, Judge Oberdorfer undoubtedly believed—along with hundreds of others who were blessed to know Judge Bryant—that the lesson of his life is a legacy most worthy of preserving. It is an exemplar of obedience to a commandment in the Old Testament book of Zechariah, chapter 7, verse 9: "Administer true justice; show mercy and compassion to one another."

EPILOGUE

"The architect Michael Graves has brought a sense of whimsy to the least whimsical of places: a federal courthouse," wrote *Washington Post* staff writer Eric M. Weiss. His article appeared in early August 2006, under the headline "A Courthouse Sprouts Curves and Color."

The $104 million, seven-story, 351,000-gross-square-foot William B. Bryant United States Courthouse Annex was nearly completed. "The most striking part of the building," said Weiss, "is the rounded, rotunda-capped portion on Constitution Avenue." He also highlighted the building's "playful roof of bow arches that resemble a series of Quonset huts," its flashes of slate blue and Cherokee red, and its large windows, which, as chief architect Thomas P. Rowe told Weiss, "represent openness, clarity and justice." Another standout was the ground-floor "sun-drenched" cafeteria "with panoramic views of the Capitol."

The annex was dedicated a few months later, on Monday, October 30, 2006. The ceremony was held in the Annex Rotunda with Douglas H. Ginsburg, chief judge of the US Court of Appeals for the DC Circuit, officiating.

Judge Bryant's friend Deputy US Marshal Kirk Bowden issued the "All rise" for Judge Ginsburg, the guest speakers, which included US Supreme Court Chief Justice John G. Roberts Jr. and Chip, along with other distinguished guests. They included Penny, Lauren, Vaughn, Beatrice, Ed, and their family, along with Fredericka Gonzalez, the daughter of Astaire's deceased brother, Dr. John W. Edwards Jr., and Diane Steed. Several members of the DePriest Fifteen were in the audience as were a host of Judge Bryant's former law clerks and a number of DC judges.

Following the presentation of the colors by the Joint Armed Forces Color Guard, the singing of the national anthem, and the retiring of the colors, the assembled resumed their seats, and Judge Ginsburg welcomed the crowd. He stated that he was "honored to be a part of this naming ceremony as it commemorates the life and work of a truly great man and judge."

Justice Roberts was the first guest speaker. "The William B. Bryant Annex will enlarge not only the space of the Prettyman Courthouse, but also the spirit of those who work within its walls," said Roberts. He had gotten to know Judge Bryant when he served on the US Court of Appeals for the DC Circuit from mid-2003 until shortly before Judge Bryant passed. Roberts told the crowd, "If you view this annex as an extension and a symbol of the growth of justice from the time the original DC courthouse building opened in 1952, then Bill Bryant stamped his name on its walls long before the government chose to do so."

Judge Hogan extolled Judge Bryant as "a true inspiration. His endowed spirit, his keen intellect, his warm personality and his legendary humility were all characteristics that defined him as a man and as a judge. I can remember his wisdom and his commitment to justice and his dignity he tried to show to everyone who appeared before him. It certainly made him our most respected judge and I think one of the most respected judges in the country."

Senator Warner recalled getting to know AUSA Bill Bryant in the early 1950s and how much he learned from him, declaring him "a professor of what I call the practical law." He recalled watching Bryant try cases. "It was a thrill." Warner went on to work for a prominent DC law firm on Fifteenth Street, NW, then became an AUSA himself, joining Bryant in the Municipal Court on Fifth Street. Warner hadn't been in his office very long when, he said, "I went out and found Bill Bryant."

"I said, hey, Bill, I know about Fifteenth Street law; I don't know about Fifth Street law. He said, 'I'll teach you.' And that he did."

When she addressed the crowd, Congresswoman Norton proclaimed that "it speaks volumes to the contributions of Judge William B. Bryant that the idea for the naming of this annex came from his own colleagues, those who knew his work best, who knew his temperament best. It speaks volumes about his contributions to the legal profession, to the bar, and to the Court on which he served."

William Benson Bryant Jr. was the final speaker.

"This great honor that you bestow upon my father today, that part of this federal courthouse here in our nation's capital will forever bear his name is such a fitting tribute to a man whose life-long career was devoted to making the principle of equal justice under the law a reality for as many people as he possibly could."

Chip spoke of his father's abiding passion for his work. "Although he was hardworking and always dedicated to doing the best job he could, he often commented that he never found his work to be difficult or tedious because he enjoyed the challenges that legal issues presented, and he loved being immersed in the law." Chip recalled being in his father's F Street office doing his homework—"and as he worked on one of his meticulously crafted legal briefs, he would pace the floor. He was a pacer. He'd start to think, he'd gather his thoughts, he'd articulate his thoughts, and that's the way some of his best legal opinions were written."

Chip spoke of how grounded his father was. "Again, although he worked very hard for all he accomplished and achieved, he always said that he felt so blessed. He took nothing in this life for granted. He was profoundly thankful for his successful career, his sharp mind and his good health. But his most cherished blessing was his relationship with my mother, Astaire. Many times he described his life with her like being on an airplane as it rolled down the runway, lifting off with a steady climb into heaven."

In sharing precious memories, Chip mentioned as well that his father was "frugal, stubbornly unpretentious, and totally down to earth. When I was a teenager, I loved cars, but my daddy drove an old 1953 Oldsmobile Super '88 which he thought was just fine." Chip begged his father to retire the Olds (turquoise on the bottom, white on top) and buy a new car, "but he said the only purpose of an automobile was to get you from point A to point B, and besides, he had other financial priorities and could not afford a new car and that I should learn that having the courage to live within one's means was respectable."

Chip added that, not long after he pleaded for a new family car, one of his dad's friends "told him that he was neither rich enough nor old enough to be so eccentric and drive that old car downtown and park it in the courthouse garage." In response, Bill took his Olds to an Earl Scheib's auto body shop for a paint job. Even after he became a judge, "he continued to drive it downtown and park it in his designated spot for several years to come. And as they say down south, 'he didn't bit mo' care.'"

On a more serious note, Chip remembered his dad as "open-minded and young at heart." He proclaimed him the "best father you could hope for."

Chip closed so beautifully with this: "I firmly believe my father is here today with us in spirit, and my family and I hope that he will remain here in your hearts and be remembered for years to come, as Judge Hogan said, the soul of this court. Thank you very much."

Following the ribbon-cutting, people headed to that sun-drenched cafeteria with its panoramic views of the Capitol for a reception and to continue their celebration of an extraordinary husband, father, grandfather, and great-grandfather, an extraordinary prosecutor and criminal defense attorney, an extraordinary teacher, and an extraordinary judge—an extraordinary soul born in a place he called "just a wide spot in the road.

SOURCE NOTES

ABBREVIATIONS

CC: *Judge William B. Bryant Centennial Celebration* (DC: William B. Bryant American Inn of Court, 2011).

Dedication: *Dedication of the William B. Bryant Annex: Monday, October 30, 2006, Annex Rotunda, United States District Courthouse, Washington DC, Chief Judge Douglas H. Ginsburg, Officiating.*

***Mallory v. US* (Court of Appeals):** *Mallory v. United States*, 236 F.2d 701, 98 US App. DC 406 (DC Cir. 1956), Casetext.com, https://casetext.com/case/ mallory -v-united-states.

***Mallory v. US* (SCOTUS):** *Mallory v. United States*, 354 U. S. 449 (1957), Oyez. https://www.oyez.org/cases/1956/521.

***PoP*:** *Presentation of Portrait of The Honorable William B. Bryant* (Washington, DC: US District Court for the District of Columbia, April 18, 1980).

Senate Hearing: US Congress, Senate. Subcommittee of the Committee on the Judiciary, *Nomination of William Benson Bryant to Be a United States District Judge for the District of Columbia*, 89th Cong., 1st sess., July 23, 1965.

***TSOOC*:** Kristen Grim Hughes, ed., *The Soul of Our Court: Recollections and Reminiscences, A Tribute to the Honorable William Benson Bryant, September 18, 1911–November 13, 2005* (Washington, DC: William B. Bryant American Inn of Court, 2006).

***US v. Mallory*:** *United States of America v. Andrew R. Mallory*, Criminal No. 543–54. United States District Court for the District of Columbia.

WBB OH: The Honorable William B. Bryant, Oral History Interviews by William B. Schultz, Esq., March 18, 1994, May 6, 1994, May 19, 1994, June 2, 1994, June 29, 1994, October 13, 1994, October 20, 1994, November 17, 1994, January 24, 1995, May 4, 1995, Oral History Project, The Historical Society of the District of Columbia Circuit, https://dcchs.org/wp-content/uploads/2019/01/Bryant -Complete-Oral-History-compressed.pdf.

PROLOGUE

3 **sixty-eight-year-old:** According to the 1900 federal census, he was born inMay 1865. Ancestry.com, *1900 United States Federal Census* [database online], Lehi, UT, USA, Ancestry.com Operations, Inc., 2004.

3 **"You crazy?":** WBB OH, 51.

3 **Playing it safe:** Ancestry.com, *1930 United States Federal Census* [database online], Provo, UT, USA, Ancestry.com Operations, Inc., 2002.

3 **"I'm not going":** WBB OH, 50.

4 **"Negro lawyers don't":** WBB OH, 51.

4 **"Papa":** WBB OH, 4.

4 **"without unnecessary delay":** Rule 5(a), Federal Rules of Criminal Procedure, https://www.federalrulesofcriminalprocedure.org/title-ii/rule-5/.

4 **"*chosen*":** at 00:37:23, Part 1, *Mallory v. US* (SCOTUS).

5 **"You said that . . . That's right, Your Honor":** at 00:37:44, Part 1, *Mallory vs. US.*

5 **"No pictures":** Miriam Ottenberg, "Court Releases Man Doomed on Rape Charge," *Evening Star* (Washington, DC), June 26, 1957, A1. All subsequent references to the *Evening Star* are to this DC newspaper.

5 **"start a new life":** "High Court Again Blasted," *Greenville (SC) News*, June 28, 1957, 28.

5 **"give greater . . . exercise of power":** "Thurmond Raps Court Reversal in Rape Case," *News and Courier* (Charleston, SC), June 28, 1957, 11B.

5 **"hooligan decisions":** Lewis Fulton Jr., "High Court Ruling Frees Criminals," *Boston Daily Record*, September 10, 1957, 22.

5 **"You have the right":** MirandaWarning.org., http://www.mirandawarning.org/whatareyourmirandarights.html.

5 **"just a wide spot in the road":** WBB OH, 1.

CHAPTER 1. WIDE SPOT IN THE ROAD

6 **"rumbling waters":** David T. King Jr., "Wetumpka Impact Crater," *Encyclopedia of Alabama*, https://encyclopediaofalabama.org/article/wetumpka-crater/.

6 **Wetumpka was rocked:** Wetumpka experienced an earthquake in both 1886 and 1887. According to Sharon Kilpatrick, Curator II/Genealogist at the Elmore County Museum, the huge one was in 1886. Email to author, February 27, 2017.

6 **Decades earlier Wetumpka:** The great fires were in 1845 and 1852. "Interesting Facts about Wetumpka," https://wetumpkaal.gov/interesting-facts-about-wetumpka/.

6 **Too, the town's pride:** Wetumpka lost out to Montgomery in 1845. "Interesting Facts."

6 **"determined":** "The Terrible Fate of a Black Brute," *Age-Herald* (Birmingham, AL), October 3, 1900, 1. In this article Townsend's given name is "Wallace," and he's sixteen.

6 **"outrage":** "The Terrible Fate."

7 **"The stake . . . to ashes":** "Negro Burned at Stake in Alabama; Confessed Planning Many Crimes," *Augusta Chronicle*, October 3, 1900, 1. In this article Townsend's given name is "Winfield."

7 **Wetumpka's population:** "Historical Population of Wetumpka City for Period 1850–2014," http://population.us/al/wetumpka/.

7 **small, brown-skinned and with high cheekbones:** Astaire A. Bryant, author interview, June 29, 2017.

7 **Lizzie was:** Ancestry.com, *1910 United States Federal Census* [database online], Lehi, UT, USA, Ancestry.com Operations, Inc., 2006. Oddly, Charlie Wood is identified as a laborer in government service.

7 Papa **Charlie, a shoemaker:** Ancestry.com, *1900 United States Federal Census* [database online], Provo, UT, USA, Ancestry.com Operations, Inc, 2004; and WBB OH, 3, 9.

7 **The baby's father:** Alberta and Benson married on February 1, 1911. Ancestry.com, *Alabama, US, County Marriage Records, 1805–1967* [database online], Lehi, UT, USA, Ancestry.com Operations, Inc., 2016. The description of Benson is taken from his WWI draft registration card. Ancestry.com, *US, World War I Draft Registration Cards, 1917–1918* [database online], Provo, UT, USA, Ancestry.com Operations, Inc, 2005. Benson's occupation before he left Wetumpka is found in the 1910 federal census. Ancestry.com, *1910 United States Federal Census* [database online], Lehi, UT, USA, Ancestry.com Operations, Inc., 2006.

7 **One day a bunch:** WBB OH, 5.

7 **"a lot of temper":** WBB OH, 4.

7 **"fortified with whiskey":** WBB OH, 4.

7 **Cap Pennington:** WBB OH, 3, 4.

7 **Charlie, born in May 1865:** Ancestry.com, *1900 United States Federal Census* [database online], Provo, UT, USA, Ancestry.com Operations, Inc., 2004.

7 **"Cap's boy":** WBB OH, 3.

8 **Charlie was a child:** In WBB OH (p. 3) Judge Bryant said that it was his understanding that Charlie's mother was a Creek woman. In the 1910–1940 federal censuses, Charlie's color or race is "B" or "Neg." This suggests that he was not very light-skinned, which he probably would have been had he been the product of white man and a non-Black Creek woman. In that case, Charlie probably would have been identified on censuses as "M" for Mulatto. Ancestry.com, *1910 United States Federal Census* [database online], Lehi, UT, USA, Ancestry.com Operations Inc, 2006; *1920 United States Federal Census* [database online], Provo, UT, USA, Ancestry.com Operations, Inc., 2010; *1930 United States Federal Census* [database online], Provo, UT, USA, Ancestry.com Operations Inc, 2002; and *1940 United States Federal Census* [database online], Provo, UT, USA, Ancestry.com Operations, Inc., 2012.

8 **Cap Pennington's displays:** WBB OH, 3.

8 **"Charlie, come on":** WBB OH, 5.

8 **"All right, goddamn it":** WBB OH, 5.

8 **After he got himself settled:** In WBB OH (p. 4), Judge Bryant said that his grandparents had five daughters and three sons. According to the 1910 census, Lizzie and Charlie Wood had five daughters and four boys. Ancestry.com, *1910 United States Federal Census* [database online], Lehi, UT, USA, Ancestry.com Operations, Inc, 2006.

CHAPTER 2. FEEL YOURSELF GROW

9 **About 30 percent:** "D.C. History Timeline: 1900–1999," Georgetown University Library, https://guides.library.georgetown.edu/c.php?g=1096877&p=8002816#:~:text=1900.

9 **"That area out there":** WBB OH, 8.

9 **1507 B Street, NE:** WBB OH, 8.

9 **They lived among:** Ancestry.com, *1920 United States Federal Census* [database online], Provo, UT, USA, Ancestry.com Operations, Inc., 2010.

9 **"My stepfather . . . or hanged":** WBB OH, 29, 30.

10 **"Before the very gates . . . negro waiters":** "Washington Is Swept by Race Riots," *New York Tribune*, July 22, 1919, 4.

10 **This was not:** The family was still at 1507 B Street, NE. In WBB OH (p. 15), Judge Bryant said that his family moved to 1320 U Street, NW, between the time that he completed third grade at Lovejoy and started fourth grade at Garnet and that he completed third grade at age nine, in 1920.

11 **"Like men we'll":** Claude McKay, "If We Must Die," Poetry Foundation, https://www.poetryfoundation.org/poems-and-poets/poems/detail/44694.

11 **"not more grudging":** William C. Anderson, "The Politicization of Black Deaths on the Campaign Trail," Truthout.org., March 19, 2016, https://truthout.org/articles/the-politicization-of-black-deaths-on-the-campaign-trail/.

11 **"Sir, you have":** W. E. B. Du Bois, "Another Open Letter to Woodrow Wilson," *Crisis* 6, no. 5 (September 1913): 232–33, https://modjourn.org/issue/bdr517516/.

12 **Scores were fired:** "Woodrow Wilson: Federal Segregation," Smithsonian National Postal Museum, https://postalmuseum.si.edu/research-articles/the-history-and-experience-of-african-americans-in-america's-postal-service-3; "Segregation in the US Government," *The Rise and Fall of Jim Crow*, Thirteen.org, https://www.thirteen.org/wnet/jimcrow/stories_events_segregation.html; and Gordon J. Davis, "What Woodrow Wilson Cost My Grandfather," *New York Times*, November 24, 2015, https://www.nytimes.com/2015/11/24/opinion/what-woodrow-wilson-cost-my-grandfather.html?_r=0-.

12 **Garnet:** In WBB OH (p. 15), Judge Bryant said that he attended Garnet-Patterson. The two schools did not merge until 1929, by which time the judge was in college.

12 **"I would always . . . get her attention":** WBB OH, 16.

12 **"I loved her":** "Hon. William B. Bryant," *New England Law Review* 27, no. 3 (Spring 1993): 677.

13 **"you could feel":** WBB OH, 15.

13 **"a little loitering":** WBB OH, 23.

13 **"out of resentment . . . own man":** Astaire A. Bryant, email to author, February 1, 2017.

13 **Dunbar High was . . . "Greatest Negro High School in the World":** JC Wright, "The New Dunbar High School, Washington, DC," *Crisis* 13, no. 5 (March 1917): 220–222.

14 **"If a Black doctor":** WBB OH, 14.

14 **"who I think would":** WBB OH, 16.

15 **"skills that were":** Edward W. Brooke, *Bridging the Divide: My Life* (New Brunswick, NJ: Rutgers University Press, 2006), 9.

15 **"Cat Thomas":** WBB OH, 42. In the oral history, Thomas was mistakenly identified as a math teacher, and his first name transcribed as "Norville."

15 **"incessantly about the evils":** WBB OH, 42.

15 **"deep hatred":** WBB OH, 23.

15 **"from the day":** WBB OH, 40.

15 **"to rub elbows":** WBB OH, 43.

15 **The inaugural celebration:** "Plan History Week," *Evening Star*, February 4, 1926, 25.

15 **"a bit irreverent . . . loved Dunbar!":** William B. Bryant Jr., email to author, April 16, 2022.

16 **"More than . . . to remember":** Alison Stewart, *First Class: The Legacy of Dunbar, America's First Black Public High School* (Chicago: Lawrence Hill Books, 2013), 149.

16 **"I tried to . . . laughed out loud":** Joseph McLaren, ed. *The Collected Works of Langston Hughes, volume 13, Autobiography: The Big Sea* (Columbia: University of Missouri, 2002), 167, 166.

17 **"the highspot . . . all over town":** Duke Ellington, *Music Is My Mistress* (New York: Da Capo Press, 1976), 23.

17 **playing one-handed:** William B. Bryant Jr., email to author, January 13, 2022.

17 **Thanks to two fantastic teachers:** WBB OH, 46.

CHAPTER 3. SCHOOLBOY

18 **Determined to go:** WBB OH, 36.

18 **"Going South":** WBB OH, 36.

18 **With no interest in:** WBB OH, 35.

19 **Depending on the course:** *Howard University Bulletin: Annual Catalogue 1928–1929* 8, no. 5, 66.

19 **Bill was able:** WBB OH, 65. I am grateful to Dr. Michael R. Winston for informing me of the apartment building's original name. Comments to author, March 3, 2022.

19 **When Bill worked at:** WBB OH, 38, 37.

19 **"No. You didn't":** WBB OH, 37.

19 **Bill was posted:** WBB OH, 38.

19 **Bill worked:** WBB OH, 38, 36, 49.

19 **The pay was sweet:** WBB OH, 36; and United Food Stores ad, *Evening Star*, August 9, 1928, 13.

19 **"There was a lot":** WBB OH, 38.

19 **Studying on the job:** WBB OH, 38.

20 **There he earned:** WBB OH, 36.

20 **"Schoolboy":** Diane Steed, interview by author, Washington, DC, June 29, 2017.

20 **"a club . . . for self and others":** Howard University, *The Bison* (Washington, DC: 1932), 87. I am grateful to Dr. Michael R. Winston for informing me that ROTC was compulsory for freshmen and sophomore male students. Comments to author, March 3, 2022.

20 **"cosmopolitan place":** WBB OH, 40.

20 **"came from . . . all the islands":** WBB OH, 39.

20 **One international student:** WBB OH, 39.

20 **"There was a whole lot . . . resented it":** WBB OH, 40.

21 **"a mecca for top-flight":** WBB OH, 44.

22 **At Howard the courses Bunche:** *Howard University Bulletin: Annual Catalogue 1928–1929* 8, no. 5, 219–21.

22 **"a feeling of growth":** David Pike, "Everyone Likes Judge William Bryant," *Washington Star*, March 20, 1977, B3.

22 **"the greatest thing":** WBB OH, 46.

22 **They included "Preparation for Trial,":** "Darrow Will Lecture at Howard University," *Evening Star*, January 1, 1931, A4.

22 **"And in college . . . attractive subject":** WBB OH, 46.

22 **As it happened:** "Hoover Delivers Howard Commencement Address in Three Minutes," *Kansas City and Topeka Plaindealer*, June 17, 1932, 2.

23 **"He had nothing to say":** WBB OH, 48.

23 **"I had worked . . . under somebody's thumb":** WBB OH, 37.

23 **"prime fool":** WBB OH, 51.

23 **tuition was $135:** J. Clay Smith Jr., *Emancipation: The Making of the Black Lawyer, 1844–1944* (Philadelphia: University of Pennsylvania Press, 1993), 35.

23 **Fairmont Street:** Ancestry.com, *US, City Directories, 1822–1995* [database online], Lehi, UT, USA, Ancestry.com Operations, Inc., 2011.

23 **"nomadic":** WBB OH, 15.

24 **In 1928 Johnson:** I am grateful to Dr. Michael R. Winston for clarifying several points in comments to author, March 3, 2022.

24–25 **"I am planning . . . current semester:** "Separate Is Not Equal: *Brown v. Board of Education*, Smithsonian National Museum of American History, http://americanhistory.si.edu/brown/history/3-organized/detail/course-syllabus.html.

25 **"The hate and scorn":** "Charles Hamilton Houston," NAACP, https://naacp.org/find-resources/history-explained/civil-rights-leaders/charles-hamilton-houston.

25 **"weren't so outraged . . . a shock to him."** WBB OH, 58.

25–26 **"no entree . . . out of the box with me":** WBB OH, 57–58.

26 **"engineer of it all":** Genna Rae McNeil, "Charles Hamilton Houston: Social Engineer for Civil Rights," in John Hope Franklin and August Meier, eds. *Black Leaders of the Twentieth Century* (Urbana: University of Illinois Press, 1982), 221.

26 **"Iron Shoes" and "Cement Pants":** Michael Kohler, "Charles Hamilton Houston and His Civil Rights Brain Trust," Boundary Stones, March 24, 2021, https://boundarystones.weta.org/2021/03/24/charles-hamilton-houston-and-his-civil-rights-brain-trust#footnote-6.

26 **"sweet man":** Juan Williams, *Eyes on the Prize: America's Civil Rights Years, 1954–1965*, 25th anniversary ed. (New York: Penguin, 1990), 7–8.

26 **"The law is a jealous mistress":** WBB OH, 49.

26 **"manna from heaven. No phone or anything":** WBB OH, 49.

26 **"You can't do this and get the law . . . from him or the school":** Joseph D. Whitaker, "Judge Bryant Struggled to Reach His High Post," *Washington Post*, April 15, 1976, A14.

27 **"so cocky":** John Spiegel, "Some Memories of Judge Bryant," *TSOOC*, 51. This and all other quotations from this article are reprinted with the permission of Judith Glasser, personal representative for John Spiegel.

27 **"had no hesitancy to fail":** WBB OH, 53.

27 **"hell of a lawyer":** WBB OH, 54.

27 **The courses Charlie Houston taught:** Genna Rae McNeil, *Groundwork: Charles Hamilton Houston and the Struggle for Civil Rights* (Philadelphia: University of Pennsylvania Press, 1984), 82.

27 **"wasn't a magical teacher":** "Hon. William B. Bryant," *New England Law Review* 27, no. 3 (Spring 1993): 679.

27 **"thoroughly prepared . . . of the pool":** WBB OH, 55.

27 **"seared your soul":** David Pike, "Everybody Likes Judge William Bryant," *Washington Star*, March 20, 1977, B3.

27 **"a lawyer's either":** Genna Rae McNeil, *Groundwork: Charles Hamilton Houston and the Struggle for Civil Rights* (Philadelphia: University of Pennsylvania Press, 1984), 84.

28 **"was obsessed with the concept . . . you failed":** WBB OH, 55.

28 **Some of the highest grades:** Joseph D. Whitaker, "Judge Bryant Struggled to Reach His High Post, *Washington Post*, April 15, 1976, A14.

28 **This petite, very pretty:** Astaire A. Bryant, author interview, June 7, 2017.

28 **"It was just like we [were]":** WBB OH, 66.

28 **The couple occasionally:** WBB OH, 66.

28 **Mostly, Bill and Astaire:** Hanging out at her house: WBB OH, 66. Frederico Sr.'s background: Astaire A. Bryant, author interview, June 7, 2017. His work at Department of the Interior: Ancestry.com, *1920 United States Federal Census* [database online], Provo, UT, USA, Ancestry.com Operations, Inc., 2010. Rebecca's race: Ancestry.com.

28 **After a two-year courtship:** WBB OH, 71, 49.

28 **Indeed, between 1929 and 1933:** "Great Depression Indicators," PBS, https://www.pbs.org/fmc/timeline/ddepression.htm.

28 **The couple:** Nickname: William B. Bryant Jr., *CC*, 57. 1034 Park Road, NW: WBB OH, 72. Judge Bryant never mentioned the name of Ed Simon's wife. The source for "Lucy" is the 1936 DC City Directory, which has the couple living at 1034 Park Road, NW, and identifies Ed as a mail carrier. Ancestry.com, *US, City Directories, 1822–1995* [database online], Lehi, UT, USA, Ancestry.com Operations, Inc., 2011. In WBB OH (p. 65), when speaking of his job at Bates Warren, Judge Bryant said that Ed "later worked at a job in the Post Office."

28–29 **He recalled:** WBB OH, 73.

29 **On Friday, June 5, 1936:** "Howard Degrees Given Graduates," *Evening Star*, June 6, 1936, A6.

29 **"I sat on":** WBB OH, 54.

CHAPTER 4. IF I CAN CUT THE MUSTARD

30 **Beatrice was the daughter:** Deborah Jones Taborn, response to author questionnaire, May 27, 2022.

30 **At the time Clauzelmin:** Her occupation: Ancestry.com, *District of Columbia, US, Select Deaths and Burials Index, 1769–1960* [database online], Lehi, UT, USA, Ancestry.com Operations, Inc., 2014. Her husband's occupation and the age of the children: Ancestry.com, *1930 United States Federal Census* [database online], Provo, UT, USA, Ancestry.com Operations, Inc., 2002.

30 **"My mother's father":** Deborah Jones Taborn, response to author questionnaire, May 27, 2022.

30 **Beatrice was ten:** Taborn, response.

30 **"My mother always":** Taborn, response.

30 **"I think my mother . . . 'inward'":** Taborn, email to author, October 5, 2022.

30–31 **Taborn reckoned:** Taborn, email.

31 **They included working:** Biography attached to Senate Hearing.

31 **According to one source:** Joseph D. Whitaker, "Judge Bryant Struggled to Reach His High Post," *Washington Post*, April 15, 1976, A14.

31 **Bryant's primary assignment:** WBB OH, 75.

31 **Bryant also sorted:** WBB OH, 75.

32 **"I told him":** WBB OH, 77.

32 **"seemed to rise":** WBB OH, 101.

32 **After Bill's job with Bunche:** Résumé attached to Senate Hearing.

32 **"It wasn't an FBI . . . what their plans were":** WBB OH, 81.

32 **"as a member of the armed":** WBB OH, 78.

33 **"got to be . . . dirty work":** WBB OH, 85.

33 **"huge . . . he was MacArthur":** WBB OH, 89.

33 **"a whole lot of respect":** WBB OH, 90.

33 **"ought to make things equal . . . the other guy has":** WBB OH, 90.

34 **"a blot on our Nation"** and **findings:** Murrey Marder, "DC Business Accused of Maintaining Negro Ghetto," *Washington Post*, December 11, 1948, 1, 8. I am grateful to Dr. Michael R. Winston for clarifying a few things about the report in comments to author, March 3, 2022.

34 **"Of course, they would":** WBB OH, 103.

34 **"When I went down . . . to do that":** WBB OH, 104.

35 **"that it wouldn't":** WBB OH, 104.

35 **Bryant shared his deep disappointment:** WBB OH, 105.

35 **Now that Astaire:** William B. Bryant Jr., email to author, September 28, 2021.

35 **It was held:** "Bar Exam Results Announced Today," *Evening Star*, August 17, 1948, A1.

35 **Bill was not present:** William B. Bryant Jr., email to author, January 13, 2022.

36 **She was named:** Astaire A. Bryant, author interview, date unknown.

36 **"I almost dropped":** WBB OH, 104.

36 **"In those days . . . represent these people":** WBB OH, 106.

36 **"Fifth Street Irregulars":** Jacob A. Stein, "Legal Spectator: Judge Bryant," *Washington Lawyer*, February 2006, reprinted in *TSOOC*, 6.

36 **"Get any cases?":** WBB OH, 106.

36 **"too shy . . . couldn't do that":** WBB OH, 106.

36–37 **"he was taking his time to . . . take your shot":** Astaire A. Bryant, email to author, January 18, 2022.

37 **"of declining . . . in their eyes":** "Chief Judge William Benson Bryant," *Howard Law Journal* 25, no. 1 (1982): 4.

37 **"The rest of the day . . . poolroom up the street":** Jacob A. Stein, "Legal Spectator: Judge Bryant," *Washington Lawyer*, February 2006, reprinted in *TSOOC*, 6.

37 **"catch-as-catch-can":** WBB OH, 144.

37 **"The pay was . . . cases to us":** Jacob A. Stein, "Legal Spectator: Judge Bryant," *Washington Lawyer*, February 2006, reprinted in *TSOOC*, 6.

37 **"sucked into . . . learned so much":** WBB OH, 116.

38 **"all of that kind of":** WBB OH, 210.

38 **"Bill quickly . . . made his point":** Jacob A. Stein, "Legal Spectator: Judge Bryant," *Washington Lawyer*, February 2006, reprinted in *TSOOC*, 6.

38 **in the case of Hilda Stroup's:** "Woman Identifies Coat Stolen Year Ago, but Fur Doesn't Fly," *Evening Star*, January 17, 1951, A15.

38 **Bryant simply used:** "Rarely Used Law Clears 2 in Traffic Death," *Evening Star*, October 27, 1950, B1.

38 **"You really ought . . . to have you":** Paul L. Friedman, *CC*, 32.

38 **"One man who":** Joseph D. Whitaker, "Judge Bryant Struggled to Reach His High Post," *Washington Post*, April 15, 1976, A14.

39 **"If I can cut":** WBB OH, 263.

39 **"Yeah, you can do it":** WBB OH, 263.

39 **"political clearance":** WBB OH, 108.

39 **On the appointed day:** In WBB OH (p. 110) Judge Bryant said only that he went to "that House Office Building." I am grateful to Office of Art and Archives, House of Representatives, for the June 10, 2022, email advising me that in the 1950s Dawson's office was in the Longworth House Office Building (vs. the Cannon House Building).

39 **"Congressman, Mr. Bryant . . . so okay":** WBB OH, 110.

39–40 **"How soon. Yesterday";** WBB OH, 111.

40 **"at least 11 local lawyers":** "William Bryant Appointed District Attorney's Aide," *Afro-American*, February 24, 1951, 6.

40 **"Mr. Bryant's appointment . . .":** "William B. Bryant Is Named Assistant U.S. Attorney," *Evening Star*, February 12, 1951, A-7. The *Star* said this occurred "today." The résumé attached to Senate hearing confirms this date.

CHAPTER 5. REPRESENTING THE GOVERNMENT, YOUR HONOR

41 **"A pathetic . . . human nature":** Joseph Paull, "Tempers Cool, Spats End at US Attorneys' 'Front Counter,'" *Washington Post*, December 27, 1951, B1.

41 **"It's all yours":** Joseph D. Whitaker, "Judge Bryant Struggled to Reach His High Post, *Washington Post*, April 15, 1976, A14.

41 **Wilson was taking:** "Warren Wilson Quits as Assistant to Fay; Takes Federal Post," *Evening Star*, October 19, 1951, A2.

41 **There were twelve AUSAs:** Joseph D. Whitaker, "Judge Bryant Struggled to Reach His High Post, *Washington Post*, April 15, 1976, A14.

42 **"I was scared":** Whitaker, "Judge Bryant."

42 **"flailing . . . otherwise sensible, congenial people . . . as big as Mr. Beck":** "Assault Case Dismissed against Former Detective," *Evening Star*, March 5, 1952, A16.

42 **In the spring of 1952:** "'Retired' Numbers Suspect Is Freed," *Evening Star*, April 17, 1952, B22.

42 **In September 1952:** "Bill Bryant Is Tough on Dope and Sex Offenders," *Afro-American*, January 9, 1954, 8.

42 **"felt that the legal profession":** C. Edward Nicholson, Esq., "Memorial—Irelan, Charles M.," Bar Association of Montgomery County, Maryland, https://www.barmont.org/page/318/Memorial-Irelan-Charles-M.htm.

43 **He was operating:** William B. Bryant Jr., email to author, July 19, 2022.

43 **"He wanted to . . . be in office":** WBB OH, 114.

43 **"little, short . . . hell of a lawyer.":** WBB OH, 118.

43 **"had not associated himself":** WBB OH, 118.

43 **"went around to a few":** WBB OH, 119.

43 **"straightforward, fair, and courageous":** WBB OH, 124.

44 **"Ready for . . . the defense":** WBB OH, 125.

44 **"What are you . . . Your Honor":** WBB OH, 125.

44 **"I guess . . . any better":** WBB OH, 125.

44 **"Tried like a seasoned":** WBB OH, 125.

44 **"The court appreciates . . .":** WBB OH, 120.

44 **"I didn't waste . . . witnesses would do it":** WBB OH, 120.

44 **"The government is satisfied":** WBB OH, 121.

44 **"trying to tell the price":** WBB OH, 191.

44 **"I think when you":** WBB OH, 190.

45 **"They have been around":** WBB OH, 190.

45 **"raised like chickens":** WBB OH, 191.

45 **"Body language . . . his voir dire":** Richard Kirkland Bowden, Oral History Interviews conducted by Joshua Klein, *Esquire*, November 28, 2007; July 30, 2008; March 6, July 2, 2009; January 19, May 6, 2010; and interview by Stephen J. Pollak, *Esquire* June 23, 2011, Oral History Project, The Historical Society of the District of Columbia Circuit, https://dcchs.org/sb_pdf/complete-oral-history-bowden/, 82.

45 **"in what he called":** Bowden, 82.

45 **"were anxious to learn . . . a magnet":** John W. Warner, *Dedication*, 13.

46 **"every day, every day, every day":** WBB OH, 136.

46 **He did not have:** Library holdings: Stephen J. Pollak, email to author, January 23, 2017.

46 **"provided white lawyers":** J. Clay Smith Jr., "Jurisprudence, Benefit, Enhancement and Protection: The Washington Bar Association Turns Seventy," May 6, 1995, unpaginated, Selected Speeches. Paper 164, Digital Howard, http://dh.howard.edu/jcs_speeches/164.

46 **annual fee of eight dollars . . . twelve dollars:** James H. Johnston, "Segregation in the Federal Courthouse in Washington DC, before and after *Brown v. Topeka Board*, *Howard Law Journal* 61, no. 1 (Fall 2017): 39.

46 **Bryant refused to pay a fee:** John McCaslin, "Inside the Beltway," *Washington Times*, December 8, 2005, reprinted in *TSOOC*, 10. In "Segregation in the Federal Courthouse," cited in the note above, James H. Johnston took issue with a 2005 W*ashington Post* article that stated that Bryant "was not allowed to use the DC Bar Association's law library. So he researched his cases with the help of a black court employee who opened the library to him after closing time." Johnston wrote: "These recollections are obviously in error. James Laughlin admitted in the brief and at oral argument in the Robinson case in 1952 that the library was integrated." This is true, but in order to use the library, Black attorneys had to pay an annual fee of eight dollars, as Johnston notes in this same article. It seems more than understandable that Bryant would refuse to pay a fee to use the library of an organization that refused Black people membership.

Johnston also wrote: "However, the suggestion that Bryant used the library "after closing time" is difficult to credit. The library was open seven nights a week until 10:30 p.m. although it closed to new users at 9:30 p.m. The night librarian in 1949, and probably later, was Charles Johnson."

Judge Bryant wasn't trying to use the library in 1949, but starting in 1952, the year Warren T. Juggins began work there. John McCaslin, cited at the top of this note, stated that he verified this story with Juggins. "He confided with me that attorney Bryant was not the only African-American lawyer he admitted to the library against the then-rules."

46 **In his quest:** Jacob A. Stein, "Legal Spectator: Judge Bryant," *Washington Lawyer*, February 2006, reprinted in *TSOOC*, 7.

47 **"The United States Attorney . . . strike foul ones":** Justice Sutherland, Opinion, *Berger v. United States*, 295 US 78 (1935), Justia, https://supreme.justia.com/cases/federal/us/295/78/case.html.

47 **Whether prosecuting a case:** "Jury to Study Civil Rights and Beating Charge," *Evening Star*, January 7, 1953, A21; "Ex-Federal Worker Tried as 'Influence Peddler,'" *Evening Star*, January 26, 1954, B1.

47 **At one point:** "Trial Halted for New Mental Examination of Arson Defendant," *Evening Star*, December 15, 1953, A3.

47 **Initially, Morey:** "Man Draws Five Years for Warehouse Fire, *Evening Star*, November 5, 1955, A3.

47 **"but what this guy . . . get rid of him":** WBB OH, 132.

47 **"feeling pretty good":** Carol Leonnig, "A Lifetime of Faith in the Law," *Washington Post*, September 15, 2004, https://www.washingtonpost.com/archive/local/2004/09/16/a-lifetime-of-faith-in-the-law/8d6a345d-84a7-440d-ad69-ad85a3654480/.

48 **"I broke out":** WBB OH, 132.

48 **"I just didn't":** WBB OH, 134.

48 **"I saw the jury come back":** WBB OH, 133.

48 **"I don't ever remember:** WBB OH, 133.

48 **"I don't like . . . to convict":** "Bill Bryant Is Tough on Dope and Sex Offenders," *Afro-American*, January 9, 1954, 8. This is the source of quotes by Bryant and by the *Afro* that follow.

48 **"Most drunkenness . . . offense":** "Bill Bryant."

48 **"as a highly competent . . . same feeling":** "Bill Bryant."

49 **"reading news magazines":** "Bill Bryant."

49 **That home was:** William B. Bryant Jr., email to author, January 13, 2022.

49 **Typically, he went home:** WBB OH, 117.

49 **On Sundays:** Astaire A. Bryant, response to author questionnaire, June 8, 2017.

49 **"instinctively":** WBB OH, 138.

49 **"the best legal mind":** WBB OH, 140.

49 **"judicious, sound . . . human touch":** Alan G. Kirk, Vice President and General Counsel, Potomac Electric Power Company in March 20, 1980, letter to Senator Thomas F. Eagleton, Chairman, Subcommittee of Governmental Efficiency and the District of Columbia, Hearing before the Committee on Governmental Affairs, United States Senate, Ninety-Sixth Congress, Second Session on Nomination of William C. Gardner to Be Associate Judge of the Superior Court of the District of Columbia, July 2, 1980 (Washington, DC: US Government Printing Office, 1980), 16.

50 **"Well, you haven those jobs":** WBB OH, 126.

50 **Still, Bryant could not resist:** WBB OH, 129.

50 **His last day:** Résumé attached to Senate Hearing.

CHAPTER 6. RAW JUSTICE

51 **"Today, education . . . unequal":** Justice Earl Warren, Opinion, *Brown v. Board of Education*, 347 U.S. 483 (1954) (USSC+), National Archives, https://www.archives.gov/milestone-documents/brown-v-board-of-education.

51 **"a lot of rejoicing":** WBB OH, 140.

51–52 **"We had the feeling":** WBB OH, 142.

52 **"Well, I can finally":** WBB OH, 142.

52 **"If segregation is unconstitutional":** Carol Anderson, *White Rage: The Unspoken Truth of Our Racial Divide* (New York: Bloomsbury 2016; reprint edition, 2017), 75.

52 **In 1948, when the Department:** Hparkins, "Executive Orders 9980 and 9981: Ending segregation in the Armed Forces and the Federal workforce," National Archives blog, May 19, 2014, https://prologue.blogs.archives.gov/2014/05/19/executive-orders-9980-and-9981-ending-segregation-in-the-armed-forces-and-the-federal-workforce/.

52 **"well-behaved":** John Kelly, "Remembering the 'Lost Laws' of Washington," *Washington Post*, February 11, 2018, https://www.washingtonpost.com/local/remembering-the-lost-laws-of-washington/2018/02/11/c0184c7c-0f33-11e8-9570-29c9830535e5_story.html#.

53 **"I propose to use":** "Annual Message to the Congress on the State of the Union, February 2nd, 1953," Eisenhower Library, https://www.eisenhowerlibrary.gov/sites/default/files/file/1953_state_of_the_union.pdf.

53 **"enlisted Hollywood moguls":** David A. Nichols, "'Unless We Progress, We Regress': How Eisenhower Broke Ground on Desegregation," Historynet.com, June 8, 2020, https://www.historynet.com/unless-we-progress-we-regress/.

52 **Pauli Murray discovered:** I am grateful to Dr. Michael R. Winston for this information in his comments to author, October 5, 2022.

53 **The firm did mostly probate:** WBB OH, 144.

53 **There were weeks**: WBB OH, 147.

53 **"We had some lean":** WBB OH, 210.

54 **Hickey Freeman:** William B. Bryant Jr., email to author, January 13, 2022.

54 **Astaire, a wizard:** Astaire A. Bryant, answers to author questionnaire, June 8, 2017, and author interview, June 7, 2017.

54 **Astaire was a bargain:** Astaire A. Bryant.

54 **As the family's money manager:** Astaire A. Bryant, answers to author questionnaire, June 8, 2017.

54 **Running her house:** Astaire A. Bryant.

54 **"convinced, early on . . . sparkle":** William C. Gardner, *PoP*, LXV.

54 **Every now and then:** WBB OH, 213.

54 **"They didn't . . . always exchanged":** Astaire A. Bryant, answers to author questionnaire, June 8, 2017.

54 **"Love many and . . . lender be":** Astaire A. Bryant, email to author, December 7, 2021.

54 **"Some folks grow up":** William B. Bryant Jr., email to author, January 13, 2022.

54 **"to deal with people":** William B. Bryant Jr., *Dedication*, 32.

55 **Penny recalled:** Astaire A. Bryant, email to author, December 7, 2021.

55 **"Damn . . . spitting mad":** Astaire A. Bryant, author interview, June 7, 2017.

55 **"Maryland Farmer . . . grown":** Astaire A. Bryant.

55 **Astaire and Bill never:** Astaire A. Bryant, author interview, June 29, 2017.

55 **"As a young boy . . . (live your life)":** William B. Bryant Jr., email to author, January 13, 2022.

55 **"she wanted . . . father's blessing":** Bryant Jr.

55 **"sitting-down day . . . Court of Appeals":** WBB OH, 141.

56 **By then his favorite:** Richard "Kirk" Bowden, *CC*, 43.

56 **"every Monday morning":** WBB OH, 144.

56 **"He didn't want . . . 'objection' all day long":** WBB OH, 198.

56 **"unless I had a record":** WBB OH. 198.

56 **"Your Honor, no questions":** Roger Adelman, *CC*, 21.

56 **"He had . . . right quick":** WBB OH, 177.

56–57 **"gifted advocate . . . doing of justice":** William C. Gardner, *PoP*, LXV.

57 **During trials:** WBB OH, 205.

57 **"I can't listen and write":** WBB OH, 205.

57 **"a poor man's stock market":** WBB OH, 147.

57 **Lefty Winston's codefendants:** WBB OH, 154; and "Defense Ready as US Rests in Bribe Trial," *Evening Star*, April 1, 1955, A21.

57 **"decided to make . . . the institution":** WBB OH, 157.

57 **"I'm levelin' . . . raw justice":** Jack Jonas "What the Bribery Jury Didn't Hear," *Evening Star*, April 10, 1955, A24.

58 **"My feet didn't":** WBB OH, 158.

58 **Whitetop Simkins had:** WBB OH, 158.

58 **In contrast, he charged:** WBB OH, 158.

58 **"It was a beautiful suit":** WBB OH, 180.

58 **"I'm in my office":** WBB OH, 159.

58–59 **"were anxious to have him":** WBB OH, 160.

59 **The oldest was:** "Policeman's Wife and Her Friend Slain," *Evening Star*, May 21, 1955, A1.

59 **"a little card-playing joint":** WBB OH, 162.

59 **Billy told Lenore:** WBB OH, 162.

59 **"with his head in her lap":** WBB OH, 162.

59 **One bullet penetrated:** "Double Slaying Laid to Park Policeman," *Washington Post*, May 22, 1955, A3; "Policeman's Wife and Her Friend Slain," *Evening Star*, May 21, 1955, A1.

59–60 **"And I knew . . . a fraud":** WBB OH, 160.

60 **"I will choose . . . a murder case":** WBB OH, 161.

60 **"good judge":** WBB OH, 124.

60 **"diminutive but fiery":** "Mental Unit Head Quits Post at 65," *Washington Post*, November 23, 1969, D10.

60 **"an ace prosecutor":** WBB OH, 163.

60 **"shot down in the street":** "Park Policeman Acquitted by Jury in Slaying of Wife and Boyfriend," *Washington Post*, October 22, 1955, 3.

60 **One of McLaughlin's witnesses:** "Park Policeman."

60 **Defense witness Dr. Amino Perretti:** "Psychiatrist Testifies on Harrison," *Evening Star*, October 21, 1955, 29.

60 **Another defense witness:** "Harrison Freed by Jury in Slaying of Wife, Friend," *Evening Star*, October, 22, 1955, A2.

60 **Defying conventional wisdom:** "Policeman Trial in 2 Slayings May End Today," *Evening Star*, October 21, 1955, A2.

61 **Bryant also put:** "Policeman Trial."

61 **"That's none of . . . that I am right":** WBB OH, 163.

61 **"Harrison sagged . . . verdict was announced":** "Park Policeman Acquitted by Jury in Slaying of Wife and Boyfriend," *Washington Post*, October 22, 1955, 3.

61 **"A couple of the [jurors]":** WBB OH, 164.

CHAPTER 7. NO COOPERATION

63 **Metzie (or Meltzie):** Ancestry.com, *1940 United States Federal Census* [database online], Provo, UT, USA, Ancestry.com Operations, Inc., 2012; and "Deaths," *Evening Star*, March 5, 1970, B7.

64 **"the demeanor of a happy leprechaun":** Ian Glass, "Order (and Speed) in the Court," *Miami News*, February 12, 1968, 3A.

64 **"notoriously one-sided":** WBB OH, 122.

64 **(Bryant also recalled):** WBB OH, 129.

64 **All we know about the jury:** *US v. Mallory*, vol. 1.1, 18.

64 **(The two alternate jurors were both men):** *US v. Mallory*, vol. 1.1, 18.

64 **She testified:** *US v. Mallory*, vol. 1.1, 45–60.

66 **He was not only brief:** *US v. Mallory*, vol. 1.1, 60–62.

66 **In redirect:** *US v. Mallory*, vol. 1.1, 62.

66 **In recross:** *US v. Mallory*, vol. 1.1, 62.

66 **The victim's husband:** *US v. Mallory*, vol. 1.1, 64–vol. 1.2, 65–75.

66 **The jury also heard:** *US v. Mallory*, vol. 1.2, 95–103.

66 **Detective Charles Mackie:** *US v. Mallory*, vol. 1.3, 125–44.

67 **"I didn't know":** *US v. Mallory*, vol. 2.1, 150.

68 **In this hearing, Detective Mackie:** *US v. Mallory*, vol. 2.1, 159–162.

68 **Deputy Coroner Richard M. Rosenberg:** *US v. Mallory*, vol. 2.1, 178–84

68 **The judge also heard from Irma Smith:** *US v. Mallory*, vol. 2.1, 185–93.

69 **She was followed by Detective Tate:** *US v. Mallory*, vol. 3.1, 193–vol 2.2, 200.

69 **"The Court finds that":** *US v. Mallory*, vol 2.2, 225.

69 **From DC General's Dr. Emanuel Stadlan:** *US v. Mallory*, vol 2.3, 312–15.

69 **On the following day:** *US v. Mallory*, vol. 3.1, 319–22.

70 **Bryant used his cross-examination:** *US v. Mallory*, vol. 3.1, 326–28.

CHAPTER 8. NEVER BEEN IN THIS POSITION

72 **Andrew Mallory's alleged confession:** *US v. Mallory*, vol 3.1, 341–47.

73 **After reading the confession:** *US v. Mallory*, vol. 3.1, 347–51.

73 **Bill Bryant's first witness:** *US v. Mallory*, vol 3.1, 355–vol 3.2, 361–65.

74 **He testified that after examining Mallory:** *US v. Mallory*, vol. 3.2., 365–85.

75 **Following the luncheon recess:** *US v. Mallory*, vol. 3.2, 400–405.

76 **"I have asked . . . the best you can":** *US v. Mallory*, 405–6. By now Bryant's co-counsel, William A. Tinney Jr., was also at the bench. He told the judge that although he had gotten a little closer to Mallory than Bryant, he had also been unable to get Mallory to tell him what he wanted to say on the witness stand. I was not able to find out exactly what Tinney's role was in the case. However, Chip remembers there was "a period of time when for several Saturdays, "Tinney," as my dad referred to him, would stop by the office." With one or both of Bryant's law partners also on the scene, they strategized and role-played. (William B. Bryant Jr., email to author, January 13, 2022.) There was a William Tinney Jr. who graduated from Howard Law in 1937.

76 **With Mallory on the stand:** *US v. Mallory*, vol 3.2. 407–vol 3.3, 423–58.

CHAPTER 9. HEART WAS JUST POUNDING

79 **Judge Holtzoff reminded the jurors:** *US v. Mallory*, vol. 4, 466–80.

79 **"very, very one-sided":** WBB OH, 123.

80 **"Are there any":** *US v. Mallory*, vol. 4, 480.

80 **"and my heart was just pounding":** WBB OH, 123.

80–81 **"I think as to . . . That is right":** *US v. Mallory*, vol. 4, 481.

81 **Julian Gensheimer:** When the judge asked "Who is the foreman of the jury?" The person who responded was identified as "Juror no. 8." When jury selection was finalized, Juror no. 8 was identified as Julian E. Gensheimer. *US v. Mallory*, vol. 4, 482, and vol. 1.1, 18.

81 **"Have we other . . . provided in this section":** *US v. Mallory*, vol. 4, 482–83.

81 **Having returned to the jury room:** *US v. Mallory*, vol. 4, 483–84.

81 **The following day:** "Jury Dooms Woman's Assailant," *Washington Post*, June 25, 1955, 1.

82 **"more prejudicial . . . new trial be granted":** *US v. Mallory*, vol. 5, 493.

82 **"properly entitled":** *US v. Mallory*, vol. 5, 494.

82 **"with his arms shackled . . . heavily bandaged":** "Youth Sentenced to Die November 11 for Criminal Attack of DC Woman," *Washington Post*, June 29, 1955, 19.

82 **"Andrew Mallory":** *US v. Mallory*, vol. 5, 495.

83 **"took the sentence calmly":** "Death Penalty Set for Rapist," *Evening Star*, June 28, 1955, B7.

83 **"He was sick . . . system of law":** Susanna McBee, "His Voice Rises at Police 'Botch-Ups,'" *Washington Post*, November 15, 1964, E2.

83–84 **"since Mallory had . . . such as it was":** *Mallory v. US* (Court of Appeal).

84 **"grossly prejudicial to . . . cannot long survive":** *Mallory v. US*.

84 **"I wasn't even . . . right quick":** WBB OH, 169.

85 **"the Supreme Court had":** Miriam Ottenberg, "Wants Question of Unreasonable Delays Settled," *Evening Star*, November 15, 1956, B1.

85 **"Oyez!":** "The Court and Its Procedures, " Supreme Court of the United States, https://www.supremecourt.gov/about/procedures.aspx.

CHAPTER 10. DELAY WAS *CHOSEN*

86 **"Mr. Chief Justice . . . important questions":** at 00:00:19, Part 1, *Mallory v. US* (SCOTUS).

86 **"the lower courts":** at 00:00:42, Part 1, *Mallory v. US.*

86 **"to that standard":** at 00:01:22, Part 1, *Mallory v. US.*

86 **Question three:** at 00:01:29, Part 1, *Mallory v. US.*

86 **Bryant proceeded:** at 00:01:51, Part 1, *Mallory v. US.*

87 **"a slight man":** Joan Biskupic, "Justice Brennan, Voice of Court's Social Revolution, Dies," *Washington Post*, Final, July 25, 1997, A1.

87 **"Now, what would That's my position":** at 00:11:54, Part 1, *Mallory v. US* (SCOTUS).

87 **"Here, in that juxtaposition":** Michael R. Winston, comment to author, March 3, 2022.

87 **"was in effect . . . that jury room.":** at 00:22: 36, Part 1, *Mallory v. US* (SCOTUS).

87 **"I think as to the question . . . further appears":** at 00:35:07, Part 1, *Mallory v. US.*

87–88 **"That's right . . . objected spontaneously":** at 00:35:21, Part 1, *Mallory v. US.*

88 **"it might have . . . I agree.":** at 00:36:23, Part 1, *Mallory v. US.*

88 **"This was an unusually direct":** William B. Schultz, comment to author, May 10, 2022.

88 **"are empowered to":** at 00:37:09, Part 1, *Mallory v. US* (SCOTUS).

88 **"circumstances over which . . . invalidate the confession":** at 00:37:19, Part 1, *Mallory v. US.*

88 **"You said that . . . That's right, Your Honor":** at 00:37:44, Part 1, *Mallory v. US.*

89 **"was about the":** at 00:40:04, Part 1, *Mallory v. US.*

89 **"Until after the . . . to *hold* him":** at 00:44:03, Part 1, *Mallory v. US.*

89 **"That's what you . . . purpose of the delay":** at 00:44:35, Part 1, *Mallory v. US.*

89 **"We'll recess":** at 00:46:59, Part 1, *Mallory v. US.*

89 **"no question . . . of illegal detention":** at 00:00:45, Part 2, *Mallory v. US* (SCOTUS).

89 **"treated kindly":** at 00:02:46, Part 2, *Mallory v. US.*

89–90 **"must be given . . . this confession":** at 00:03:35, Part 2, *Mallory v. US.*

90 **"The inference at . . . the janitor's apartment.":** at 00:04:56, Part 2, *Mallory v. US.*

90 **"a reasonable suspicion":** at 00:05:31, Part 2, *Mallory v. US.*

90 **"When did the . . . six o'clock":** at 00:10:22, Part 2, *Mallory v. US.*

90 **"Anything in the record":** at 00:11:00, Part 2, *Mallory v. US.*

90 **"there's nothing in the record":** at 00:12:52, Part 2, *Mallory v. US.*

90 **"the certainty or . . . which were introduced":** at 00:21:00, Part 2, *Mallory v. US.*

90 **"Suppose you took":** at 00:21:43, Part 2, *Mallory v. US.*

91 **"met the general":** at 00:22:37, Part 2, *Mallory v. US.*

91 **"The reason the police . . . ultimately did confess.":** at 00:25:49, Part 2, *Mallory v. US.*

91 **"with the underlying . . . secreted away":** at 00:27:34, Part 2, *Mallory v. US.*

91 **"Mr. Barrett,":** at 00:28:40, Part 2, *Mallory v. US.*

91 **"drastic change":** at 00:29:10, Part 2, *Mallory v. US.*

91 **"The McNabb Rule":** at 00:29:16, Part 2, *Mallory v. US.*

91–92 **"a good example . . . interest of society":** at 00:30:09, Part 2, *Mallory v. US.*

92 **"So, what do you . . . the word 'necessary'":** at 00:33:27, Part 2, *Mallory v. US.*

92 **"The central concept":** at 00:43:28, Part 2, *Mallory v. US.*

92 **"Normally I would . . . is the difference?":** at 00:48:13, Part 2, *Mallory v. US.*

92 **"the search stands":** at 00:50:59, Part 2, *Mallory v. US.*

92 **"arguing then that":** at 00:54:27, Part 2, *Mallory v. US.*

92 **"If the authorities":** at 01:06:38, Part 2, *Mallory v. US.*

93 **"And Mr. Bryant . . . It's my honor":** at 01:06:49, Part 2, *Mallory v. US.*

93 **Mrs. Mallory sent him:** WBB OH, 204.

93 **"We cannot sanction":** Justice Frankfurter, Opinion, *Mallory v. US*, 354 US 449 (1957), Justia, https://supreme.justia.com/cases/federal/us/354/449/#tab-opinion-1941572.

94–95 **"most significant . . . advocacy":** Supreme Court Historical Society, https://supremecourthistory.org/oral-arguments/significant-oral-arguments-the-warren-court/.

94 **"I do not . . . at some point":** William B. Bryant Jr., email to author, January 13, 2022.

94 **"was really undeserving . . . *McNabb* and *Upshaw*":** WBB OH, 130.

95 **"finally broke down":** WBB OH, 171.

95 **"I just knew":** Susanna McBee, "His Voice Rises at Police 'Botch-Ups,'" *Washington Post*, November 15, 1964, E2.

95 **"If he got involved":** Theodore R. Newman Jr., author interview, August 12, 2022.

96 **"stripped of all":** Jack C. Landau, "Killough Freed Reluctantly in Murder Case," *Washington Post*, October 9, 1964, A3.

96 **Judge Newman remembered:** Theodore R. Newman Jr., author interview, August 12, 2022.

96 **"he didn't know how":** Newman Jr.

96 **He used to tease:** Newman Jr.

96 **He advised Newman:** Newman Jr.

97 **Bryant also schooled Newman:** Newman Jr.

97 **"one mile rule . . . on safe ground":** Newman Jr.

97 **"The central feature . . . invest in others":** Theodore R. Newman Jr., email to author, August 9, 2022.

CHAPTER 11. A MORAL ISSUE

98 **"botch up their investigations . . . he sees as injustice":** Susanna McBee, "His Voice Rises at Police 'Botch-Ups,'" *Washington Post*, November 15, 1964, E2.

98 **One was Jasper Brown:** The source for his township is the 1950 federal census, Ancestry.com, *1950 United States Federal Census* [database online], Lehi, UT, USA, Ancestry.com Operations, Inc., 2022. The source for his involvement with the NAACP is WBB OH, 181. The source for the desegregation of schools is James Ross and WC Burton, "Shooting Follows Mixing at School," *Greensboro Daily News*, January 23, 1963, A1, A5.

98 **"There were about three . . . bumped him":** WBB OH, 182.

99 **"Yeah, I'll try it":** WBB OH, 183.

99 **"for being meaner than hell":** WBB OH, 188.

99 **"I figured I":** WBB OH, 185.

99 **"the better part of":** WBB OH, 185.

99 **Other sources:** "Brown to Leave Caswell County," *Greensboro Daily News*, January 10, 1964, A4.

99 **"madder than . . . was wronged":** WBB OH, 188.

99 **"they froze him out":** Thomas Little quoted in Doug Struck, "Southern Change: It Sometimes Gallops, Often Crawls: Racial Views Have Evolved in NC Town," *Baltimore Sun*, November 22, 1984, 34A.

99 **"I would have felt":** WBB OH, 204.

100 **"as a clear abuse . . . lawful means":** "The Southern Manifesto," American RadioWorks, http://americanradioworks.publicradio.org/features/marshall/manifesto.html.

100 **leaving some 1,700 Black children:** Katy June-Friesen, "Massive Resistance in a Small Town: Before and after *Brown* in Prince Edward County, Virginia," *Humanities* 34, no. 5 (September/October 2013), https://www.neh.gov/humanities/2013/septemberoctober/feature/massive-resistance-in-small-town.

100 **"was a total news junkie":** William B. Bryant Jr., email to author, October 6, 2022.

101 **"It makes me sick":** Michael Jay Friedman, *Free at Last: The US Civil Rights Movement* (US State Department, 2008), 43, https://tr.usembassy.gov/wp-content/uploads/sites/91/free_at_last.pdf.

101 **"We are confronted . . . are free":** "Televised Address to the Nation on Civil Rights," John F. Kennedy Presidential Library and Museum, https://www.jfklibrary.org/learn/about-jfk/historic-speeches/televised-address-to-the-nation-on-civil-rights.

102 **On this glorious:** Astaire A. Bryant, answers to author questionnaire, June 8, 2017.

102 **"without being killed":** Theodore R. Newman Jr., author interview, August 12, 2022.

102 **And the three:** Newman Jr., author interview.

102 **"the order of the day":** Martin Luther King Jr., "A Look to 1964," *Amsterdam News*, January 4, 1964, 6.

102–3 **"We believe that . . . forbids it":** "July 2, 1964: Remarks upon Signing the Civil Rights Bill," Millercenter.org, https://millercenter.org/the-presidency/presidential-speeches/july-2-1964-remarks-upon-signing-civil-rights-bill.

103 **"race, color":** Transcript of Civil Rights Act (1964), National Archives, https://www.archives.gov/milestone-documents/civil-rights-act.

CHAPTER 12. BEST EFFORT

104 **"for what seemed . . . buddies about it":** William B. Bryant Jr., email to author, September 28, 2021.

104 **"I wanted a complete":** Bryant Jr, email.

105 **"It became obvious . . . and the Robinsons":** Bryant Jr.

105 **Bryant thought someone:** WBB OH, 218.

105 **Johnson was hosting:** Entry for July 15, 1965, 6, 7, "Lyndon B. Johnson's Daily Diary Collection," July 15, 1965, 6, 7, LBJ Presidential Library, http://www.lbjlibrary.net/collections/daily-diary.html.

105 **"And what's your country? . . . eleven months":** WBB OH, 219.

106 **"looked bad":** WBB OH, 219.

106 **Years later, he wondered:** WBB OH, 217.

106 **"The cost to the community":** "Police Arrests for Investigation—Unconstitutional Practice," 88th Cong., 1st sess., *Congressional Record* 109, pt. 11 (August 14, 1963), S 14874, https://www.govinfo.gov/content/pkg/GPO-CRECB-1963-pt11/pdf/GPO-CRECB-1963-pt11-8-1.pdf.

106 **In his 1974 book:** Joseph C. Goulden, *The Benchwarmers: The Private World of the Powerful Federal Judges* (New York: Weybright and Talley, 1974), 287. Goulden also wrote that sponsors included labor leader A. Philip Randolph and President Johnson's friend Abe Fortas, who served as a US Supreme Court associate justice 1965–1969.

107 **A few years earlier:** WBB OH, 215.

107 **"We don't know . . . still together":** William B. Bryant Jr., *Dedication*, 31.

107 **Bryant had also:** WBB OH, 216.

107 **Judge Newman recalled:** Theodore R. Newman Jr., author interview, August 12, 2022.

107 **"his greatest joy was trying":** Newman Jr.

107 **"When the word got out":** WBB OH, 148.

107 **"in clover":** WBB OH, 212.

107 **If confirmed by the Senate:** WBB OH, 212.

108 **"were usually appointed":** Joseph D. Whitaker, "Judge Bryant Struggled to Reach His High Post," *Washington Post*, April 15, 1976, A14.

108 **"was tangled with far-flung":** Joseph C. Goulden, *The Benchwarmers: The Private World of the Powerful Federal Judges* (New York: Weybright and Talley, 1974), 285. In WBB OH (p. 146) Judge Bryant said that he spent one year on this case.

108 **"Do you think . . . that kind of guy":** Goulden, *Benchwarmers*, 285. In WBB OH (pp. 146 and 212), Judge Bryant stated that he charged $32,000.

108 **"is more than . . . by law":** Michael R. Winston, comments to author, March 3, 2022.

108 **"Because of his background":** Joseph C. Goulden, *The Benchwarmers: The Private World of the Powerful Federal Judges* (New York: Weybright and Talley, 1974), 287.

109 **And so, on the morning:** Senate Hearing, 1. The hearing was held in what was then called the New Senate Office Building. Completed in 1958, it was named for Senator Everett Dirksen of Illinois until 1972. For clarifying something about the hearing, I am grateful to Yashi Gunawardena, who in October 2021 was staff assistant, Senate Judiciary Committee, Senator Richard J. Durbin, chair.

109 **"The Conscience of the Senate":** "Philip A. Hart: A Featured Biography," US Senate, https://www.senate.gov/senators/FeaturedBios/Featured_Bio_Hart.htm.

109 **"May I ask . . . the nominee":** Philip A. Hart, Senate Hearing, 2.

109 **"exceptionally well qualified . . . outstanding attorneys":** Paul F. McCardle, Senate Hearing, 4.

109–10 **"unquestionable legal . . . committee assignments":** Fredrick H. Evans, Senate Hearing, 5.

110 **"I know from . . . personal character":** Joseph C. Waddy, Senate Hearing, 7.

110 **Penny was at:** Astaire A. Bryant, email to author, September 24, 2021.

110 **"If my folks":** William B. Bryant Jr., email to author, September 28, 2021.

110 **"I have appeared . . . courtroom tactics":** John J. Carmody, Senate Hearing, 8–9.

111 **After Carmody:** Hart, Senate Hearing, 9.

111 **"Sir, at the risk . . . effort":** William B. Bryant, Senate Hearing, 12.

111 **"Next time . . . very much, sir":** Hart and Bryant, Senate Hearing, 15.

111 **"a criminal case dynamo . . . attitude toward it":** "Newest Federal Judge Criminal Dynamo," *Afro-American*, July 24, 1965, 14.

112 **For example, . . . "He liked pecans a lot":** Astaire A. Bryant, response to author questionnaire, June 8, 2017.

112 **At the time:** "Senate Confirms Nominations of Gasch and Bryant," *Evening Star*, August 12, 1965, B9; Dom Banafede, "Who Will Judge the Judges?," *Corpus Christi Caller-Times*, February 27, 1966, 2B. The first article said, "There now are seven Negro federal judges in the nation." The second article, which appeared six months after Bryant's confirmation, reported that at the time of publication, "there are 78 circuit judges and 303 district judge on regular active service."

113 **"You know . . . right from wrong":** Carol Leonnig, "A Lifetime of Faith in the Law," *Washington Post*, September 15, 2004, https://www.washingtonpost.com/archive/local/2004/09/16/a-lifetime-of-faith-in-the-law/8d6a345d-84a7-440d-ad69-ad85a3654480/.

CHAPTER 13. DAY AFTER DAY, TRYING CASES

114 **"wry sense of humor":** "Judge McGuire Busy as New Chief of Court," *Evening Star*, September 22, 1961, B3.

114 **"hectic . . . kind of business":** WBB OH, 223.

115 **During these hectic days, the cases:** "Youth Found to Be 17, Averts Adult Sentence," *Evening Star*, January 15, 1966, A5; "Arson Verdict Raises Query on Confession Exclusion, *Evening Star*, August 26, 1966, C6; "Girl Completes Testimony in Rape Trial of 5," *Evening Star*, April 5, 1966, B4; William Basham, "Autopsy Facts Revealed, Lawyer Asks Full Report," *Sunday Star*, December 12, 1965, D7.

115 **"Every day from":** WBB OH, 223.

115 **"tagged as the . . . guilty pleas":** William Basham, "Rotating Sentencing Panel Brings End of 'Judge Shopping' in District," *Sunday Star*, March 31, 1968, B1.

115 **"had distinguished . . . a defendant":** Basham, "Rotating Sentencing."

115 **Agonizing over:** Basham, "Rotating Sentencing."

115 **"pays closer attention":** Leonard Downie Jr. "Judge-Shoppers Hunt Bargain Terms," *Washington Post*, January 26, 1967, A6.

115 **In cases of:** Downie Jr., "Judge-Shoppers."

115 **More than any:** Downie Jr., "Rotating Sentencing."

116 **"Most favor either 'fair'":** William Basham, "Rotating Sentencing Panel Brings End of 'Judge Shopping' in District," *Sunday Star*, March 31, 1968, B1.

116 **"the right to walk . . . off property":** Basham, "Rotating Sentencing."

116 **"Whatever impulses":** Basham, "Rotating Sentencing."

116 **"wheel syndrome . . . nearest penitentiary":** Basham, "Rotating Sentencing."

117 **"We got terrible":** David Welna, "Remembering North Korea's Audacious Capture of the USS *Pueblo*," *All Things Considered*, January 23, 2018, https://www.npr.org/2018/01/23/580076540/looking-at-the-saga-of-the-uss-pueblo-50-years-later/.

117 **Between the start of the Tet:** "Tet Offensive," Brittanica.com, https://www.britannica.com/topic/Tet-Offensive; "Tet Offensive: Turning Point in

Vietnam War," *New York Times*, January 31, 1988, 14, https://www.nytimes.com/1988/01/31/world/tet-offensive-turning-point-in-vietnam-war.html.

117 **"A nation that continues":** Martin Luther King Jr, "Beyond Vietnam: A Time to Break the Silence," April 4, 1967, American Rhetoric, https://www.americanrhetoric.com/speeches/mlkatimetobreaksilence.htm.

118 **"Beep, beep!":** Joe Heim, "Echoes of the Past Reverberated in Howard University Student Occupation," *Washington Post*, April 7, 2018. https://www.washingtonpost.com/local/education/echoes-of-the-past-reverberated-in-howard-university-student-occupation/2018/04/07/17e438be-38e0-11e8-acd5-35eac230e514_story.html.

119 **"If the human race . . . at least stay his hand":** "Twenty-Seven People Worth Saving," *Esquire*, October 1968, 180.

119 **"the man behind . . . financial sacrifice":** "Twenty-Seven," 181.

119 **Astaire Bryant was engaged:** William B. Bryant, email to author, September 28, 2021.

120 **"distract motorists":** Carl Bernstein, "Court Voids Rules on White House Protests," *Washington Post*, April 28, 1969, A4.

120 **". . . injured shrubs":** Bernstein, "Court Voids."

120 **"rights to freedom":** Bernstein, "Court Voids."

120 **"between 10,000 and 30,000":** Bernstein, "Court Voids."

120 **"Despite the large numbers":** Bernstein, "Court Voids."

120 **"in the interest of":** Bernstein, "Court Voids."

120 **"thousands of tourists . . . number of demonstrators":** Bernstein, "Court Voids."

120 **Eventually the DOI:** Mary M. Cheh, "Demonstrations, Security Zones, and First Amendment Protection of Special Places," *University of the District of Columbia Law Review* 8, no. 1 (September 30, 2004): 55–56.

121 **"would be forced to swim":** Judge William B. Bryant, Opinion, *Hodgson v. United Mine Workers of America*, 344 F. Supp. 17 (D.D.C. 1972), Justia, https://law.justia.com/cases/federal/district-courts/FSupp/344/17/2303340/. This is the source for all other Judge Bryant quotes in the UMWA case.

122 **"strongest order":** Jim Mann, "Rules Set for Reins on UMW," *Washington Post*, June 17, 1972, A1.

122 **On July 11:** "Deaths," *Evening Star*, July 14, 1970, B5.

122 **"At the time of her death":** Astaire A. Bryant, email to author, January 18, 2022.

122 **"My father, of course":** Astaire A. Bryant email.

122 **Bill knew that Benson:** On his being a World War I vet: Ancestry.com, *US, Veterans' Gravesites, ca.1775–2019* [database online], Lehi, UT, USA, Ancestry.com Operations, Inc., 2006. On the nickname "Buddy": WBB OH, 7.

123 **He also knew:** WBB OH, 7.

123 **Benson was:** Born on January 9, 1889, he died on October 7, 1967. Ancestry.com, *US, Veterans' Gravesites*, ca. 1775–2019 [database online], Lehi, UT, USA, Ancestry.com Operations, Inc., 2006.

123 **"He got off the phone . . . his own family":** William B. Bryant Jr., email to author, December 21, 2023.

CHAPTER 14. IS IT RIGHT? IS IT RIGHT?

124 **When Alberta passed:** William B. Bryant Jr., email to author, January 13, 2022 and William B. Bryant Jr., comments to author, April 11, 2022. Unless otherwise noted, these are the sources for information about home life.

125 **"complete with . . . that Christmas":** William B. Bryant Jr., email to author, January 13, 2022.

125 **One favorite:** Astaire A. Bryant, response to author questionnaire, June 8, 2017.

125 **"I was ten":** William B. Bryant Jr., email to author, April 6, 2022.

125 **Later, Bill sometimes:** Astaire A. Bryant, response to author questionnaire, June 8, 2017.

125 **Bill and Astaire . . . "hardly ever fried":** William B. Bryant Jr., email to author, April 6, 2022.

125 **They included get-togethers:** Bryant Jr., email. While he did recall that Inez Dabney worked for the federal government (email to author, April 11, 22), he did not recall Edna Artis's occupation. The source for that is the 1940 census, Ancestry.com, *1940 United States Federal Census* [database online], Provo, UT, USA, Ancestry.com Operations, Inc., 2012.

125 **"My dad definitely":** William B. Bryant Jr., email to author, April 6, 2022.

126 **"and I loved . . . my mom":** Bryant Jr., email.

126 **"We were among":** William B. Bryant Jr., email to author, January 13, 2022.

126 **Brookland was home:** I am grateful to Dr. Michael R. Winston for this information. Comments to author, May 27, 2022.

126 **"my parents decided":** William B. Bryant Jr., email to author, January 13, 2022. Unless otherwise noted, this is the source for all that follows on the Northampton Street home.

127 **"many of my father's signature":** William B. Bryant Jr., email to author, January 13, 2022.

127 **"I killed a lot of plants":** William B. Schultz, author interview, May 3, 2017.

127 **"some of the regulars":** William B. Bryant Jr., email to author, January 13, 2022.

128 **"complained that he":** Ernest Holsendolph, "ACLU Wins $12-Million Suit. For War Protesters at Capitol," *New York Times*, January 17, 1975, 1.

128 **"award by a jury":** Holsendolph, "ACLU Wins."

129 **Eventually the total:** Saundra Torry, "19 Years Later, Suit by Vietnam War Protesters Is Finally at Peace," *Washington Post*, November, 18, 1990,

https:// www.washingtonpost.com/archive/business/1990/11/19/19-years-later-suit-by-vietnam-war-protesters-is-finally-at-peace/fc586539-a765-4b31-98d8-a1637203ed9a/.

129 **"his love of justice":** John W. Nields Jr., Oral History Interviews by Elizabeth Cavanagh, Esq., September 27, 2017, March 20, April 24, May 22, July 10, and October 22, 2018, Oral History Project, The Historical Society of the District of Columbia Circuit, https://dcchs.org/sb_pdf/nields-complete/ 104.

129 **Judge Bryant ruled:** Thomas W. Lippmann, "Drafted Graduate Student Wins Deferment until End of Semester," *Washington Post*, March 12, 1969, A18.

129 **"solely because of hair":** "Court Bars C&P Firing of Men for Long Hair," *Evening Star*, December 11, 1970, B4.

129 **According to the *Washington Post*:** Sanford J. Ungar, "Judge Frees Youth Denied DC Hearing," *Washington Post*, November 19, 1970, A1.

129 **"bumps on his face . . . one eye":** Ungar, "Judge Frees Youth," A16.

129 **this overcrowded, crime-ridden:** Winston Groom, "Receiving Home's Fitness Challenged," *Evening Star*, September 22, 1970, B1.

129–30 **"There is . . . 'a scar over the eye.'":** Sanford J. Ungar, "Judge Frees Youth Denied DC Hearing," *Washington Post*, November 19, 1970, A16.

130 **Another case that surely:** Barry Kalb, "Court Tells Owners to Heat House Now for Welfare Clients," Barry Kalb, *Evening Star*, January 14, 1971, B1, B4.

130 **"I saw an unforgettable":** Harry W. Goldberg, "Judge Bryant's Compassion," *Washington Post*, November 29, 2005, A20.

130 **Judge Bryant ordered:** David Pike, "Man Struck by Tree Awarded $975,000—May Be a Record," *Washington Star*, March 6, 1976, D1, D2.

131 **The US Court of Appeals:** Allan Frank, "$975,000 Verdict Upheld for Man Struck by Tree," *Washington Star*, June 28, 1978, B2.

131 **"a walking travesty":** Wiley A. Branton, *PoP*, LXIII.

131 **"Assistance of Counsel":** Sixth Amendment, National Constitution Center, https://constitutioncenter.org/the-constitution/amendments/amendment-vi.

131 **"After you look . . . 'Is it right? Is it right?'":** Wiley A. Branton, *PoP*, LXIV.

CHAPTER 15. A VERY DISTINCTIVE DIGNITY

132 **"one of four":** Timothy S. Robinson, "Bryant Is 1st Black Judge to Head US Court Here," *Washington Post*, March 20, 1977, B1.

132 **"After watching heroin":** David Pike, "US Court's New Chief Judge Favors Decriminalizing Heroin," *Washington Star*, March 20, 1977, B1.

132 **"If addicts were":** Pike, "US Court's." Unless otherwise noted, this is the source of Judge Bryant quotes that follow.

133 **"I'm sure that organized":** Pike, "US Court's," B2.

133 **"Other judges . . . by Rap. Inc.":** Pike, "US Court's," B2.

133 **"One judge said":** Pike, "US Court's," B2.

134 **"a lawyer's lawyer . . . as a person":** David Pike, "Everybody Likes Judge William Bryant," *Washington Star*, March 20, 1977, B1.

134 **"is the most human . . . world he wants":** Pike, "Everybody Likes," B3.

134 **"This has some significance:"** Pike, "Everybody Likes," B3. This is the source of Judge Bryant quotes that follow unless otherwise noted.

135 **"his eyes twinkling":** Pike, "Everybody Likes," B3.

135 **Several months after Bryant:** Washington Bar Association, Inc. and Washington Bar Association Educational Foundation, Inc. Law Day 2022 program, https://washingtonbar.org/wp-content/uploads/2022/05/2022-Law-Day-Program.pdf.

135 **"You always knew . . . was gold":** Joyce Hens Green, author interview, June 26, 2017.

136 **"was whether there . . . follow the flag?":** Daniel A. Rezneck, "He Sought Mercy, He Did Justice," *Legal Times*, November 21, 2005, reprinted in *TSOOC*, 22. This is the source for Rezneck quotes that follow unless otherwise noted.

136 **"Dr. Mead, will you":** Rezneck, "He Sought Mercy," 22.

137 **"American Samoa has its Constitution":** Memorandum Opinion and Order, *King v. Andrus*, 452 F. Supp. 11 (D.D.C. 1977), Justia, https://law.justia.com/cases/federal/district-courts/FSupp/452/11/2302257/. Unless otherwise noted, this is the source of Judge Bryant quotes in this case.

138 **Gilbert Morgan:** "Killer of 3 in Home Pleads Insanity," *Evening Star*, March 24, 1978, E2.

138 **California congressman Richard:** Toni House, "Ex-Rep. Hanna Gets 6 to 30 Months for Role in Korea Scandal," *Washington Star*, April 24, 1978, 2nd ed., A1.

138 **Folksinger-activist Joan Baez's:** "Score One for Joan," *Washington Star*, November 4, 1978, A2.

138 **Jim "Yazoo" Smith':** Paul Attner, "Smith v. Redskins: Ruling May End 11-Year Fight," *Washington Post*, December 30, 1981, D1.

138 **"burly, 250-pounder":** Timothy S. Robinson, "Linwood Gray Is Acquitted on Drug Charges," *Washington Post*, July 19, 1979, A1.

138 **"major tax case . . . to the community":** Timothy S. Robinson, "Linwood Gray Sentenced on Tax Evasion Charge," *Washington Post*, August 18, 1979, C3.

139 **"He didn't like it . . . bother me'":** Diane Steed, author interview, June 29, 2017.

139 **"A black-bag job":** WBB OH, 238–39.

139 **"Nixon testified . . . over my mouth":** WBB OH, 239.

139 **"All you had":** WBB OH, 241.

140 **"spontaneous . . . nothing you can do":** WBB OH, 241.

140 **Felt was fined:** Laura A. Kiernan, "Ex-FBI Men Felt, Miller Draw Fines," *Washington Post*, December 16, 1980, https://www.washingtonpost.com/archive/politics/1980/12/16/ex-fbi-men-felt-miller-draw-fines/173d4d29-b5a5-46f8-8303-9d5bae88c9cd/. In WBB OH (p. 240), Judge Bryant said that he fined Felt $10,000 and Miller $7,500.

140 **"the convictions . . . damn little":** WBB OH, 240.

140–41 **"and our nation . . . threatening our nation":** Ronald Reagan, "Statement on Granting Pardons to W. Mark Felt and Edward S. Miller," April 15, 1981, Ronald Reagan Presidential Library and Museum, https://www.reaganlibrary.gov/archives/speech/statement-granting-pardons-w-mark-felt-and-edward-s-miller-0.

141 **"all smiles and beaming":** William B. Bryant Jr., email to author, February 12, 2022.

141 **Initially he was:** Bryant Jr. email.

142 **Like Bryant, he:** Richard Pearson, "John L. Smith, Chief Judge of US District Court, Dies," *Washington Post*, September 6, 1992, https://www.washingtonpost.com/archive/local/1992/09/06/john-l-smith-chief-judge-of-us-district-court-dies/e63e63dc-8d30-4a91-bef8-92eb063a2bd9/.

142 **Judge Bazelon sometimes took:** William B. Schultz, comment to author, May 8, 2022.

142 **"Mr. K's," a dining room:** Philip Taubman, "Milton Kronheim's, Where the Justices Adjourn for Lunch," *New York Times*, July 15, 1979, 36.

142 **"Even before . . . he touches":** David L. Bazelon, *PoP*, LIX–LX, LXI.

143 **"I don't . . . relax or something":** Wiley A. Branton, *PoP*, LXIII.

143 **"as a brother . . . and as a talker.":** William C. Gardner, *PoP*, LXIV, LXV.

143 **"invariably leaves one":** Henry F. Greene, *PoP*, LXVIII.

144 **"Bill, would you say a few words?":** John Lewis Smith, *PoP*, LXVIII.

144 **Judge Bryant, thus far:** William B. Bryant Jr., email to author, February 12, 2022.

144 **"Ever since I found out . . . Thank you very much":** William B. Bryant, *PoP*, LXVIII.

144 **"I think he must've":** William B. Bryant Jr., email to author, February 12, 2022.

CHAPTER 16. FEEL THEMSELVES GROW

145 **"is not looking back . . . last week'":** Laura A. Kiernan, "Bryant Steps Down Today as Chief Judge of US District Court," *Washington Post*, September 18, 1981, B4.

145 **"There is no end":** William B. Schultz, "A Modest Servant of Law and Life," *Washington Post*, November 18, 2005, A23.

145 **Judge Bryant took senior status:** William B. Schultz, comment to author, May 8, 2022.

145–46 **"Judge Bryant wasn't . . . understood the Constitution":** Carol Leonnig, "A Lifetime of Faith in the Law," *Washington Post*, September 15, 2004, https://www.washingtonpost.com/archive/local/2004/09/16/a-lifetime-of-faith-in-the-law/8d6a345d-84a7-440d-ad69-ad85a3654480/.

146 **"Congressman Kelly presented":** William B. Bryant, "Memorandum on Due Process and Other Post Trial Motions," *United States v. Kelly*, 539 F. Supp. 363 (D.D.C. 1982), Justia, https://law.justia.com/cases/federal/district-courts/FSupp/539/363/2151546/.

146 **"It has an odor . . . repulsive":** Laura A. Kiernan, "Abscam Defenses Disputing Convictions Get Help—From Justice Dept.," *Washington Post*, January 12, 1981, A3.

147 **"The function of . . . actions":** William B. Bryant, "Memorandum on Due Process and Other Post Trial Motions," *United States v. Kelly*, 539 F. Supp. 363 (D.D.C. 1982), Justia, https://law.justia.com/cases/federal/district-courts/FSupp/539/363/2151546/.

147 **"Considering the genuine":** George MacKinnon, Opinion, *UNITED STATES of America, Appellant, v. Richard KELLY*. No. 82–1660, Openjurist.org, https://openjurist.org/707/f2d/1460/united-states-v-kelly.

147 **"The importuning of":** Ruth Bader Ginsburg, Opinion, Openjurist.org, https://openjurist.org/707/f2d/1460/united-states-v-kelly.

148 **"What the government . . . a crime":** Al Kamen, "Ex-Rep Kelly Sentenced in Abscam Case," *Washington Post*, January 13, 1984, A5.

148 **"lived for almost 20 years":** Lucy Morgan, "Richard Kelly: 1924–2005: A Political Career Defined by Abscam," *Tampa Bay Times*, August 25, 2005, B1.

148 **"Don't ask a 'why':** Roger Adelman, *CC*, 20.

148 **"The old folks would say":** Adelman, *CC*, 20.

149 **"just get in and get out":** Adelman, *CC*, 21.

149 **"He tracked":** Adelman, *CC*, 21.

149 **"Do you really":** Adelman, *CC*, 21.

149 **"Well, why don't . . . High praise":** Adelman, *CC*, 21.

149 **"And I'd tell him":** Adelman, *CC*, 21.

149–50 **"Oh, yes, your Honor . . . he's guilty":** Adelman, *CC*, 23, 24.

150 **"Judge Bryant decided . . . a lawyer":** Beth Perovich Gesner, "Recollections of Judge Bryant," Historical Society of the District of Columbia Circuit, n.d., 1–2.

150 **Her son Alan:** Alan M. Freeman, "A Lasting Impression," *TSOOC*, 35. This information and quotations from this article are reprinted with the permission of Alan M. Freeman.

150–51 **"I was . . . a few minutes":** Carol Garfiel Freeman, "He Was Understanding and Kind," *TSOOC*, 27. Reprinted with the permission of Carol G. Freeman.

151 **"allowing me . . . in my mind":** Alan M. Freeman, "A Lasting Impression," *TSOOC*, 35.

151 **"robbed judges":** Ned Miltenberg, "An Angel with a Sense of Mirth," *TSOOC*, 57. This and all other quotations from this article are reprinted with the permission of Ned Miltenberg.

152 **"to promote civility":** "Message from the Board," William B. Bryant American Inn of Court, https://inns.innsofcourt.org/for-members/inns/the-william-b-bryant-american-inn-of-court/message-from-the-board/.

152 **"There was not":** Richard "Kirk" Bowden, *CC*, 46.

152 **"Young man":** Bowden, *CC*, 41.

152 **"I got to sit":** Bowden, *CC*, 44.

153 **"simplify the most":** Kirk Bowden, "I Was Blessed to Have Had This Prince of a Man as a Friend," reprinted in *TSOOC*, 15.

153 **"retains a mixture":** David Pike, "Everybody Likes Judge William Bryant," *Washington Star*, March 20, 1977, B3.

153 **"dynamic had to":** Diane Steed, author interview, June 29, 2017.

153 **For years, no degrees:** Steed; and William B. Bryant Jr., email to author, March 8, 2022.

153 **a 1965 DC Public Service Award:** DPAAC Staff, "Bryant, William" (2016), *Manuscript Division Finding Aids*. 239, https://dh.howard.edu/finaid_manu/239.

153 **"not a priority for him":** William B. Bryant Jr., email to author, March 8, 2022.

153 **Judge Bryant, who tended:** David Pike, "Everybody Likes Judge William Bryant," *Washington Star*, March 20, 1977, B3.

153 **"He didn't want":** Diane Steed, author interview, June 29, 2017.

154 **Judge Bryant came in under . . . "law and fairness":** Diane Steed, email to author, February 22, 2022.

154 **"the way other people":** Diane Steed, author interview, June 29, 2017.

154 **"He treated me . . . all family":** Steed, author interview.

154 **"decisions he was":** Lynne Bernabei, "A Society Is Judged by How It Treats the Most Vulnerable," *TSOOC*, 38. Reprinted with the permission of Lynne Bernabei.

154 **"very precise":** Diane Steed, author interview, June 29, 2017.

154 **"models of clarity":** "Chief Judge William Benson Bryant," *Howard Law Journal* 25, no. 1 (1982): 2.

155 **"vivid memories . . . world in general":** William B. Schultz, *CC*, 10.

155 **"was a total racist . . . to get the job done":** William B. Schultz, author interview, May 3, 2017.

155 **"Judge Bryant encouraged":** Schultz, comment to author, February 1, 2024.

155 **"in a relatively minor . . . makes mistakes":** Ned Miltenberg, "An Angel with a Sense of Mirth," *TSOOC*, 56.

156 **"a big case . . . short recess":** John Spiegel, "Some Memories of Judge Bryant," *TSOOC*, 51.

157 **"tears began to":** Spiegel, "Some Memories."

157 **"Very early . . . legal career":** Robert P. Watkins III, "A Teacher Affects Eternity," *TSOOC*, 20. Reprinted with the permission of Robert P. Watkins III.

157 **"a pivotal moment":** Robert P. Watkins III, Esquire, Oral History Interviews by James McKeown, Esquire, February 5, March 5, May 9, June 19, July 26, August 21, and September 19, 2019, Oral History Project, The Historical Society of the District of Columbia Circuit, https://dcchs.org/sb_pdf/watkins-all/, 65.

158 **"I reeled . . . my critique":** William R. Hyde Jr., "A Lost Ball in High Weeds," *TSOOC*, 43. Reprinted with the permission of William R. Hyde Jr., Esq.

158 **"It goes . . . comes first":** Gesner, "Recollections of Judge Bryant," Historical Society of the District of Columbia Circuit, n.d., 1.

158–59 **"I'll always hold . . . chambers":** Beth Perovich Gesner, "I Will Always Smile When I Think of Him," *TSOOC*, 55. Reprinted with the permission of Hon. Beth Perovich Gesner.

159 **"Go to the US":** Paul L. Friedman, *CC*, 31.

159 **"there was nothing better":** Friedman, *CC*, 35.

159 **"And because Judge Bryant":** Friedman, *CC*, 36.

160 **"He welcomed . . . what he thought":** James Robertson, *CC*, 37.

160 **"Jim, a district judge":** Reminiscences of James Robertson, Interview by Myron A. Farber on January 29 and January 30, 2013, The Rule of Law Oral History Project, Columbia Center for Oral History, Columbia University, http://www.columbia.edu/cu/libraries/inside/ccoh_assets/ccoh_10491112_transcript.pdf, 76.

160 **"In the land":** William B. Bryant, *TSOOC*, 30.

160 **"It's hard to take":** William B. Bryant, *TSOOC*, 31.

160 **"Whenever you try":** William B. Bryant, *TSOOC*, 34.

160 **"Where a worm":** William B. Bryant, *TSOOC*, 30.

161 **"When he thought":** Paul L. Friedman, *CC*, 35–36.

161 **"stand in line":** Ned Miltenberg, "An Angel with a Sense of Mirth," *TSOOC*, 57.

161 **"I'll wait my turn":** Vernon E. Jordan Jr., "Eulogy," delivered at the funeral services for Judge William B. Bryant held at the Dunbarton Chapel, Howard University School of Law, reprinted in *TSOOC*, 77.

CHAPTER 17. I'LL BE THERE

162 **This Black men's golf:** "Pro-Duffers DC History," DC Pro-Duffers.org, http://dcproduffers.org/duffers-history/; William "Rick" Hyde Jr., "African-American Golf before Eldrick 'Tiger" Woods' Urban One interview, January 9, 2020, transcript provided by William R. Hyde Jr., email to author, June 10, 2022.

162–63 **"practiced more . . . all the time":** William R. Hyde Jr., email to author, June 10, 2022.

163 **"often compared . . . Lee Elder":** Kirk Bowden, "I Was Blessed to Have Had This Prince of a Man as a Friend," reprinted in *TSOOC*, 16.

163 **"It was literary":** Tara Bahrampour, "A Club of Their Own: The Story of a Secret Poker Society Started by Pioneering African Americans," *Washington Post*, September 8, 2018, https://www.washingtonpost.com/news/inspired-life/wp/2018/09/08/the-story-behind-the-76-year-old-secret-poker-club-started-by-prominent-black-men-in-d-c/.

163 **"godfather of daycare":** "Thomas Taylor," *DIGDC*, https://digdc.dclibrary.org/islandora/object/dcplislandora%3A268439.

163 **"always hunting":** Tara Bahrampour, "A Club of Their Own: The Story of a Secret Poker Society Started by Pioneering African Americans," *Washington Post*, September 8, 2018, https://www.washingtonpost.com/news/inspired-life/wp/2018/09/08/the-story-behind-the-76-year-old-secret-poker-club-started-by-prominent-black-men-in-d-c/.

163 **Those others:** Bryant family Brookland Literary and Hunting Club ephemera provided by Astaire A. Bryant and William B. Bryant Jr.

164 **At the start:** Michael R. Winston, email to author, April 7, 2022.

164 **"was the most intent":** Winston, email.

165 **"equanimity . . . in bold relief":** Michael R. Winston, *CC*, 52.

165 **"was a pleasure":** Colbert I. King, "Celebrating the Pride of a Pioneer," *Washington Post*, November 19, 2005, A25.

166 **"Vernon and my dad":** William B. Bryant Jr., email to author, February 13, 2022.

166 **Christmas after Christmas:** Astaire A. Bryant, email to author, February 13, 2022.

166 **Whenever the dapper:** William B. Bryant Jr., email to author, February 20, 2022.

166 **"Vernon would call":** Bryant Jr., email.

166 **"Where? What time? I'll be there":** Vernon E. Jordan Jr., "Eulogy," delivered at the funeral services for Judge William B. Bryant held at the Dunbarton Chapel, Howard University School of Law, reprinted in *TSOOC*, 78.

166 **"thoroughly enjoyed the sermons":** William B. Bryant Jr., email to author, February 20, 2022.

166 **"a rumbling":** Robert D. McFadden, "Rev. Gardner C. Taylor, Powerful Voice for Civil Rights, Dies at 96," *New York Times*, April 6, 2015, https://www.nytimes.com/2015/04/07/us/rev-gardner-c-taylor-powerful-voice-for-civil-rights-dies-at-96.html.

166 **"allegations against Jordan . . . criminal charge":** "Vernon Jordan," Pew Research Center: Journalism & Media Staff, October 20, 1998, https://www.pewresearch.org/journalism/1998/10/20/vernon-jordan/.

166 **"Every night, . . . alright?'":** Vernon E. Jordan Jr., "Eulogy," delivered at the funeral services for Judge William B. Bryant held at the Dunbarton Chapel, Howard University School of Law, reprinted in *TSOOC*, 78.

167 **"would call my dad":** Astaire A. Bryant, email to author, February 13, 2022.

167 **"He really enjoyed":** William B. Bryant Jr., email to author, April 6, 2022.

167 **"We all squeezed":** William B. Bryant Jr., email to author, April 6, 2022.

167 **At one point:** Astaire A. Bryant, email to author, February 22, 2022.

168 **"It was good":** Vaughn Stebbins, author interview, May 15, 2022. Unless otherwise noted, this is the source of all quotes and information provided by Vaughn Stebbins.

168 **"Knowing that the waffles":** Lauren Stebbins, author interview, May 26, 2022. Unless otherwise noted, this is the source of all quotes and information provided by Lauren Stebbins.

169 **During any given summer:** William B. Bryant Jr., email to author, April 7, 2022.

170 **As for the couple's:** William B. Bryant Jr., email to author, April 6, 2022.

169 **"chatted, laughed":** Deborah Jones Taborn, response to author questionnaire, May 27, 2022.

170 **"My parents. on their porch":** William B. Bryant Jr., email to author, April 6, 2022.

170 **"She was conscious brought to tears":** William B. Bryant Jr., email to author, June 7, 2022. Unless otherwise noted, this is the source for the rest of his comments and information in this chapter on his mother's stroke, recovery, subsequent illness, and death.

170 **"he didn't wear":** Diane Steed, author interview, June 15, 2022.

171 **"Judge Bryant came in":** Diane Steed, author interview, June 29, 2017.

171 **For some time:** William B. Bryant Jr., email to author, June 7, 2022.

171 **After Astaire had the stroke:** William B. Bryant Jr., email to author, June 7, 2022 (activities); Astaire A. Bryant, email to author, July 19, 2022 (golfing outfit); William B. Schultz, comment to author, September 24, 2022 (law clerks' gift of golf clubs).

171 **"at the urging of Vernon . . . you pay for":** William B. Bryant Jr., email to author, July 19, 2022.

172 **By then their number one:** William B. Bryant Jr., email to author, April 6, 2022.

172 **As Bill carried on**: William B. Bryant Jr., email to author, June 7, 2022.

172 **"She never looked":** Lauren Stebbins, author interview, May 26, 2022.

172 **"He said he wasn't":** Diane Steed, author interview, June 29, 2017.

173 **On September 22:** "Death Notices," *Washington Post*, September 20, 1997, C4. The information was confirmed by the family.

173 **"We did not dwell":** William B. Bryant Jr., email to author, June 7, 2022.

173 **"did sometimes go":** William B. Bryant Jr., email to author, April 6, 2022.

173 **"I remember one Friday night":** Deborah Jones Taborn, response to author questionnaire, May 27, 2022.

173 **Many a Friday:** Lauren Stebbins, author interview, May 26, 2022.

173 **"Papa, you gotta. Every moment of it":** Stebbins, author interview.

174 **Vernon Jordan called:** William B. Bryant Jr., email to author, February 13, 2022.

174 **Moreover, for several years:** Astaire A. Bryant, email to author, February 13, 2022.

174 **"Astaire's poinsettia":** Vernon E. Jordan Jr., "Eulogy," delivered at the funeral services for Judge William B. Bryant held at the Dunbarton Chapel, Howard University School of Law, reprinted in *TSOOC*, 78.

174 **Sonia Avalos was also:** Astaire A. Bryant and William B. Bryant Jr., emails to author, June 8, 2024.

174 **After his beloved:** Diane Steed, author interview, June 29, 2017. Astaire A. Bryant was present and said that her dad sometimes visited the grave in the evening.

174 **Early on:** William Benson Bryant Jr., email to author, June 7, 2022.

CHAPTER 18. NOT TO BE TOLERATED IN A CIVILIZED SOCIETY

175 **After he lost his wife:** Diane Steed, author interview, June 15, 2022.

175 **He also kept:** Astaire A. Bryant, author interview, June 7, 2017.

176 **"When he was 89 years old . . . wanted to drive":** William B. Bryant Jr., email to author, July 12, 2022.

176 **"would always reply":** William B. Bryant Jr., *Dedication*, 30.

176 **"often asked former clerks":** William B. Schultz, comment to author, September 27, 2022.

176 **"The day I became . . . left the sky":** *Tribute: The Honorable William B. Bryant, United States District Judge for the District of Columbia*, District of Columbia Circuit Judicial Conference, Farmington, Pennsylvania, June 6–9, 2006, 7.

177 **"you could damn near":** WBB OH, 232.

177 **On November 5, 1975, in *Campbell*:** Judge Bryant, Memorandum and Order, *Campbell v. McGruder*, 416 F. Supp. 100 (D.D.C. 1975), Justia, https://law.justia.com/cases/federal/district-courts/FSupp/416/100/1501136/. This is the source for all information and quotes on the order.

178 **In an earlier order (March):** JY Smith, "Officials Rebuked on Jail," *Washington Post*, April 2, 1975, C1.

178 **"These conditions . . . human being":** *Inmates, DC Jail v. Jackson*, 416 F. Supp. 119 (D.D.C. 1976), Justia.com, https://law.justia.com/cases/federal/district-courts/FSupp/416/119/1501176/.

179 **"was permitted to talk":** Mary Ann Kuhn, "Plight of Jail Told in Court," *Evening Star*, October 12, 1972, B1.

179 **"I feel I'm being":** Kuhn, "Plight of Jail."

179 **sentenced by Bryant:** Ronald Taylor and B. D. Colen, "6 Implore Judge to End Faults at Jail," *Washington Post*, October 12, 1972, A9. In this source McCoy's first name is Albert.

179 **"They don't think we're people":** Mary Ann Kuhn, "Plight of Jail Told in Court," *Evening Star*, October 12, 1972, B1. In this source McCoy's first name is Alvin.

179 **"You take a 16-year-old kid":** Ronald Taylor and B. D. Colen, "6 Implore Judge to End Faults at Jail," *Washington Post*, October 12, 1972, A9.

179 **"only be brought":** Taylor and Colen, "6 Implore," A9.

179 **"I wrote you . . . I tried":** Taylor and Colen, "6 Implore," A9.

179 **Judge Bryant promised:** Taylor and Colen, "6 Implore," A9.

179 **And by the time:** Mary Ann Kuhn, "Plight of Jail Told in Court," *Evening Star*, October 12, 1972, B1.

180 **In the summer of 1985:** Michael Hedges, "US Judge Orders DC Jail to Cut Population by 1,000," *Washington Times*, July 16, 1985, 1A.

180 **"massive overcrowding . . . have intensified":** Hedges, "US Judge," 1A, 8A.

180 **What he saw literally:** William B. Bryant Jr., comment to author, July 18, 2022.

180 **"fouled with urine . . . wanton pain":** Michael Hedges, "US Judge," 8A.

180 **"They were quiet":** William B. Schultz, comment to author, July 17, 2022.

180 **"long-standing pattern . . . and negligent":** Jonathan M. Smith, "Enforcing Corrections-Related Court Orders in the District of Columbia," *University of the District of Columbia Law Review* 2, no. 2 (March 31, 1994): 246, 245, https://digitalcommons.law.udc.edu/cgi/viewcontent.cgi?article=1256&context=udclr.

180 **"quality of medical services":** Smith, 245.

180 **"the mental health care":** Smith.

180 **"the Big Dipper":** Tony Locy, "US Judge Seizes Control of DC Jail Medical Care," *Washington Post*, July 12, 1995, https://www.washingtonpost.com/archive/local/1995/07/12/us-judge-seizes-control-of-dc-jail-medical-care/9662be67-8ac0-4bf6-946f-1cd148304152/.

181 **"action came as":** Locy, "US Judge."

181 **The judge's action also:** Yesim Sayin, "Twenty Years after the Revitalization Act, the District of Columbia Is a Different City," DC Policy Center, December 19, 2017, https://www.dcpolicycenter.org/publications/twenty-years-revitalization-act-district-columbia-different-city/.

181 **As the *Post* reported . . . "the third judge . . . Complex":** Tony Locy, "US Judge Seizes Control of DC Jail Medical Care," *Washington Post*, July 12, 1995, https://www.washingtonpost.com/archive/local/1995/07/12/us-judge-seizes-control-of-dc-jail-medical-care/9662be67-8ac0-4bf6-946f-1cd148304152/.

181 **"I have some concern":** Locy, "US Judge."

181 **"called the judge's action":** Locy, "US Judge."

181 **In early 1995:** Howard Schneider and David A. Vise, "Barry Says DC Deficit Now $722 Million," *Washington Post*, February 2, 1995, https://www.washington post.com/archive/politics/1995/02/02/barry-says-dc-deficit-now-722-million/f96ef7a6-c2ef-4119-8ab6-01d996dda154/.

182 **"Ending one of":** Department of Corrections, "Court Terminates 32-Year Oversight of DC Jail," March 25, 2003, https://doc.dc.gov/release/court-terminates-32-year-oversight-dc-jail.

182 **"a number of":** Department of Corrections.

CHAPTER 19. A GOOD FIGHT

183 **"I came home . . . more money":** Eleanor Holmes Norton, *Dedication*, 22.

183 **"one of the brightest . . . long on reputation":** WBB OH, 211.

183–84 **"I know Judge Bryant . . . life at the bar":** Eleanor Holmes Norton, "Judge William B. Bryant Annex to the E. Barrett Prettyman Federal Building and United States Courthouse" 108th Cong., 2nd sess., *Congressional Record*, vol. 150, no. 61, May 5, 2004 (Washington, DC: US Government Printing Office): E753.

184 **"There are so many":** Carol Leonnig, "A Lifetime of Faith in the Law," *Washington Post*, September 15, 2004, https://www.washingtonpost.com/archive/local/2004/09/16/a-lifetime-of-faith-in-the-law/8d6a345d-84a7-440d-ad69-ad85a3654480/.

184 **In March 2005:** Press Release, "Norton, Leahy and District Court Judges Ask Congress to Name New Annex for First African American Chief Judge Here," March 1, 2005, https://norton.house.gov/media-center/press-releases/march-1-2005-norton-leahy-and-district-court-judges-ask-congress-to-name.

184 **"Prior to the current":** "Excerpts from the Comments of Senator John Warner," reprinted in *TSOOC*, 64.

184 **He was found:** William B. Bryant Jr., email to author, January 13, 2022.

185 **"In Judge Bryant's closed":** Eleanor Holmes Norton, "Norton Mourns Passing of Judge William Bryant," November 14, 2005, https://norton.house.gov/media-center/press-releases/november-14-2005-norton-mourns-passing-of-judge-william-bryant.

185 **"the soul of the court":** Yvonne Shinhoster Lamb, "Pioneering DC Judge Beat Racial Odds with Wisdom," *Washington Post*, November 15, 2005, A1, https://www.washingtonpost.com/archive/politics/2005/11/15/pioneering-dc-judge-beat-racial-odds-with-wisdom/21f1645e-e352-4671-8403-363ba062f6ac/.

185 **Penny, Chip . . . other hymns:** William B. Bryant Jr., email to author, February 13, 2022.

185 **Penny, Chip, Lauren:** William B. Bryant Jr., comment to author, July 18, 2022.

185–86 **"Bill Schultz . . . about himself'":** Henry F. Greene, "Tribute to Judge Bryant on Behalf of His Law Clerks," delivered at the funeral services for Judge William Bryant held at the Dunbarton Chapel, Howard University School of Law, reprinted in *TSOOC*, 68–69. Reprinted with the permission of Henry F. Greene.

186 **"He was a special . . . we shall miss him":** Thomas F. Hogan, "An Attempt to Show the Sun with a Lantern," delivered at the funeral services for Judge William B. Bryant held at the Dunbarton Chapel, Howard University School of Law, reprinted in *TSOOC*, 71–72. Reprinted with the permission of Thomas F. Hogan.

186 **"growing thin":** Paul Schwartzman, "DC Judge's Humility, Humor Recalled," *Washington Post*, November 19, 2005, B3.

186 **"from a podium . . . the judge himself":** Schwartzman, "DC Judge's."

186–87 **"To measure the life . . . I'm ready":** Vernon E. Jordan Jr., "Eulogy," delivered at the funeral services for Judge William B. Bryant held at the Dunbarton Chapel, Howard University School of Law, reprinted in *TSOOC*, 77–79.

187 **"We do not expect":** James T. Haley, *Afro-American Encyclopaedia: or, The Thoughts, Doings, and Sayings of the Race; Illustrated with Beautiful Half-Tone Engravings* (Nashville, TN: Haley and Florida, c. 1895): 410.

188 **"It is unlikely":** Louis F. Oberdorfer, "Standing against the Winds That Blow," *Tribute: The Honorable William B Bryant, United States District Judge for the District of Columbia* (District of Columbia Circuit Judicial Conference, Farmington, Pennsylvania, June 6–9, 2006): 16.

188 **"Administer true justice":** The Holy Bible, Zechariah 7:9 (NIV).

EPILOGUE

189 **"The architect":** Eric M. Weiss, "A Courthouse Sprouts Curves and Color," *Washington Post*, August 2, 2006, https://www.washingtonpost.com/archive/local/2006/08/03/a-courthouse-sprouts-curves-and-color-span-classbankheadfanciful-annex-to-federal-structure-is-nearly-finishedspan/31750c07-8e08-4c46-baf5-9dda6dbd8c82/.

189 **"The most . . . views of the Capitol":** Weiss, "A Courthouse."

189 **Judge Bryant's friend:** *Dedication*, 2.

189 **They included:** William B. Bryant Jr., comment to author, July 18, 2021.

189 **Several members:** Bryant Jr., comment.

190 **"honored to be":** Douglas H. Ginsburg, *Dedication*, 5.

190 **"The William B. Bryant . . . chose to do so":** John G. Roberts Jr., *Dedication*, 6, 7.

190 **"a true inspiration":** Thomas F. Hogan, *Dedication*, 9.

190 **"a professor of . . . And that he did":** John W. Warner, *Dedication*, 13.

190 **"it speaks volumes":** Eleanor Holmes Norton, *Dedication*, 20.

191 **"This great honor . . . Thank you very much":** William B. Bryant Jr., *Dedication*, 28–33.

INDEX

ABOUT THE AUTHOR

Tonya Bolden has authored, coauthored, and edited more than fifty books for readers of various ages. Many of her titles have garnered starred reviews from *Kirkus Reviews*, *Publishers Weekly*, and other publications. Her numerous awards include a Children's Book Guild of Washington, DC's Nonfiction Award for her body of work. This magna cum laude baccalaureate of Princeton University with a master's degree from Columbia University lives in New York City. To learn more about her work, visit tonyaboldenbooks.com.

FSC
www.fsc.org
MIX
Papier | Fördert gute Waldnutzung
FSC® C083411

Kolibri 360 GmbH
Ferdinand-Jühlke-Straße 7
99095 Erfurt, Deutschland
produktsicherheit@kolibri360.de